A TIGER LOOSE ON AN ICE FLOE

The Indian Ferozepore Brigade on the Western Front 1914–1915

David Snape

Helion & Company

Helion & Company Limited
Unit 8 Amherst Business Centre
Budbrooke Road
Warwick
CV34 5WE
England
Tel. 01926 499 619
Email: info@helion.co.uk
Website: www.helion.co.uk
Twitter: @helionbooks
Visit our blog at blog.helion.co.uk

Published by Helion & Company 2023
Designed and typeset by Mach 3 Solutions (www.mach3solutions.co.uk)
Cover designed by Paul Hewitt, Battlefield Design (www.battlefield-design.co.uk)

ISBN 978-1-915113-69-6

British Library Cataloguing-in-Publication Data.
A catalogue record for this book is available from the British Library.

For details of other military history titles published by Helion & Company Limited contact the above address or visit our website: http://www.helion.co.uk.

We always welcome receipt of book proposals from prospective authors.

Contents

List of Illustrations

List of Maps

Throughout the First World War the Indian Army relied on volunteers to fill its ranks. This was a strength and a weakness.
The poster, written in Hindi, states:
"This soldier defends India. He protects his home and family. The best way to help your family is to join the army."

Preface

Whilst researching for a MA dissertation as very mature student at the University of Wolverhampton, I discovered the War Diaries of the Indian Corps in France. Although they were written by the Corps' British Officers, they provided an insight into the struggles which their Indian troops faced during mobilisation, embarkation and their arrival on the Western Front in September 1914. These Sepoys and Sowars provided a much-needed support to an exhausted BEF and enabled the Allies to check the German "race to the sea". The conditions in which they fought were completely new and, sometimes terrifying even though many of the Indians had considerable fighting experience in their homeland. They had been deprived of modern weaponry because of the Indian Government's penury and were organised differently from their British counterparts but had considerable skill in improvisation which proved extremely useful on the Western Front.

Throughout the War the Indian Army was manned solely by volunteers which was both a strength and a weakness. They received considerable criticism from certain quarters of the British Army but the BEF owed them a great debt. This book tries to illustrate their contribution to the fighting in France and Belgium during the years 1914-15 by using the words of those who were there. It also attempts to use examples of their efforts to illustrate the big picture of events as supplied by the Official Histories.

I would like to thank Helion & Company for allowing me to work on this book and my editor, Dr Michael LoCicero, for his invaluable help in bringing it to print. I dedicate this book to my late wife, Jill, who could never understand my fascination with all things military, but was prepared to read my work and offer helpful suggestions.

David Snape
Northamptonshire 2023

Introduction

It was, moreover, with confidence and pride that I was able to offer to his Majesty the first and largest military force of British and Indian troops for service in Europe that has ever left the shores of India. I am confident that the honour of this land and of the British Empire may be safely entrusted to our brave soldiers, and that they will acquit themselves nobly and ever maintain their high traditions of military chivalry and courage. To the people of India I would say at this time, let us display to the world an attitude of unity, of self-sacrifice, and of unswerving confidence under all circumstances, in the justice of our cause and in the assurance that God will defend the right.[1]

It was with these words that Lord Hardinge informed the members of his Council and the people of India that he had formally offered the Army in India to serve in the First World War. Hardinge had resisted the idea that his army would be forced to serve outside the subcontinent and one suspects there were some members of the Council who felt that the Viceroy had his tongue in his cheek when he described his confidence in the offer. Hardinge's first responsibility was the defence of India both from external threat and internal civil unrest.

Removing a large body of troops would place both these things at risk. However, the Force which was sent from India, denominate the Indian Expeditionary Force A (IEFA), which might suggest that, as it transpired, there would be a B, C etc.

Although Hardinge had previously been reluctant to contemplate the Indian Army serving on foreign battlefields, the support from the Rulers of Indian States was unstinting and *The Times* Correspondent in Bombay was able to report that this assistance had been offered as early as 6 August 1914.[2]

Charles Hardinge, 1st Baron Hardinge was Viceroy of India from 1910 to 1916. He had entered the Diplomatic service in 1880 and was appointed Ambassador to Russia in 1904 and permanent Under Secretary for Foreign Affairs in 1906, he was raised to the peerage and appointed Viceroy of India in 1910. His government reversed Lord Curzon's unpopular partition of Bengal and took the occasion of the December 1911

1 Lord Hardinge of Penshurst, Viceroy of India, address to the Viceroy's Council. See *The Times History of the* War, Vol. 1, pp. 164-165.

2 *The Times History of the War*, p. 164.

visit of King George V and his Queen to announce the transfer of the capital of India from Calcutta to New Delhi.

On Hardinge's return to Great Britain in 1916, he was again appointed Permanent Under Secretary for Foreign Affairs. His offer to resign from public life because of the criticism of his contribution to the arrangements for the first part of the Mesopotamian Campaign which ended with the British surrender at Kut, was refused. Hardinge became British Ambassador to Paris in 1920 and he retired in 1922

Charles Hardinge, 1st Baron Hardinge of Penshurst
Viceroy of India 1910-16.

This volume attempts to recount the experiences of the IEFA, later to be designated The Indian Corps, from its mobilisation to its departure from France, by examining its War Diaries. Each Battalion was required to keep an account of its day-today activities. They were written by hand and mostly in pencil. These Diaries also contained a number of type-written documents which were formal reports to High Command or orders which Senior Officers circulated to those units under their command. Some Diaries provided a general picture of activities whilst others went into great detail and sometimes named individual casualties amongst the rank and file rather than just amongst officers as was most common. Some are bland but others include an occasional criticism of the orders they had received or the activities of other Units. The clarity of handwriting varies but the Diaries are generally easy to read.

In order to provide a focus, the book concentrates on the Diaries of one of the Brigades of the Indian Corps, The Ferozepore Brigade. However, to analyse how this section of the Indian Corps fits into the bigger picture, reference is made to the work of Edmonds in his multi-volume history of military operations in France and Belgium. In addition, and, on a lesser scale, the works of Merewether and Smith, *The Indian Corps in France,* and Lieutenant General James Willcocks', the Corps Commander, *With the Indians,* provide something of a biased self-evaluation of the Corps' performance in the first two years of conflict on the Western Front.

It is hard to imagine the confusion, concern and impact which the ordinary Sepoy and Sowar endured during those years. The criticisms which have been made of their performance misconception and time have obscured the level of the Indian Corps' achievements through false comparisons and misapprehension have resulted in looking through a glass darkly rather than face to face through the Diaries. Whilst not ignoring the difficulties which the Indian Corps faced both through its individual soldiers to its commander, it is hoped that this account, in a small way, addresses this imbalance by concentrating on the individual voices of its Battalions.

Sir Pratap Singh; Commander of the Jodhpur Lancers and supporter of the Imperial War Effort. Lieutenant-General Sir Pratap Singh, GCB, GCSI, GCVO was the Maharaja of the princely state of Idar (Gujarat). By the time of the First World War Sir Patrap had served in a number of campaigns in India including the Second Afghan War and the Tirah Campaign. He had commanded a contingent during the Boxer Rebellion. When war broke out in Europe, Lieutenant General Singh General went to France in command of the Jodhpur Lancers until 1918 even though he was in his seventies.

1

The Indian Army in 1914

The Indian Army formed the largest body of Empire troops outside the British Isles and, at the outbreak of war, consisted of 193,901 Indian combatants, 76,953 British soldiers and 45,630 non-combatants.[1] It had existed for two purposes; the defence of India from possible Russian attack on the Northwest Frontier and to assist the civil power in keeping order. It was created in 1895 by a combination of the Armies of the East India Company and the Princely States but was later subjected to a number of significant reforms by then General Herbert Horatio Kitchener during his tenure as Commander in Chief of India between 1902 and 1909. He decreed that the Indian Army would be 'a force recruited locally and permanently based in India, together with its expatriate British officers.'[2] Kitchener was keen to ensure that the Indian Army's emphasis moved from internal security to external defence in order to prepare it to protect the subcontinent against a Russian European army.[3] The composition of the Indian army was roughly 40 percent Muslim, a similar percentage of Hindu and around nineteen percent Sikh. Many were not actually 'Indian' as such but rather South Asian.

Much of the Army's activity involved fighting to maintain the security of the Khyber region which linked Afghanistan and India and would be a likely route for

1 The National Archives (Henceforth TNA) MUN 5/176/1143/16. Memorandum on India's Contribution to the War in Men, Material and Money August 1914 to November 1918. No two accounts can agree on the exact number of men which made up the Indian Army but this was the official figure at the time of the publication of the Memorandum.

2 Timothy Moreman, 'Lord Kitchener, the General Staff and the Army in India, 1902-14' in David French & Brian Holden Reid (eds.), *British General Staff: Reform and Innovation* (London: Routledge, 2004) pp. 58-62.

3 Charles Townshend, *When God Made Hell: The British Invasion of Mesopotamia and the Creation of Iraq, 1914-1921* (London: Faber and Faber, 2011) p. 25. David Snape, 'With a master's eye he saw what was needed and did it.' Kitchener's Indian Army Reforms 1902-1909, *Soldiers of the Queen, Journal of the Victorian Military Society*, Issue 170, May 2018.

an invading Russian Army.[4] There its opponents were the many different tribes who inhabited the region and, although many were supposedly subservient to the Emir of Afghanistan, most cherished their independent life. They were excellent guerrilla fighters and brilliant in the use of terrain. In terms of the contemporary standards of warfare they were poorly armed and, though tough opponents, did not provide the European combat experience which the Indian Army would need when confronting the Russians.

When in August 1914. the Viceroy, Lord Charles Hardinge, declared war on Germany on behalf of the subcontinent and there was an outpouring of support from many quarters. Over three quarters (21 out of 27) of the Princes' Imperial Service Troops contingents, whose purpose was mainly ceremonial or policing duties were mustered and a proportion of these men had been trained to standards similar to that of the British Indian Army. The Princes themselves were also keen to show their support in other ways and made large donations to the cause such as that of the Maharajah of Mysore who gave 60 Lakhs of rupees.[5] Some Princes were not content to simply offer financial support and, like the septuagenarian Regent-Maharajah, Major General Sir Pratap Singh, Commander of the Jodhpur Lancers, they were prepared to personally go to war. Encouraging recruitment became a competitive feature of the early months of the war and rich landowners vied with each other to provide more and more men for the war effort. Numbers soon exceeded the Army's ability to train and arm these *volunteers* but, such was the extent of their commitment, that Lord Hardinge, in September 1914 was able to report that 700 princes had offered assistance in a variety of ways.[6]

Throughout the First World War the Indian Army continued to rely upon volunteers. This was because of Imperial policy, fundamental social divisions in Indian society and the previously relatively small need to conscript recruits given the potential number of volunteers and the role of the Indian Army as determined before 1914 as outlined above.[7]

Army recruitment could involve a number of strategies. A Battalion might send a recruiting party to certain districts from which previous volunteers had come. Battalion officers, who were in contact with military pensioners. might ask them to suggest candidates or men on leave might bring back friends or acquaintances from their village. Many Sepoys preferred this system of local recruitment since it was a

4 Major General Charles Metcalfe MacGregor, *The Defence of India; a Strategic Study* (Simla, Government Central Branch Press, 1884).

5 £40,000. Over 4.5 Million in today's value.

6 Philip Mason, *A Matter of Honour: An Account of the Indian Army, Its Officers and Men* (London: Macmillan, 1978) p. 408.

7 Roy Kaushik, Race and Recruitment in the Indian Army 1880-1918 in *Modern Asian Studies*, Vol. 47, No. 4, 2013, p. 1310.

way of providing employment for their neighbours and an income for their families.[8]

In spite of its importance to the British war strategy, the Indian Army suffered considerably from events in its history. There were erroneous theories about the fighting capabilities of different Indian ethnic groups and the concentration on the original rationale for its existence as identified by Kitchener. This dynamic significantly affected the development of the Indian Army but, by 1914, it had developed a unified sense of identity, a feeling of exclusivity and extensive experience in mountain warfare as has already been described. It had, however, no experience of large-scale operations or the sustained nature of European industrial warfare.[9] In addition, it did not have a structure by which it could prepare sufficient reserves if there was a high casualty rate. Although this is an important criticism as an official review of the Army conducted shortly after the end of the First World War by the Government of India declared, it must be remembered that such a conflict as a World War had not really been envisaged by Britain and, even if it had been considered, there was a reluctance to accept that the Indian Army would be a part of it.[10] Indeed, there was an understanding amongst European countries that native troops would not be used against European forces outside the indigenous- peoples' lands.

General Sir Garrett O'Moore Creagh, V.C.
Commander in Chief of the Indian Army
1909-1914.

The Indian Army's role of defence and civil control had determined its training and there was little realisation that it might have to serve abroad. Accordingly, all units

8 David Omissi, *The Sepoy and the Raj: The Indian Army, 1860–1940* (Houndmills: Macmillan, 1994), p. 21. Sepoy = Infantryman.

9 Robert Johnson, "I shall die arms in hand, wearing the Warriors' Clothes": 'Mobilisation and Initial Operations of the Indian Army in France and Flanders' in *British Journal for Military History*, Vol. 2, Issue 2, February 2016, p. 109.

10 Government of India, *The Army in India and its Evolution* (Calcutta: Superintendent Government, Government Publishing, 1924), p. 219.

received instruction and experience in defending India's borders and keeping order in the country.

General Sir Garrett O'Moore Creagh VC, GCB, GCSI was born in County Clare, Ireland in 1848, won his Victoria Cross in the Second Afghan War. After a distinguished career he commanded the British Forces during the Boxer Rebellion and succeeded Lord Kitchener as as Commander-in-Chief, India. O'Moore Creagh, and Douglas Haig, Chief of the Indian General Staff from 1909 to 1911, believed that, should there be a world war in which the Indian Army would be required to deploy on European battlefields, such an event would require massive increases in funding and recruitment. However, Lord Hardinge, Viceroy from 1910 to 1916, believed that, if there was such a war, it would not be India's concern.[11] He argued that O'Moore Creagh's views were, 'in complete opposition to the international politics of the day.[12] The Viceroy correctly believed that the numbers of recruits required such circumstances would be too great for the current Indian recruitment system and ordered Haig to destroy his plans for preparing the Indian Army for service abroad.[13] Haig only pretended to do so.[14] Creagh, resigned in frustration; he had lacked sufficient vigour for his role, but he was succeeded by Beauchamp Duff, who was to prove even more compliant and came to be seen by some as merely an office clerk.[15]

Such a dismissive judgement would seem at first sight to be somewhat harsh. General Sir Beauchamp Duff GCB, GCSI, KCVO, CIE, KStJ, a member of an aristocratic Scottish Family, had been destined for the army from an early age and graduated from the Royal Military Academy, Woolwich, in 1874. Commissioned into the Royal Artillery, he served in the Afghan War and then transferred to the Indian Staff Corps His abilities as an outstanding officer marked him out as one of the Indian Army's high flyers and he attended a course at the Staff College from 1887 to 1889 from which he passed out in first place. He was immediately appointed as Military Attaché to the Viceroy. When Lord Kitchener was appointed Commander in Chief of the Indian Army, Duff continued to rise and hold a number of senior posts becoming Chief of the Indian General Staff in 1906. On 22 October 1913, Duff replaced General O'Moore Creagh as Commander-in-Chief, India. His appointment was a change to the normal practice as the post was normally held by a British Army officer and, such a decision was a tribute to Beauchamp Duff, who was part of the Indian Army, and, as the first such an appointment was a indication to his perceived abilities. It was under Duff's overall leadership that the Mespotamia Campaign was

11 George Morton Jack, *The Indian Army on the Western Front* (Cambridge: CUP, 2014)
12 Cambridge University Library, CUL/MD, Hardinge Papers, Letter to G. Allen, 12 January 1914.
13 Townshend, When *God Made Hell*, p. 26.
14 Gary Sheffield, *Douglas Haig: From Somme to Victory* (London: Aurum Press, 2016) p. 62.
15 Ron Wilcox, *Battles on the Tigris: The Mesopotamian Campaign of the First World War* (Barnsley: Pen & Sword 2006) p. 68. Stanley L. Menezes, Fidelity *and Honour: The Indian Army from the Seventeenth to the Twenty-First Century* (New Delhi: OUP, 1999) p. 243.

initiated, which in spite of Townsend's brilliant beginning it ended in disaster with the surrender at Kut al Amara. This had been an entirely Indian Army affair and the ailing Beauchamp Duff was relieved of his post in October 1916. The shame proved too much and he committed suicide in early 1918. Hardinge's short sighted intransigence would condemn the Indian Army to a series of impromptu and calamitous missions such as Townshend's drive to Baghdad.[16]

The 'Army in India Committee' of 1912-1913 recommended that the field army should be made up of seven infantry divisions, and five cavalry brigades which would be sufficient troops to deal with both Afghanistan and the Frontier Tribes until the Home Country was able to send reinforcements.[17] Such was the order of battle of the Indian Army when it was mobilised in 1914 but much of the previously agreed equipment essential for this reorganisation had yet to be distributed because of poor finances and, perhaps, because of the continuing reluctance to accept India would play a major part in a European war.

However, in 1913 the Government of India, forced to acknowledge that a European war was a distinct possibility, agreed to offer Britain two infantry divisions and two cavalry brigades for overseas service should they be needed. It believed that sending more troops would place the security of India, always its first concern, in jeopardy. It did not again consider the deployment of the Army in India, which consisted of both British and Indian Battalions, overseas until 30th July 1914 when it informed the Army Council that, in the case of a serious European war, it could only actually supply two divisions of infantry and one cavalry brigade without risking the security of the sub-continent. In spite of India's much lauded public support when war was declared as has been previously described, it was this reduced allocation which was accepted by the Home Country since it had few alternative sources which could quickly support the BEF.[18] One should not forget, however, that, as time progressed, many additional Indian troops were sent to fight in the various theatres of the war and, surprisingly, in spite of this dramatic drain on the Indian Army's ability to recruit, all these men continued to be volunteers for whom a military career was both honourable and earned the gratitude of the King Emperor. As Edmonds points out, no effort was made to make India the eastern military base of the British Empire by establishing the industrial capabilities in the country which would be needed to do so or creating the essential stocks of materiel required except in relatively unimportant items such as limited quantities of artillery and small arms ammunition as well as boots, saddles and horse harness.[19]

16 Morton-Jack, *The Indian Army*, pp. 112-113.
17 Brigadier General Sir James Edmonds, *Military Operations, France and Belgium, 1914, Vol. 1* (London: MacMillan & Co, 1920), p. 12. Henceforth Edmonds 1914, Vol 1.
18 Asquith's Guildhall speech quoted in Vedica Kant, *If I die here who will remember me? India and the First World War* (New Delhi, Roli Books, 2014) p. 30 and Johnson, 'I shall die arms in hand, wearing the Warriors Clothes', p. 108.
19 Edmonds, 1914, Vol. 1. p. 14.

The Viceroy, Hardinge, possessed a limited strategic vision which was to restrict his war policy to his own domain. He was extremely conscious and jealous of his independent authority and, although he acquiesced to many requests from the War Office, such as the return of most of the British pre-war Battalions which were serving as part of the Army in India, he was determined to defend his status against all comers. Protocol demanded that only one British Government Office, the India Office, had the right to deal directly with the Indian Army's Headquarters at Simla but Kitchener, the newly appointed Secretary of State for War, who had maintained many connections with the subcontinent, and perhaps forgetting he was now a creature of politics rather than a soldier, attempted to side-step this restriction by sending telegrams directly to his protégée, Beauchamp Duff, who had served under him as Chief of the General Staff, India. This underhand attempt to bypass formal methods of communication was quickly labelled by Hardinge as 'unconstitutional' even though it might have proved to be more efficient.[20] Similarly, when war was declared, Hardinge protested that British Indian officers, either on leave or training in Britain, were retained by the Home Army without prior consultation. The British Government's motives for making this decision are obvious but it deprived the Indian Army of some of its brightest young officers and left Beauchamp Duff 'absolutely crippled';[21] not surprisingly since the number of those retained amounted to 253 officers.[22] Half of the 47 reserve officers were also 'swept up' in the British mobilisation.[23] The Indian Army Officer Reserve was something of a Cinderella organisation. As Major Crum wrote, ' No serious attempt was made to recruit for the Reserve, the only standard of military knowledge required was a certificate of proficiency such as granted to a Captain of Volunteer Forces in India, and only in the case of cavalry was a yearly training of 14 days insisted on.'[24] Similarly, the Reserve of other ranks was a somewhat hit or miss affair. The British Army had a well organised system whereby men who had served their normal seven years with the colours were required to be prepared for a recall for the next five years. In this way, at the outbreak of the War, Battalions were quickly brought up to combat strength. In the Indian Army the normal period of service was 20 to 25 years and, when a Sepoy retired, he was often passed his usefulness. In addition being numbered amongst the reserve was entirely voluntary for retired Sepoys. Those men who did volunteer

20 Morton-Jack, *The Indian Army,* p. 282. Frederick, James. Moberley, *The Campaign in Mesopotamia 1914-1918, Vol. 2* (London: HMSO, 1923-27), pp. 29-30.
21 British Library, Indian Office Records. LM/16/17/16/22: Collection of private Telegrams between the Secretary of State for India and the Viceroy, prior to the Outbreak of War with Turkey', Telegram from the Viceroy to the Secretary of State, 14 August 1914. (Henceforth BL/IOR).
22 TNA MUN 5/176/1143/16: Memorandum on India's contribution to the war in men, material and money, p. 7.
23 Johnson, 'I shall die arms in hand', p. 112.
24 W. E. Crum, 'The Indian Army Reserve of Officers'in the *Journal of the United Service Institution of India,* Vol. XLV, 1916, p. 282.

trained with the linked Battalion for two months every two years, but their military value was negligible. In total, at the outbreak of the War there were some 31,923 men in the Indian reserve.[25] Such men were described as 'a motley collection,' of whom 'many were quite unfit for active service.'[26] Merewether and Smith agreed that many of the reservists were 'entirely incapable of undergoing the rigours of a winter campaign in Europe.[27] An accusation which was also levelled at those Battalions who did serve on the Western Front.

At the start of the war in 1914 the Indian Army had no intermediate chain of command and its headquarters was weighed down with minor administrative and bureaucratic details. Divisional commanders were responsible not only for their active formations, but also for India's internal security and also recruiting troops within their respective areas. On mobilisation, Divisional Staffs took to the field, leaving little or no-one to maintain the local administration and carry out recruitment. Support services were insufficient, and many troops intended for a field force were not moved from their old stations into the areas of their new Divisional Command which had obvious disruptive consequences. This inadequate and inefficient organisation was clearly demonstrated when Indian Expeditionary Force A (IEFA) needed good quality reinforcements after First Ypres, and was to become a problem which was to persist throughout the Indian Corps' service in France and ultimately resulted in the withdrawal of the Indian infantry from the Western Front in 1915. IEFD which was to serve in Mesopotamia, also suffered from similar poor administration which was further complicated because, as the Mesopotamia Commission pointed out, Beauchamp Duff, who had overall responsibility for the campaign, did not visit Mesopotamia or even went to Bombay, (Mumbai), the IEFD's port of departure, but relied on telegrams from officers who were often reluctant to reveal the real conditions under which the soldiers IEFD fought and died.[28]

Promotion in the Indian Army was often gained as a result of seniority rather than solely on ability. In 1914 the average age of Indian Brigadiers and Divisional Commanders was roughly seven years greater than in the Home Army. Accepting an Indian commission was seen by some as professional suicide [29] by junior British officers and the sub-continent was viewed as a military backwater.[30] Such a view might have

25 Anon, *The Army inn India and its Evolution* (Calcutta, Superintendent of Government Printing, 1924 p. 126.

26 G. Pigot, *History of the 1st Battalion, 14th Punjab Regiment, Sherdil-ki-Paltan (late XIX Punjabis)* (New Delhi: Roxy Printing Press, 1946), p. 98.

27 John W. B Merewether & Frederick Smith, The *Indian Corps in France* (London, John Murray, 1918) p. 465.

28 BL/IOR/L/PS/20/57, *Mesopotamia Commission. Report of the Commission Appointed by Act of Parliament to Enquire into the Operations of War in Mesopotamia, together with a Special Report by Commander J Wedgwood, DSO, MP, and Appendices* (London: HMSO, 1917).

29 Imperial War Museum, DS/MISC/2: Henderson Papers p. 12.

30 Morton-Jack, *The Indian Army on the Western Front*, p. 116.

discouraged the most able and ambitious young officers from accepting an Indian appointment since professional expertise, as indicated by the suffix p.s.c.,[31] was held to be of little value as Horace Smith-Dorrien, who was later to command II Corps in 1914, was to discover in 1891 when no one on the Indian Army Headquarters Staff, from the highest to the lowest, could boast such a qualification.[32] In his *Separate Report*, issued as addendum to the *Report* of *the Mesopotamia Commission*,[33] Commander Wedgwood argued that The Indian Army's Reserve System was totally inadequate as only 43 officers were available at the outbreak of the War.[34] Townshend went as far as to describe them as being 'untrained civilians'.[35] Attempts in the first year of the War to find suitably qualified men in Britain to train as officers for the Indian Army failed miserably as only six were found with the necessary Indian and military experience. Wedgewood also commented that the inefficiency of Indian Army's senior officers was demonstrated when 21 general officers had to be removed during the Mesopotamia Campaign.[36] In addition, the IEFA had many of its original commanders replaced during its short deployment on the Western Front as some senior Indian officers who holding on to the posts in order to gain a pension found themselves severely challenged by modern industrial warfare.

The Indian Army's British officers were not true members of the British Army, but, as young subalterns had to serve for a year with a Regular Army Battalion as part of their training before gaining a permanent commission within the Indian Army *per se*. Many of them had been born in Britain and came from middle class families and saw India as offering both opportunity for a military career as well as an affordable standard of living. Those who had been born in India often came from families in which the military tradition was strong.[37] They were seen as having qualities of leadership which no Indian or even Anglo-Indian could possess and because of this fallacious view; racial purity was seen as important.[38] Twelve to each infantry Battalion of approximately 750 Indian soldiers, these officers were required to communicate with their men in their native language and their initial home leave was not permitted until a new subaltern had become so proficient. Since at least nine languages were spoken within the Indian Army, Urdu was chosen as its *lingua franca*.[39] The need for officers

31 Passed Staff College.
32 H. Smith-Dorrien, *Memories of Forty-Eight Years' Service* (London: John Murray, 1925), p. 72.
33 BL/IOR/L/PS/20/57: Mesopotamia Commission, *Wedgwood, Separate Report, pp. 121-132.*
34 *Wedgwood, Separate Report, p. 121.*
35 E Latter, 'The Indian Army' in the *Journal of the Society for Army Historical Research, Vol. LXXII No 291, Autumn 1994,* p. 172.
36 Wedgwood, *Separate Report, p. 121.* See comments on removal of senior IEFA officers.
37 George Morton-Jack, *The Indian Army on the Western Front) p. 2.*
38 George MacMunn, *The Martial Races of India* (London: Sampson Low, 1933) pp. 270-71. The Indian Medical Service was an exception.
39 Trench, *The Indian Army,* p. 15.

to become close to their men was even more important that in British Battalions and may have been a further attempt to prevent another rebellion by encouraging a Company to be like a tight community.

British Battalions have often been described as family units, but in the Indian Army, in spite of the greater social division between officers and men, rapport was even closer. Officers spent much of their spare time with their men and developed personal relationships with them upon which the Army came to depend. In this respect the Indian Army was not entirely unique as there were similar relationships in the British Army. The pre-war British Regular Army has correctly been described as being 'recruited from the bottom of society' but 'led from the top'.[40] This applied to an even greater extent to the Indian Army. Its recruits were mostly illiterate peasant farmers who joined up in their late teens for a period of long service with the promise of a regular wage, a pension and a grant of land on retirement. The pay, however, was small; eleven Rupees at the outset of the War,[41] but, as David Omissi pointed out, even this small amount would be valued by relatives in India who had few alternative sources of income.[42]

As the War progressed Indian soldiers became aware of the better pay of their allies and there was some resentment as to the pittance they received and, consequently, it was increased.[43] Professor Gary Sheffield, when describing the pre-war British Army, argued that the core of the British officers' creed was *noblesse oblige*; the belief that privilege entailed responsibility for one's men.[44] The paternalism in both the pre-war Home Army and the Indian Army meant there were many similarities but also significant differences. 'Temporary Officers' in the Home Army received a crash course in their duties. This included the expectation that they would adopt paternalistic attitudes towards their men. Since many such officers had served in the ranks, they were well aware, from their own experience, that caring for one's men was important to a unit's morale.[45] However, British Temporary officers spoke the same language as their men, but new officers in the Indian Army were required to learn to address their men in their native tongue and none were recruited from the ranks.

There are alternative views, however, about the quality of British Indian officers. Some commentators argued that they were often unambitious and thought that the very best type of British Indian Army officer was 'not vastly clever' but 'very sound'.[46]

40 J. F. C Fuller, *The Army in My Time* (London: Rich & Cowan 1935), p. 6.
41 David Omissi (ed.), *Indian Voices of the Great War* (London: Viking 2014,) p. 20.
42 Omissi, *Indian Voices,* p. 1.
43 BL/IOR:L/MIL/5/825/1f. 66: Memorandum from Censor of Indian mail re Indian troops' dissatisfaction with pay. 12 February 1915 and Kant, *If I die here ... p. 118.*
44 Gary Sheffield, *Command and Morale. The British Army on the Western Front 1914-1918* (Barnsley: Praetorian Press 2014), p. 176.
45 Sheffield, *Command and Morale,* p. 179.
46 Henry Villiers-Stuart quoted in Robert Maxwell, *Villiers-Stuart Goes to War* (Edinburgh: Pentland Press, 1989) p. 26.

This assessment was confirmed by the *Indian United Services Institute Journal* of 1914 which expressed surprise at 'the somewhat low standard' of those Majors who took the *Tactical Fitness for Command' Examination.*[47] However, Anthony Chevenix Trench points out that 20 of the top 25 students at the Royal Military College Sandhurst in 1913 opted to join the Indian Army.[48] This impressive statistic was partly because the chances of gaining a commission in the Indian Army depended not simply on the marks registered on admission to the Military College as in the case of Claude Auchinleck in 1903[49] After the Second Boer War, however, gaining an Indian commission depended on the marks gained in the final examination.

In 1908 Bernard Montgomery, a future Field Marshal, was 'bitterly disappointed' not to have achieved a sufficiently high enough mark to gain a commission in the Indian Army which had been his original intention.[50] In Montgomery's case it was perhaps his questionable behaviour at Sandhurst which contributed to his final outcome.[51] It was true that an Indian commission in the late Victorian and Edwardian Indian Army tended to make a smaller drain on a young officer's resources than one at Home and this might have been an attraction to

The Young Bernard Montgomery in 1915.

47 *Journal of the United Services Institution of India*, 1914, pp. 437-438
48 Charles Chenevix Trench, The *Indian Army and the King's Enemies; 1900-1947* (London: Thames & Hudson, 1980) *p. 25.*
49 Philip. Warner, *Auchinleck: The Lonely Soldier* (London: Buchan and Enright, 1981). p. 13.
50 Bernard Law Montgomery, The *Memoirs of Field-Marshal the Viscount Montgomery of Alamein, K. G. (London: Collins, 1958). p. 26.*
51 Tony Heathcote, *The British Field Marshals 1736–1997.* (Barnsley: Pen & Sword, 1999), p. 213.

potential officers with no or somewhat meagre independent means. An Indian Army commission, however, did provide plenty of opportunities for action since the Indian Army was almost constantly engaged in short, bloody, punitive expeditions against the Khyber tribes.

The exceptions to this initially perceived lack of professionalism were the officers of the Mountain Artillery, who held British Army commissions and were on attachment. They had both the skill to manage their guns and to command their units. Charles Townshend cites an example of how an Australian artillery officer was able to work with an Indian battery since it used normal English commands and retained a strict adherence to the standard drill book.[52] Perhaps this says as much about the Mountain Artillery gunners as to the flexibility of the Australian officer. Similarly, when the 2/8th Gurkhas had all its senior officers killed or wounded,[53] Lieutenant General James Willcocks, Commander of the Indian Corps, sent Major Tomkins, an officer of 28th Punjabis who spoke no Gurkhali, to command them. Both he and the Viceroy Commissioned Officer (V.C.O.) spoke Urdu and he therefore was able to successfully command the Battalion until a more suitably qualified Gurkha officer could be found.[54]

VCOs, known as "Indian officers" or "Native officers", were treated almost in all respects as British commissioned officers, but only had genuine authority over Indian troops. They viewed the Battalion and Company as their family even more than their British counterparts as, for example, did Risaldar-Major Mir Jafar Khan, a 50-year-old Pathan, who offered a typical example of the loyalty and affection for his Battalion which had developed over a lifetime of service. In reaction to a rumour that he was to be sent back to India after 33 years with 4th (Hodson's) Horse,[55] he wrote to a friend in 1916, that for him, the pleasure of seeing home again would 'be as nothing to the sorrow I should feel at having to part from the Battalion'.[56] Although vastly experienced and reasonably fluent in English, Subedars and Risaldars were expected to obey the orders of inexperienced junior British officers, though the latter would have been foolish not to consult the Subedar Sahib for advice.[57] V.C.O.s had a prestige greater than that attached to their official status and often sorted out problems in the ranks without the knowledge of their British officers. They were also capable of speaking frankly to junior British officers whom they thought were in danger of letting down their Battalion.[58] Willcocks, although a great supporter of the Indian Army, argued

52 Townshend, *Die in Battle*, p. 171.
53 TNA: WO95/3946: 7th Indian (Meerut) Division, 20th (Garhwal) Indian Infantry Brigade, 2/8th Battalion, Gurkha Rifles War Diary, 30/10/1914.
54 Corrigan, *Sepoys in the Trenches*, p. *82*.
55 The Duke of Cambridge's Own Lancers.
56 Risaldar-Mir Jafar to Abdul Wahid Khan, 23 May 1916 in Omissi, *Indian Voices*, p. 188-189.
57 Trench, *Indian Army*, p. 16.
58 Lieutenant A.G. Raw's Diary quoted in Trench, *Indian Army*, pp. 16-25.

that Indian Officers could not be relied upon in command positions because of lack of training or temperament,[59] and begged future governments not to replace the British Officer with them.[60] In spite of this lack of trust in Indian officers, many examples of them taking command in exceptional circumstances can be found especially on the Western Front.[61] There were also many similar examples in the previous history of the Indian Army.[62] Their supposed lack of temperament was, in fact, a product of the belief that they were so by nature and this could not be changed. Their lack of training was a partial outcome of this view and ensured their lack of command experience sometimes did affect their performance when British Officers had been killed and wounded, which frequently occurred during action on the Western Front. As Philip Mason argued when discussing Field Marshal Lord Roberts' attitude to V.C.O.s, ' he (Roberts) was less than fair to Indian Officers when he held it against them when they turned to a British officer for support in time of difficulty. They had been taught to do just that; they were subordinates.'[63] Similarly, the lack of training and the low expectations of the Sepoy was compensated, it was believed, by their trust in their British officers and so there is little wonder that poor performance in such situations became a self-fulfilling prophecy.

In spite of Hardinge's assertion that the Indian Army was absolutely ready by the standards of the time,[64] these norms were inadequate for a conflict like that of 1914.[65] Such criticism could equally be levelled against the BEF but at least it had begun tentative planning for a continental war against Germany as early as 1910 and had made a number of strategic and tactical improvements because of its experiences in the Boer War.[66] This criticism, however, was certainly more applicable to the Indian Army.[67] Commander Wedgwood, of the Mesopotamia Commission, which reviewed the performance the Indian Expeditionary Force D during the Mesopotamia Campaign,[68] was extremely critical of the training of the pre-war Indian Army which he described as consisting of 'mid-Victorian manœuvres'

59 James Willcocks, *With the Indians in France* (London: Constable and Co. Ltd., 1920). p. 6.
60 Willcocks, *With the Indians,* p. 344.
61 Townshend, Die in Battle, pp. 170-172
62 Thomas Woseley, Haig, The Indian Army 1885 to 1919 in *The Cambridge History of India* (Cambridge, CUP, 1932) Vol. 6, p. 396
63 Mason, *A Matter of Honour*, p. 348.
64 Charles Hardinge, *My Indian Years* (London, John Murray, 1948), *pp.* 98 & 103.
65 Townshend, *When God Made Hell,* p. 26.
66 For a consideration of how the Boer War had helped refocus the BEF from being a Victorian to a Modern Army See Spencer Jones. *From Boer War to World War: Tactical Reform of the British Army, 1902-1914.* (Oklahoma, University of Oklahoma Press, 2013).
67 The War Office, *Report of the Committee on the Lessons of the Great War* (London. HMSO, 1932) p. 8. Tim. Travers, *The Killing Ground* (Barnsley. Pen & Sword, [1987] 2003), pp. 53-54
68 For an examination of the preparations which Britain undertook to prepare for war see J. Gooch, *The Plans of War. The General Staff and British Military Strategy, 1900-1916* (New York, John Wiley and Son Inc, 1974).

carried out without the modern accoutrements of war. He even suggested that the Army in Southern India had undertaken no manœuvres at all.[69] Unlike the BEF, which had gained some experience of large troop manoeuvres and the coordination of infantry and artillery during the Second Boer War, the Indian Army, as a whole, had little or no knowledge of the type of large-scale operations in which it was about to take part.[70]

However, this view was not held by all such as George Nathaniel Curzon, Marquess of Kedleston, who was Viceroy for India between 1899-1905. Curzon was born in 1859 and became Assistant Private Secretary to Lord Salisbury in 1885 and the following year entered Parliament as Member for Southport in South-West Lancashire.[4] His maiden speech, which was chiefly an attack on home rule and Irish nationalism, was regarded in much the same way as his oratory at the Oxford Union: brilliant and eloquent but also presumptuous and rather too self-assured. He was Under-Secretary of State for India in 1891–92 and Under-Secretary of State for Foreign Affairs in 1895–98. Curzon resigned as Viceroy of India in 1905 after a political dispute as to whom should be in charge of the Indian Army with the British military commander Lord Kitchener. During the First World War, Curzon served as leader of the House of Lords and a member of the War Cabinet and he still regarded himself as something of an authority in military matters. In his introduction to Merewether and Smith's *The Indian Corps*, the ex-Viceroy argued that it was a mistake to think that the Indian Army was' raised, trained and equipped for service in India alone or on its frontiers and that the call for external warfare was therefore both novel and disconcerting.'[71]

He backed this claim by citing a number of instances where the Indian Army did see active service abroad. His examples included the Ashanti Wars, the Boxer Rebellion and the Boer War. In doing so, however, Curzon mainly refers to the British Battalions which served as part of the Army in India which consisted of both British Battalions and Indian Battalions. The only genuine example of an Indian Battalion serving overseas was during the Boxer Rebellion of 1900 which had small resemblance to the fighting on the Western Front. Curzon also claims that the Indian Army's third function after defending the frontier and aiding the Civil power was to be 'ready at a moment's notice' for Imperial service in other parts of the globe.'[72] He also asserted that the Indian Army had 'long been one of the most important units in the scheme of British Imperial deference, always ready, of admirable efficiency and assured valour.'[73] It would seem that Curzon was again referring to the British Battalions which served

69 J.C. Wedgwood, *Separate Report*.
70 General Sir Ian Hamilton quoted in Maxwell, *Villiers-Stuart on the Frontier* (Edinburgh: Pentland Press, 1988), p. 155.
71 George Nathaniel Curzon, 'Introduction' in Merewether and Smith, *The Indian Corps*, p. ix.
72 Curzon, 'Introduction', Merewether and Smith, *The Indian Corps*, p. x.
73 Curzon, 'Introduction', Merewether and Smith, *The Indian Corps*, p. x.

George Nathaniel Curzon, Marquess of Kedleston, Viceroy for India 1899-1905.

in India as, although it was to prove that the Army in India was ready to deploy as will be shown from its ability to mobilise rapidly and it did prove its valour, there were many examples where its lack of efficiency became very clear. Perhaps behind his vigorous defence of the Indian Army lay the criticism of the Indian Battalions' operations in France and Curzon was attempting to make sure that the blame for poor performance would not be placed at his door since he had been a previous Viceroy.

Indeed Curzon's successor Hardinge believed that India was unlikely to be involved in a European war and his Liberal Party tendencies ensured that he kept military expenditure to a minimum.[74] General James Willcocks, who was to command the Indian Corps in France in 1914, argued that the Government of India regarded military expenditure to be of small importance.[75] The Mesopotamia Commission was later to agree, and devoted a lengthy section of its report to the 'Atmosphere of Economy up to the date of the War and the effect upon military preparation in India.'[76]

A prime example of this parsimony, coupled with socio-political thinking of the time, can be found in the way in which Indian Battalions were armed. The principle seemed to have been to supply the Indians with weapons inferior to those used by the British troops but superior to those used by the hostile tribes against which they fought on the Frontier. This not only reduced costs but also ensured that the British troops stationed in India always had weapon superiority in case there was a repetition of the events of 1857. In addition, heavy artillery was never entrusted to Indians but always operated by British Battalions. In fairness the mountain artillery which was the backbone of the Indian Army was skilfully used and most suitable for the Frontier warfare in which it was engaged but it became quickly obvious that it was unsuitable for use on the European battlefield and, as the War Office as to discover, difficult to replace without the help of Indian armament factories.

The fact that Britain turned to the subcontinent for help was considered by some as a very risky gamble. Sending Indian troops to fight on the Western Front was 'a very hazardous experiment' since the concentration of the fighting would test the mettle of British soldiers let alone his inferior Indian counterpart.[77] The desperate situation which Britain found itself after its declaration of war on Germany led it to violate an agreement amongst the European powers not to use colonial troops against 'white' units in a European war. Many feared the spectre of miscegenation between natives and white women who would find the natives exotic, erotic and irresistible.[78] Such fears grew considerably when wounded Indian soldiers were sent to convalesce in Britain, which is one reason why they were segregated and treated separately from the British wounded.[79] The families of Sepoys serving in France, especially the wives, were also worried about the temptations which their husbands and sons would face. In some cases this was a justified fear: 'I have heard about your amours with French women and how the officers forbid it.'[80]

74 Briton C. Busch, *Hardinge of Penshurst* (Hamden: Archon, 1980), p. 237.
75 James W. Willcocks, *With the Indians,* p. 4.
76 BL IOR/L/PS/20/57 *Mesopotamia Commission*, Section D Para. 38, p. 105.
77 Merewether and Frederick Smith, *The Indian Corps,* p. 479.
78 Phillipa Levine, *Prostitution, Race and Politics. Policing Venereal Disease in the British Empire* (New York, Routledge, 2003) p. 161.
79 Levine, *Prostitution,* Chapter 6.
80 Farrier Major Khan to Walid Mahomed Khan, 16th Lancers serving in France Quoted in Kant, *If I die here …* p. 46.

A further reluctance to dispatch Indian troops to France by some observers of the subcontinent was linked to the role of the Indian Army in policing the country. With so many troops out of the India and Britain occupied with a European war, would the opponents of British rule seize the opportunity to rebel? The spectre of the Great Mutiny loomed large in the minds of the Military and political leaders of the day but the thought of the 'contemptible little army' crossing bayonets with the German military machine made the gamble seem the only option. So vital was the Indian Army to Britain that Field Marshal Kitchener, having set out his plans for the rapid recruitment of Britons at the beginning of the War, told Marshals Joffre and Foche that, 'On 1 July 1915 you will have a million British soldiers in France. Before that date you will have practically none.'[81]

In fact many Indian nationalists were in favour of the subcontinent playing a part in the War. They believed that it would offer India bargaining power in demanding greater freedom from Britain. Rather than independence, what was hoped for was Home Rule with a similar government structure to that of Britain's dominions of Canada and Australia. As the Congress Party's leader, Bal Gangadhar Tilak, said, "Purchase war debentures but look at them as title deeds of Home Rule". Things did improve, in 1917, the Secretary of State for India, Edwin Montagu, declared that British policy in India was now aimed at increasing Indians in every branch of the administration, and gradually developing self-governing institutions, with a view to eventually producing a responsible government in India becoming an integral part of the British Empire. His intentions were embodied in the 1919 Government of India Act, planned after a lengthy visit to India in 1917-18. Unfortunately, the Act produced a violent reaction in the sub-continent but later Montagu's approach resulted in a period of calm

Aware of these complexities Britain's determination to accommodate the various religious and other Indian practices was to form an important part of Sepoys' material conditions of service or *Rizzat*[82] and significantly impacted upon the Indian Army's organisation making the work of the Indian Quartermaster's Department, charged with its supply, much more complicated than his British counterpart.[83]

It also caused further complications since Indian Battalions might consist of men of a single class, or ethnic group, such as the Gurkhas or, alternatively, of Companies of mixed classes; each with different requirements. For example, 57th (Wilde's) Rifles was made up of companies of Sikhs, Dogras, Pathans and Punjabi Musulmans.[84] Whilst these arrangements were thought to prevent classes combining in revolt, it caused command issues since it was thought that a man of one ethnic group could

81 Kitchener Quoted in John Pollock, *Kitchener: the Road to Omdurman* (London: Constable 1998) p. 413

82 Stanley, *Die in Battle*, p. 26

83 Nicholas. Gardner, 'British Prestige and the Mesopotamia Campaign, 1914–1916' in *The Historian*, Vol. 77, Issue 2, Summer, 2015, p. 269

84 Contemporary term for Moslems

not be put in charge of those of another. This practice prevented a unified system of promotion and also required Battalions to have different diets. It has been suggested, however, that the division created between Sepoys of different classes was often reduced by their close association in the army. Men saw themselves as comrades rather than from different classes.[85] Though important at the War's beginning, the 'Martial Race Theory' became less tenable as the War progressed and the need for recruits increased

85 Mason, *A Matter of Honour*, p. 361

2

The Ferozepore Brigade

The Ferozepore Brigade was created in late 1904 as one of the many reforms undertaken by Kitchener, when he was Commander in Chief, India.[1] and its first commander was Major General Walter Kitchener, the C-in-C's brother who had been recently made a Companion of the Order of the Bath for his services in South Africa. Walter left India to become Governor and C-in-C of Bermuda in 1908.[2] By 1914 The Ferozepore Brigade was part of the 3rd (Lahore) Division which consisted of the Ferozepore Brigade, the Jullundur Brigade which was based at Dalhousie the Sirhind Brigade, based at Kasauli, and the Ambala Cavalry Brigade based at Ambala. This Division was part of the Northern Army of India and had its headquarters at Dalhousie.[3] It was commanded by Lieutenant General Henry Buckley Burlton Watkins CB, who had entered the Indian Army in 1878 and had seen extensive service in Afghanistan and had been part of the Tochi Field Force in 1897-98 as a Deputy Assistant Adjutant General of the 1st Brigade and also in the Bazaar Valley Field Force of 1908 during which he had commanded the 3rd Brigade which had been held in reserve. Both campaigns were commanded by James Willcocks. Watkins had also served as Deputy Secretary in the Military Department of the Government of India. and was created a Companion of the Bath in the Birthday Honours of June 1906.[4]

The Ferozepore Brigade, part of the Lahore Division, was commanded in 1914 by Brigadier General Raleigh Gilbert Egerton CB. Egerton had fought in no less than six Indian Campaigns[5] and was described as a 'die-hard cavalry man'. He held the belief that the cavalry troopers had superior intellect when compared with those

1 Henceforth C-in-C.
2 Walter died as a result of complications after an operation for appendicitis operation. See *The New York Times*, 8 March 1912.
3 War Office, *The Monthly Army List* (London, 31 July 1914) p. 70.
4 David Snape,
5 Hazara Expedition in 1888, the Isazai Expedition in 1892, Waziristan Campaign 1894 and 1895. Chitral Campaign in 1895 and the Dongola Campaign in 1896

Major General Henry Buckley Burlton Watkins CB Commander of the Lahore Division.

Cap Badge of the 1st Battalion Connaught Rangers.

who were in charge of mechanical transport.[6] As was the custom with Indian Army Brigades, Egerton's Ferozepore Brigade included a British Regular Army Battalion on a 14-year tour and three Indian Battalions.[7]

The 1st Battalion Connaught Rangers, the British Regular Army battalion in the Ferozepore Brigade, was created by an amalgamation of the 88th Battalion of Foot (Connaught Rangers) and the 94th Battalion of Foot. The 88th had been deployed to India in 1857 in response to the Indian Mutiny and served there until 1870. After service in South Africa in 1877, during which the Battalion saw action in the 9th Xhosa War and in the Anglo-Zulu War, it returned to India in 1879.

The 94th Battalion of Foot embarked for South Africa in spring 1879 and saw action at the Battle of Ulundi in July of that year. The Battalion then marched into the Transvaal and took part in Sir Garnet Wolseley's successful attack on

6 Lord Anglesey, *A History of the British Cavalry: Volume 8: 1816-1919 The Western Front* (Barnsley, Pen and Sword, 1995) p. 318.

7 1st Connaught Rangers; 9th Bhopal Infantry; 57th Wilde's Rifles (Frontier Force) and 129th The (Duke of Connaught's) Baluchis.

Sekhukhune's stronghold on 28 November 1879. The Battalion also saw service in the First Boer War.

Newly amalgamated, the 1st Battalion, Connaught Rangers, recruited mainly in the west of Ireland and saw extensive service in the Second Boer War fighting at Colenso, Spion Kop and Tugela Heights before finally returning to India in 1903. In 1914 it was commanded by Major General Hurdis Secundus Lalande Ravenshaw, who had been commissioned into the East Yorkshire Battalion in December 1888. Seeking action, in August 1890 Ravenshaw transferred to the Devonshire Battalion which was sent to India where he served in the Chitral Relief Column in 1895, the Malakand Campaign of 1897 and the Tirah Campaign of 1897-98. He also saw action in the Second Boer War and was involved in the Relief of Ladysmith. On his return to England in 1902 Ravenshaw was made Adjutant of The Military College, Sandhurst, a post which he occupied until 1907. At the outbreak of the War, Ravenshaw was brought out of semi-retirement at the age of 63 to command the Connaught Rangers.

The 9th Bhopal Infantry had been created from the Bhopal Battalion as part of the Kitchener Indian Army Reforms in 1903. Its Colonel in Chief in 1914 was the Nawab of Bhopal, Hajjah Nawab Begum Dame Sultan Jahan, who could trace her family line back to the time of the Moghul empire. The Battalion was divided into 'Class Companies' which meant that Sepoys of a similar ethnicity and religion were grouped together into individual Companies. Other Battalions in the Indian Army were made up of solely one Class or ethnic group. The 9th Bhopal Infantry comprised of two Companies of Sikhs,[8] two of Rajputs,[9] two of Brahmans[10] and two of Musalmans. This structure reflected the composition of the Indian Army as being 'a mosaic of ethnic groups.'[11] One purpose of this arrangement was to improve morale within the Companies or Battalions as well as the *esprit de corps* of each individual fighting unit. The structure of the 9th Bhopal Infantry also reflected the erroneous *Martial Race Theory* which proposed that certain Indian ethnic groups were more military in character than others and it was from the former that volunteers were mainly recruited. The latter were regarded as possessing few soldierly qualities but, the Theory promoted those races, such as the Gurkha, Punjabi Moslems and Pathans, which had stayed loyal during the Great Mutiny as potential recruits. The 9th Bhopal Infantry was made up of the descendants of men who had stayed loyal to the British in 1857 and was thus a paradigm for the Indian Army. In 1914 three quarters of the Infantry in the Indian Army came from these ethnic groups. The *Martial Race Theory* was simply a self-fulfilling prophecy which, even before the outbreak of the War, was being questioned but, since it was a significant feature in the Indian Army in 1914, it cannot be ignored.

8 Followers of the teaching of Guru Nanak from the Punjab.
9 Hindus from northern and western India.
10 High Class Hindus.
11 DeWitt C. Ellinwood, 'Ethnic Aspects of the Indian Army in World War 1', in Indian History Congress, *Proceedings of the Indian History Congress* (1978), Vol. 39, Volume I pp. 823.

However war-like some Indian soldiers were thought to be, it was assumed that they would perform less well than Battalions of the British Regular Army alongside which they served.[12] Such lack of expectation affected the Indian Army's deployment and meant they were held back when the going became increasingly hard. Ian Hamilton, whose command included the Indian Expeditionary Force (IEFG) in Gallipoli, had previously, and perhaps typically, underestimated the abilities of Indian soldiers to use modern sophisticated weaponry and argued that a Sepoy 'would never be able to use the back sight of his rifle or learn numeric figures'; a perfect example of the tendency to underestimate the Sepoys' capabilities. Given this belief, it is a credit to the Indian Army's personnel that it was able to adapt to industrial warfare as well as they did.[13]

Class Companies may enable members of different Indian ethnic groups to serve within the same Battalion, but they did cause considerable difficulties for both for the command and the Quartermaster structures. The problem of providing food for Indian troops was illustrated in a Memorandum from the Headquarters Section of the Meerut Division produced in November 1914.[14] The Memorandum complained that food was packed into trains for the whole Division and not separated for each Brigade. The dietary requirements of different Classes varied, and a considerable amount of time had to be spent separating the individual Division's requirements from the bulk of supplies. The Memorandum uses the problem of 'bread' as an example. There were three types of bread consumed by the different Battalions in the Meerut Brigade. Bread, Atta flour which was made into Chapatis and biscuits. In the case of Meerut Division, most of its Battalions required Atta, three Battalions needed rations which composed of half bread and half Atta, one Battalion only wanted biscuit. The Memorandum concluded that, when the division was in action with little time for cooking these arrangements had to be much improved.

British Officers, as has been explained, were expected to be fluent in Urdu which was 'the Indian Army's *lingua franca*'.[15] They were also expected to be competent in the specific languages spoken by their men. In a Class Company Battalion there could be two or three different languages. Officers spent much of their spare time with their men and developed personal relationships with them upon which the Indian Army depended. This close relationship could be a weakness. If such officers were killed or wounded and replaced by strangers who were unfamiliar with the men, the Indian soldiers might 'be utterly lost'.[16] Such a conclusion of the effects of the loss of British officers was described by Charles De Vere Townshend with reference the siege of Kut

12 Kent E. Calder, *The Sepoy* (London: John Murray, 1919), p. 104.
13 Robert. Maxwell, *Villiers-Stuart on the Frontier* (Edinburgh: The Pentland Press 1989), p. 155.
14 TNA WO 95/3932, Meerut Division, Headquarters Branches and Services, Adjutant and Quartermaster General, War Diary, Appendix 3, No. 10/3 Q. 11 November 1914.
15 Charles. Chevenix Trench, *The Indian Army and the King's Enemies 1900–1947* (London: Thames and Hudson, 1988) p. 15.
16 Trench, *The Indian Army*, p. 15.

during the Mesopotamia Campaign; 'the loss of British Regular officers endangered the defence of Kut'.[17] Field Marshal Lord Roberts, a hero of British India and one of the advocates of the *Martial Race Theory* described it quite succinctly shortly before his death which was caused by pneumonia after inspecting Indian troops in France. 'No one had a higher regard for them [the Sepoy] than I have, but they have their limits ... with British officers they fight splendidly, without them they cannot do much.'[18]

Modern historians such as Omissi[19] and Stanley[20] have argued that the bond between the Sepoy and his British Officers was not as significant as the latter would have liked to believe. The fact that so many British officers were killed, and the Sepoys continued to fight under the command of their V.C.O.s would suggest that that Omissi and Stanley are, at the very least, partially correct. Despite the mutual respect between officers and Sepoys, it probably was difficult for the former to really appreciate the true feelings of the latter. The view that Indian soldiers were somehow more unreliable and less confident than their British equivalent was a product of the belief that Sepoys were lacking in moral fibre even if they were from the martial races. For example, until 1911 Indians could not be awarded the Victoria Cross for acts of bravery similar to those of their British counterparts which suggests that even their most courageous deeds were not believed comparable to those of British soldiers.

Badge of the 9th Bhopal Infantry.

In August 1914, the 9th Bhopal Infantry, nicknamed *The Bo-Peeps,* and commanded by Lieutenant Colonel Charles Francis Dobbie, was stationed at Faizabad, having returned the previous month from service in Rangoon, Burma. Dobbie, who had initially been commissioned in the Yorkshire Light Infantry, had served with the Battalion for many years but was a sick man even before the Battalion was ordered to be mobilised, in spite of which, he was determined to lead his men into action. His second in command was Lieutenant Colonel Henry Lawrence Anderson[21] who had been recently promoted. Dobie and Anderson seemed to have worked closely together sharing command responsibilities.

17 E. Latter, 'The Indian Army', *Journal of the Society for Army Historical research*, Vol. LXXII, No. 291, Autumn 1994, p. 170.
18 Field Marshal Lord Roberts quoted in James W. Willcocks, *The Romance of Soldiering and Sport* (London: Cassell, 1925) pp. 282-283.
19 David Omissi (ed.), *Indian Voices of the Great War* (London: Viking 2014, [1999]), p. 20. *The Sepoy and the Raj*, p. 106.
20 Peter Stanley, Die *in Battle Do not Despair*; *the Indians in Gallipoli 1915* (Solihull: Helion & Co., 2015), pp. 32-33.
21 Anderson, who had been born in Lucknow, had first been commissioned in the Yorkshire Light Infantry in August 1888 and joined the Indian Army in April 1890. Lewis A. Clutterbuck et al, *The Bond of Sacrifice: Biographical record of all British officers who fell in the Great War, Vol. 1* (London: Anglo-African Publishing Contractors, 1916), p. 1.

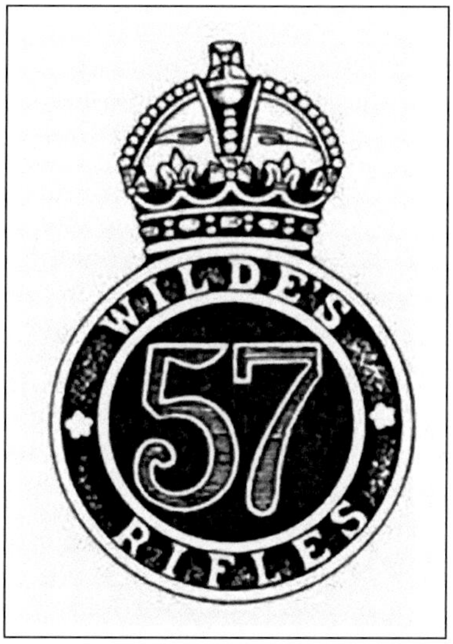

Cap Badge of the 57th (Wilde's) Rifles Frontier Force.

The 57th (Wilde's) Rifles (Frontier Force) was formed from the 4th Battalion of Punjab Infantry which had distinguished itself in the attacks on Delhi and Lucknow during the Indian Mutiny in 1857. It also earned the first Indian Army's overseas battle honour in 1900 when it helped quell the Boxer rebellion in China. In 1903 the 4th became the 57th (Wilde's) Rifles (Frontier Force) as a result of the Kitchener Reforms. Like the 9th Bhopal Battalion, the 57th Wilde's Rifles was also a 'Class Company' Battalion and consisted of two Companies of Sikhs, two of Dogras,[22] two of Punjabi Musalmans and two of Afridi Pathans.[23] Stationed at Ferozepore in 1914 it was commanded by Lieutenant Colonel Frederick William Barton Gray, who, like the other Battalion commanders, had seen much active service in campaigns such as Waziristan in 1895, the Mohmand Campaign in 1898, for which he had been mentioned in despatches, and China in 1900

The Brigade Commander, Brigadier General Egerton, inspected the Battalion in 1914 and his conclusions were as follows:[24]

Drill	Very Much Improved
Manoeuvre	Very Satisfactory
Physical Training	Very Satisfactory
Signalling	Satisfactory
Musketry	Requires Attention
Discipline and Conduct	Very Good
Arms and Equipment	The rifles are very old and well cared for. Equipment complete and serviceable.
Health	Good
Recruits	Well Selected
Personnel	Very Satisfactory
Interior Economy	Very efficiently maintained. Due economy is exercised with regards to recruits' outfits.
General Efficiency	The general standard of efficiency is quite satisfactory, and the Battalion is fit for service.

22 From the country between the Punjab and Kashmir.
23 From the area of the Khyber Pass.
24 IOR/L/MIL/7/17023: Confidential Review Reports on Indian Army Units 1913-1924.

General James Willcocks, describe the 57th has having exceptionally good officers and a fine class of Indian officers and men all round.[25]

The Badge of the Duke of Connaughts 129th Baluchis.

The 129th The Duke of Connaught's Own (D.O.C) Baluchis, like the other two Indian Battalions in the Ferozepore Brigade, owed its title to the Army nomenclature reforms in 1903 when all Bombay Units added 100 to their designation. It had been originally raised as the Baluch Battalion in 1846 and had changed its name on no less than nine occasions. In 1883 Prince Arthur, the Duke of Connaught, the third son of Queen Victoria, was appointed its Colonel in Chief which was the origin of its title. Another Class Company Battalion, the 129th Baluchis consisted of two Companies of Punjabi Musalmans, three Companies of Masuds and three Companies of other Pathans. The C-in-C India, O'Moore Creagh, who had been a previous commanding officer of the Battalion, became its Colonel in Chief in 1912. In 1914 it was stationed at Ferozepore and commanded by Lieutenant Colonel William Melvill Southey. As a young officer Southey was busy collecting both experience and certificates. He gained qualifications in Army Signalling, a certificate in musketry, and a certificate of proficiency in Pashtu. He saw service in Uganda in 1898-1899, during which Campaign he was mentioned in despatches, the Somaliland Campaign in 1908-1910 and so had experienced beyond the shores of India. In late January 1914, the Battalion was also inspected by Brigadier General Egerton, the Brigade Commander and his assessment was as follows:[26]

Turn Out	Smart
Drill	Very Satisfactory
Manoeuvre	Very Satisfactory
Interior Economy	Very Satisfactory. Due economy is practised as regards recruits' outfits
General Efficiency	The instruction and training of the Battalion are very carefully carried out, with most satisfactory results in all respects, Discipline is well maintained, and the health of the men is very good. Battalion is fit for service.

25 Willcocks, *With the Indians*, p. 34.
26 IOR/L/MIL/7/17023: *Confidential Review Reports on Indian Army Units 1913–1924.*

3

Mobilisation: August – September 1914

Herbert Asquith, the British Prime Minister at the outbreak of the First World War, sealed the Indian Army's fate for the next four years when, he announced that Britain was entering a struggle which required not only the resources of the United Kingdom but that of the vast Empire, of which it was the centre, must also be 'thrown into the scale'.[1]

The Indian Army's normal role in defending outbreaks of rebellion in the distant parts of the subcontinent required rapid mobilisation as well as the ability to move quickly to the scene of the conflict.[2] Although this new fight was thousands of miles away, the principle was the same. The orders for mobilisation were received by the Indian Expeditionary Force A, which would become known as the Indian Corps at 1100 hours on 8 August 1914.[3] However, the 129th Baluchis were informed that war with Germany had been declared on 6 August, or 'broken out' as the Battalion War Diary described it.[4] It is interesting that the *'Clear the Line'* Cypher Message which contained the Order indicates that although the procedure for mobilisation was to follow the plan set out in 1913, it was also to include changes which had been communicated as recently as 5 August 1914. Clearly, the Indian Army Staff anticipated that the declaration of War would be made, and that India would be involved.

The *'Clear the Line'* Message was followed by a telegram on 11 August which detailed arrangements for both veterinary and hospital organisation.[5] Hospitals were to be of

1 Asquith address to the House of Commons quoted in John A. Spender and Cyril Asquith, *Life of Herbert Henry Asquith, Vol. 2* (London: Hutchinson 1932), pp. 114-115.
2 Keith Jeffrey, 'An English Barrack in the Oriental Seas? India in the aftermath of the First World War', in *Modern Asian Studies,* Vol. 15: 3 1989, p. 369.
3 TNA WO 95/3923: 3 Indian (Ferozepore) Division, Infantry Brigade, 1st Battalion Connaught Rangers War Diary, 8 August 1914.
4 TNA WO 95/3924: 3 Indian (Ferozepore) Division, Infantry Brigade, 129th (D.C.O.) Baluchis War Diary, 6 August 1914.
5 TNA WO 95/3911: Telegram No, 959/1, From General Officer Commanding to General Officers Commanding 3rd Division, 11 August 1914.

Herbert Henry Asquith: Prime Minister of Great Britain, 1908-16.

two types; Section Hospitals with 100 beds and General Hospitals of 500 beds. There would also be two X Ray Sections transferred from the Dehra Dun Brigade. The telegram also addressed the problem of transport and stated that only first line transport would accompany the Force but additionally, there would be mules which were part of the Maxim Gun Sections. Army carts essential for the transportation of baggage would be distributed at the port of embarkation.

Every Battalion in the Indian Army had large numbers of followers whose job it was to carry out the menial tasks prohibited to Sowars or Sepoys because of their religion or assumed superior status.[6] Followers included sweepers, cooks, watercarriers, grooms, and smiths. They were meant to serve in the rear but the duties of some, such as the water carriers, brought them to the Front and, as can be seen on the memorials at Neuve Chapelle and Basra, many perished in war. The 1st Indian Cavalry Division, for example, had 1,551 followers divided into two categories: public and private. The public followers were on the payroll of the Division and those designated private were employed by officers as personal servants. These men were vital to the performance of the Indian Army, but they were extra mouths to feed and bodies to transport though their contribution to its fighting performance may have been slight. However, they were an important feature of the Indian Army as is conveyed in Kipling's poem *Gunga Din* which describes the life of a follower, whose principal task was to devotedly bring water to soldiers even at the height of battle:

Though I've belted you and flayed you,
By the livin' Gawd that made you,
You're a better man than I am, Gunga Din![7]

Sir Beauchamp Duff, C-in-C Indian Army, although more of an administrator than an experienced warrior, was conscious of the need both for followers to be included in the mobilisation but also the necessity of restricting their numbers, ordered that none of the British Battalions should take them and that the number of Batmen, the British officers' personal servants, should be reduced to one each. In addition, officers were only allowed two chargers. Men were to be issued with one blanket and the Battalions should take their tents since, at the very least, these would be required to accommodate the men at the port of embarkation. The British infantry and cavalry Battalions were to be issued with 300 rounds of ammunition per man whilst the Indian units would be only allotted 200 rounds, but additional ammunition would be distributed at the ports of embarkation. Finally, Staff officers concerned with mobilisation and equipment were informed that they did not need, as was the usual custom, to prepay for the telegrams they were ordered to send by their Divisional Commanders.

6 Sowar = Cavalry trooper.
7 Rudy*ard Kipling's Verse* (Toronto: Copp Clark Ltd, 1919), p. 806.

General Sir Beauchamp Duff, C-in-C India 1913-17.

The 3rd (Ferozepore) Division War Diary notes that the mobilisation orders were received by telephone, a further indication of the need for a rapid response. Detailed orders were not received until 11th August by the Baluchis,[8] Major General Townshend expressed surprise at such urgency, since the two Commanders-in-Chief immediately before the war had lacked so much dynamism.[9] In contrast, Johnson correctly points out that the pre-war plan for war mobilisation worked extremely well.[10] The Indian Battalions, in addition to mobilising, undertook energetic recruiting in order to provide a future ten percent reserve as per the Mobilisation Plan.[11] The 4th (Prince Albert Victor's) Rajputs which was also expected to be part the Ferozepore Brigade in time of war was not, however, directed to mobilise.[12] This was possibly because it was stationed at Multan, over 300 kilometres from Ferozepore. Its place was taken by the 9th Bhopal Infantry. Beauchamp Duff was assisted in the mammoth task by two experienced officers, Percy Lake and George Fitzpatrick.

Lake had followed Haig and as Chief of the Indian Army General Staff in 1912 and brought extensive combat and administrative experience to his role of modernising the Indian General Staff. Lake had held a number of posts including Chief of the General Staff in Canada and General Officer Commanding the 7th Indian Division. Later in the War, Lake was to relieve General John Nixon for his failure to relieve the siege of Kut but was also to be removed for his own failure to do so.

George Fitzpatrick, an Anglo-Canadian who served as Director of Military Operations in India from 1914 to 1916 when he succeeded Lake as Chief of the General Staff. Inspite of the expertise which Lake and Kirkpatrick brought to the

8 TNA WO 95/3924 3 Indian (Ferozepore) Division, Infantry Brigade 129 (D.C.O.) Baluchis War Diary, 6 August 1914.
9 Major General Charles Townshend, quoted in Stanley, *Die in Battle. Do Not Despair*, p. 30. He was referring to O'Moore Creagh and Beauchamp Duff.
10 Johnson, *"I shall die arms in hand"*, p. 111.
11 TNA WO 95/3924: 129 (D.C.O.) Baluchis War Diary, August 1914.
12 TNA WO 95/3922: 3 Indian (Lahore) Division, 7 (Ferozepore) Infantry Brigade, Brigade Headquarters War Diary, 8 August 1914.

George V: The King Emperor.

task, there were some problems with mobilisation caused by the bureaucracy which bedevilled much of the Indian Army's existence; but in this it was not unique.[13] For example, the 9th Bhopal Infantry found it difficult to dispatch the detailed messages regarding the mobilisation as it was a Sunday and the local Postmaster was ' quite incapable of any helpful action.'[14] Many Sepoys were on leave in August 1914 and the Battalion Diary described how men, who were in the Punjab, were ordered to return but the problems with the Postal Services seems to have delayed their arrival. The 9th felt obliged to report the problem to Division when it was asked for a progress report and the Diary records men consequently arriving in dribs and drabs for three days.[15]

The 9th Bhopal Infantry left their base at Faizabad with 800 other ranks, 8 British Officers and 18 V.C.O.s and 39 Followers at 1845 hours on 15 August and arrived at Karachi at 1000 hours on August 19 having been joined on the way by an additional 114 soldiers of various kinds. Egerton was keen to see the quality of the men who were to serve under him and inspected the Battalion on 21 August.

On 22 August, in order to ensure that the Indian Army knew why they were fighting, Egerton ordered that both British and Indian Battalions, officers and men alike, were informed of the messages of King George V and Field Marshal Kitchener which stressed that it was the duty of the Army to fight for the Empire and to support its Belgian and French Allies. Kitchener, always conscious of the need to maintain soldiers' morals, reminded them that they should be 'invariably considerate, courteous and kind,' during their service abroad.[16] On the 23 August half of the Bhopals, together with the 129th Baluchis, were ordered to travel to Keamari Port, Karachi, and prepare to embark on the SS *Ellenga* which was owned by the British India Steam Navigation Company. The train journey of the two double Companies of the Bhopals to the port was not without incident. A Sepoy, Kale Khan, fell from the train sustaining injuries and had to be replaced. There were a number of other examples of men being injured or falling sick such as that of Naik Asl Baiz [17] who contracted pneumonia and requiring to be replaced by men from other Battalions in order to ensure that the embarking force was at maximum strength.[18] In Naik Baiz case, his replacement came from the 127th Baluchis which had previously provided the 129th with a double company to bring it up to strength. This is an example of the Indian Army linking Battalions and was to prove useful later in the War when casualty replacements were required.

13 Cuthbert A.L. Graham, *A History of Indian Mountain Artillery* (Aldershot, Gale and Poldon 1957) p. 127.
14 TNA WO 95/3923, 3 Indian (Lahore) Division, 7 (Ferozepore) Infantry Brigade 9th Battalion Bhopal Infantry War Diary, 9 August 1914.
15 TNA WO 95/3923: 3 Indian (Lahore) Division, 7 (Ferozepore) Infantry Brigade 9th Battalion Bhopal Infantry, War Diary, 10 August 1914.
16 *Sind Gazette*, 17 August 1914, Reuters Telegrams.
17 Naik = Corporal.
18 TNA WO 95/3924: 3 Indian (Lahore) Division, 7 (Ferozepore) Infantry Brigade, 9th Battalion Bhopal Infantry War Diary, 23 August 1914.

As with the other units of the Brigade, the 129th Baluchis received general mobilisation orders on 8 August which instructed the Battalion to recall those men on furlough. The war diarist expressed a little frustration by stating that although orders to mobilise was received on the 8th, detailed instructions as what to do were not received until the 11th, thus delaying the procedure by three days. The Battalion was also instructed to call in all its reservists and also required to submit the names of all British Officers who were on leave but not in India to the Divisional Headquarters. The reason why these names were required would soon become obvious to the Indian Army for when war was declared, as has previously described, British Indian Officers in Britain, either on leave or training, were retained by the Home Army. By asking for details of these men the Army discovered the additional number of officers who would be available.

The 129th was understrength and needed to rapidly attempt to reach its 'Peace time' strength of 816 and on 10 August a further 20 recruits were attested; a ceremony during which newly trained recruits swore allegiance to the Indian Government. Further recruiting parties were despatched and preparations were put in place to train new men. Again, the war diarist points out that the fact that the Battalion was made up of different Class Companies and this made recruiting more difficult since the Recruiting Officers must be aware into which Company a recruit would be placed according to his class and recruiting could not be a case of 'come one come all'. The outbreak of cholera at the Kohat Recruiting Centre in the Khyber District further complicated matters and, consequently, there was some confusion as to where the recruits from Kohat were to assemble. The Diary of the 129th gives a genuine feel of the energy and excitement which was required in this initial phase of mobilisation and, not surprisingly, hints at some disorganisation as the Battalion moved to its wartime status.

A Lance Naik of the 129th (DOC) Baluchis in Parade Dress 1911.

The five officers from the Connaught Rangers headquarters, who were on

local leave in India including Brigadier General Egerton and the Brigade Major, Captain Sangster, were immediately recalled; two of whom arrived back on the following day. By the afternoon of the 9 August, men were being medically examined and machine gun mules and officers' chargers were checked. The Medical Officer (MO), Captain John Boyd, recorded that the men of the Connaught Rangers were told that preference for serving overseas would be given to those men who had been recently inoculated against enteric fever as well all those who had volunteered.[19] An army may march on its stomach, but the officers of the Connaught Rangers knew that that the Battalion would also extensively march on its feet and the Rangers' boots were fitted with nails and metal toe plates. Various other preparations were made and by 15 August, the seventh day of mobilisation, the Battalion was ready. Fifteen officers and 878 other ranks of the Connaught Rangers entrained on 17 August, bound for Karachi. Such had been the intensity of the unusual preparations, ten men had to be left at Ferozepore suffering from severe heat stroke through over exertion in the sun: three of these subsequently died.

The War Diary of the 57th (Wilde's) Rifles (Frontier Force) tells us little about the preparations to leave Ferozepore which it did on 21 August by special train arriving in Karachi on Sunday 23 August 'without special incident'.[20] Lieutenant Colonel Gray must have been very satisfied to receive a compliment from the G.O.C who inspected them on their arrival. The Battalion had arrived at Karachi with 8 British Officers, 17 Indian Officers and 719 rank and file. In addition, there was a total of 24 Public or Battalion followers, 18 private followers including two which were described as manservants. The Battalion brought with it 18 Officers' Chargers and 12 Machine Gun mules. Its War Diary also recorded that the Medical Officer accompanying the Battalion was Captain Kanwar Indarjit Singh of the Indian Medical Service (IMS). IMS doctors were both British and Indian but the latter were in the minority.[21] The IMS was the only branch of the Indian Army where Indian officers held British Army Commissions. Candidates for entry into the IMS in 1911 had to be in possession of a registrable medical qualification and certificate of attendance at a course in ophthalmology of at least three months' duration. On arrival in France the IMS not only treated the sick and wounded but also were responsible to ensuring drinking water was safe, the management of trench latrines, monitoring sites designated for the slaughtering of animals and clearing woods which had been fouled by poilus.[22] They were particularly concerned with the exposure of Sepoys to unfamiliar western diseases

19 TNA WO 95/3923: 3 Indian (Lahore) Division, 7 (Ferozepore) Infantry Brigade War Diary 1st Connaught Rangers Medical Officer War Diary, 8 August 1914.

20 TNA WO 95/3923: 3 Indian (Lahore) Division, 7 (Ferozepore) Infantry Brigade, 57th Wilde's Rifles 23 August to 1 September 1914 War Diary, 23 August 1914.

21 Merewether and Frederick Smith, *The Indian Corps*, p.494

22 TNA WO 95/3917: 3 Indian (Lahore) Division, Headquarters Branches and Services, Royal Army Medical Services Assistant Director Medical Services, War Diary, 3 October 1914. (Poilu = French infantryman).

such as mumps and, in particular, measles against which the troops had no immunity. They also were occupied in treating malaria and enteric fever which had followed the troops from India.[23] Captain Singh, as will be recorded later. well deserves the mention he received. Later that day Jemadar Ibrahim arrived with a detachment of 80 other ranks and three additional Followers which brought the Rifles' numbers up to their war time strength together with the required additional ten per cent reserve.

Preparations were in hand to transport the Indian Expeditionary Force to Europe from the ports of Bombay and Karachi and the officer responsible for the mammoth undertaking was Rear Admiral Richard H. Pierse who had been appointed C-in-C, East Indies Station in 1913.

Peirse had joined the Royal Navy in 1873 and, in 1885, had developed a new concept which was to become the fire-control system used in all ships with large guns. Promoted to Captain in 1900, he commanded HMS *Dido* during the Second Boer War. Peirse was appointed C-in-C East Indies Station in 1913 and then promoted to Vice Admiral in October 1914, During the First World War he took part in the attack on Smyrna in 1915, in which he outgunned the Turkish Fleet. He continued in his role on the East Indies Station until December 1915. A meticulous planner, Pierse and his staff produced an extremely detailed set of orders dictating how the IEF's convoys were to be conducted. They set out not only the dates of departure and nature of the convoy, which was made up of s 23 transports and the nine naval ships which would escort it, but it also dealt with details such as what to do if a man went overboard, how to react if there was fog, how to use semaphore and the code to use for morse messages by wireless.

By the evening of the 23 August the whole of the Ferozepore Brigade had arrived at Karachi and, according to the Brigade Headquarters' Diary, was ready to embark;[24] a truly remarkable feat of organisation in 15 days. The Connaught Rangers encamped at the Karachi Racecourse where further preparations were made for its departure which included the issue of three months' pay.[25] A number of men re-joined the Battalion at this point and this brought the Connaught's numbers up to 16 officers and 903 other ranks. The Connaughts embarked on the T.S.S. *Edavana,* another British India Steam Navigation Company vessel on which they were joined by the 1st Battalion Manchester Regiment which was part of the Jullundur Brigade. It was intended that they would be the first troops to embark from Karachi on 25 August as part of the

23 TNA WO 95/3917: Assistant Director Medical Services War Diary, 3 October 1914, TNA WO 95/ 3935: Assistant Director Medical Services War Diary, 25 October 1914, TNA WO 95/3917: Assistant Director Medical Services War Diary, Appendix XXX, January 1915.

24 TNA WO 95/3922: 3 Indian (Lahore) Division, 7 (Ferozepore) Infantry Brigade, Brigade Headquarters War Diary, 23 August 1914.

25 C.C. Jackson, G. D. Martin, & H. Smith, *History of the 4th Battalion 16th Punjab Regiment* (Aldershot, Gale & Polden Ltd, 1931) p. 37.

1st Division; 17 days after the order to mobilise.[26] This embarkation was not without delay, however. The first units of the Connaught's arrived at the docks at 1030 hours but the final contingent did not reach them until 2100 hours. During the intervening period the troops were left sitting on the dockside in the sun which resulted in several men reporting sick the following day. To make matters worse, the conditions on the *Edavana* were poor and insanitary. Initially, as well as the 1872 troops there were 30 head of cattle, described as being of inferior quality, and 400 sheep.[27] The latter were removed before the ship sailed which improved matters slightly. In addition the Machine Gun Section, consisting of 16 men, also left the ship but were then ordered to return before it embarked. The chaos continued when 120 sheep were reloaded on the *Edavana*. When the original herd of sheep had been removed, soldiers had occupied the space which they had vacated but the new woolly arrivals caused men and sheep to share the same space and they were forced to sleep side by side.[28] Although the initial mobilisation had gone very well because of experience and sound planning, the actual embarkation was not so smooth, probably since it was the first time it had be practised in these particular circumstances. Such were the concerns of the Connaught Rangers' Medical Officer that he prepared a special report about the unhealthy conditions on board. The Report was handed in when the ship arrived at Cairo; a military example of closing the gate too late. On 28 August, the ship moved to mid-stream to await the rest of the convoy

Read Admiral Richard Henry Peirse. Commander-in-Chief, East Indies Station.

The *Edavana* finally set sail at 1500 hours on 29 August and the Medical Officer's frustration continued to grow because the ship's bakers became so badly affected by seasickness that they were unable to produce a sufficient supply of good bread. When

26 TNA WO 95/3930: 7 Indian (Meerut) Division Headquarters. Branches and Services General Staff War Diary, 8 August 1914.

27 The *Edavana* was only licensed to carry 1,072 for voyages over 48 hours duration.

28 TNA WO 95/3923: Medical Officer's Diary, 29 August 1914.

the doctor suggested that biscuits be issued instead, he was told 'there were none on board'.[29] It was not until four days later that the bread situation, and that of the bakers, improved.

The *Edavana*, built in Glasgow by Barclay, Curle & Co. Ltd in 1911, left Karachi Docks on 29 August and joined a large convoy of seven other troopships which was escorted by R.I.M.S. *Northbrooke*; another Glasgow built vessel. No one on board the *Edavana*, even the senior officers, knew where the convoy was bound.[30] The men were ordered to wear their newly modified boots in order to prepare their feet for the conditions to come wherever that might be.

The War Diary of the Connaught Rangers says nothing about the eight-day sea voyage to Aden where the *Edavana* docked to load coal and water, The time it spent in Aden was very short and on the following day (8 September), the ship set off for Suez. This journey took five days and, on arrival at the port, the Battalion entrained to journey to Cairo where they were lodged in Abbessea Barracks. Here they were joined by their Commanding Officer, Colonel Ravenshaw who had come out of semi-retirement and who was accompanied by their Roman Catholic Chaplain, Reverend Father Frederick Peal who was described as 'a true type of Irish priest'.[31] Peal, also described as a' bearded elder chaplain',[32] would serve with the Connaught Rangers in Mesopotamia, and was later to produce a small book about his experiences entitled *War Jottings*.[33]

The Divisional War Diary is more informative with regard to the voyage. Division troops embarked from Karachi on 25 August aboard the SS *City of Glasgow* which had been built at Glasgow in 1906 and had a top speed of 11 knots.[34] The Convoy set course for the Kuria Muria Islands; a group of five islands in the Arabian Sea, close to the coast of Arabia which belonged to Great Britain but were a dependency of Aden. The islands were well known for the large amounts of guano which could be extracted and used as fertiliser. It seems, perhaps unsurprisingly, that there were few inhabitants on the islands and no indication of there being any resources for the convoy. It is probable that the islands were simply a rendezvous or catch-up point for the fleet which was made up of ships capable of different speeds. The sea was rough but there was another cause for concern. Radio messages had been detected from the German cruiser *Königsberg*, which was some 506 miles south of Bombay. Clearly there appeared to be a danger that the German navy might intercept the convoy and, on the 27 August, two days into the voyage, RMIS *Dufferin*, one of the convoy's escorts,

29 TNA WO 95/3923: Medical Officer's Diary, 29 August 1914.
30 Shrabrani Basu, *For King and Another Country: Indian Soldiers on the Western Front, 1914–18* (London: Bloomsbury Publishing, 2015) pp. 31-32.
31 Public Record Office Northern Ireland, McRory Papers, Diary Book 1, p. 59
32 Imperial War Museum Collection HU 81657, Connaught Rangers in Mesopotamia, 1914-
33 Fred Peal, *War Jottings* (Calcutta: Catholic Orphan Press, 1916).
34 The *City of Glasgow* was torpedoed and sank in September 1918 off the coast of Ireland.

'beat to quarters' indicating that it suspected enemy presence. As was the usual practice, orders were given for the convoy to scatter and each ship to make its own way. *The City of Glasgow,* however, was ordered to accompany the SS *Kirkfield,* since the latter was without a wireless. In behaving in this way the ships were following the instructions of Rear Admiral Pierse, which decreed that ships without wireless should pair with ones which had. The pair should then communicate between themselves by semaphore using a signal lamp. The *Dufferin* steamed off towards the east in strong winds and heavy seas; possibly in the hope of contacting a distant enemy.[35]

At 2000 hours on the following evening, the *City of Glasgow* received a new order from HMIS *Dufferin* which required it to change course, and to rendezvous 45 miles from the Kuria Murias. The two ships, *Dufferin* and *Kirkfield,* were faced with a strong headwind and heavy seas and missed the appointed rendezvous time with the *Dufferin* since they were 14 miles off course. However, at 2200 hours, the *City of Glasgow* reached the designated point and joined four ships from the convoy's 'Echelon A' which had sailed from Karachi as well as the eight ships which made up the 'Echelon B' which had sailed from Bombay and were being escorted by HMS *Swiftsure,* a pre-dreadnought battleship, and HMS *Duke of Edinburgh,* a cruiser. Both ships had participated earlier in the month in the pursuit of the German ships the *Goeben* and the *Breslau* which had shelled French naval bases on 28 July, then entered the Mediterranean and escaped to Istanbul. Both British ships were later to survive the Battle of Jutland in 1916.

The weather improved over the next few days and HMS *Edinburgh* left the convoy sailing in the direction of Aden but 'heading for an unknown destination'.[36] There seemed to be a small failure in the organisation at this point as although the captains of the troop-carrying ships were given the code word to the cypher in which secret messages were to be encoded, they were not giving instructions as to its use. On the following day, 2 September, at 1015 hours, the Lahore Division was informed for the first time, its true destination: Marseilles. Although the journey's end had been kept secret, the Reuters News Agency had previously identified that it would be France since it had quoted a statement by Lord Kitchener, the Secretary of State for War, made in the House of Commons on 28 August, that two Indian divisions were being sent to France. The convoy was ordered to make the journey to France via Suez where the mountain batteries and their ammunition were to be disembarked This clearly indicated that such lightweight artillery was deemed to be more useful in Egypt than on the battlefields of Europe.

Having escorted the convoy thus far the *Swiftsure* left to return to Aden and its Captain, Edward Albert McKenna, sent this farewell message to his charges:

35 The *Dufferin* was one of the British vessels sent on an expedition in 1917 into the Red Sea to assist in the Arab Revolt.

36 TNA WO 95/3991: 3 Indian (Lahore) Division, Headquarters, Branches and Services, General Staff War Diary, 1 September 1914.

> In saying farewell to the Expeditionary Force he wishes them all good fortune and trusts that our troops from India may soon be given an opportunity of adding fresh laurels to their already brilliant record.[37]

The *City of Glasgow* continued towards Suez and the weather remained fine. Headquarters were concerned about a missing ship, the *Castalia,* which had become detached form the convoy. It was with some relief that the Captain of HMS *Black Prince,* the armoured cruiser escorting the convoy, was able to inform them that the *Castalia* was safe and sound and under the care of the light cruiser, HMS *Chatham,* and about a day in the *Glasgow's* wake.[38] Realising that some of these exchanges of information might be of use to an eavesdropping enemy, the *Black Prince*'s Captain suggested that future messages should be in code. However, it transpired that only he had Naval codes and the Military could not translate his coded messages.

On 9 September The *City of Glasgow* arrived at Suez and, the Headquarters Section of the Lahore Division, was met by General Staff Officer (Grade 1) Colonel T. E. O'Leary. O'Leary had seen considerable active service especially in the Boer War and had previous experience as a transport officer. He bore orders that the infantry should disembark and proceed to Cairo, but the mounted units should remain onboard the *City of Glasgow* which was to proceed to Alexandria where the horses would be disembarked and exercised. Having reached Cairo, the Headquarters of the Lahore Division established itself at the Grand Continental Hotel, a favourite of the rich and famous which had previously included Conan Doyle and Lawrence of Arabia.

Turning their attention to the likely conditions in Western Europe, the IEFA Headquarters telegraphed the Commander in Chief India suggesting that the standard topee helmet worn by British soldiers in India was not appropriate for the European climate and requested that the troops be issued with cloth caps. Headquarters also issued a detailed set of instructions to the various Commanding Officers of the Lahore Division which contained directions about exercising the troops and the need to warn them of the prevalence of venereal disease in Egypt. Care should also be taken to ensure that the animals did not eat sand with their food which could cause sand colic which, in the worst cases, caused a complete obstruction of the large bowel which would be fatal. This should be prevented, directed the instruction, by putting the animal's food on blankets.[39] On the same evening the remaining transports arrived at Suez.

On the 15 September it was announced that Sir James Willcocks had been appointed as the Commander of the newly named Indian Corps which was to be divided into two Divisions: the Lahore Division and the Meerut Division. Willcocks had been born in India on April Fool's Day 1857. Early in his career he had specialised

37 TNA WO 95/3991: 3 Indian (Lahore) Division, Headquarters, Branches and Services, General Staff War Diary, 5 September 1914
38 HMS *Black Prince* was sunk with all hands during the Battle of Jutland.
39 TNA WO 95/3991: 3rd Indian (Lahore) Division, Headquarters, Branches and Services War Diary, General Staff Appendix I (19), issued 11 September 1914.

as a transport officer but when the opportunity arose for him to become a permanent member of the Commissariat and Transport Department, he declined the offer in favour of being the Adjutant of his Battalion.[40] He had then served extensively in a number of wars and punitive expeditions such as commanding the Bazar Valley Field Force and the Mohmand Field Force both in 1908. Promoted Lieutenant General he took command of the Northern Army of India in 1910

The 129th Baluchis arrived at the docks at Kiamari for departure to Europe and began to board HMT *Ellenga*.

The War Diary gives an interesting breakdown of the composition of the Baluchis at this point as follows: 8 British Officers, 1 Medical Officer and an Assistant Surgeon, 18 V.C.O.s, 77 NCOs, and 732 Privates. In addition to these were 81 Followers of various kinds.[41] In an age of little mechanisation, the 129th Baluchis also loaded 13 horses which were probably Officers' chargers, 12 Machinegun mules, 69 transport mules, 13 Ammunition Train Carts which were needed to cope with the 851,200 rounds of ammunition together the 20 round pouches which each Sepoy carried for their rifles. The Baluchis' war diarist clearly had an eye for detail.

If the men of the 129th Baluchis were expecting a blissful cruise they were soon disappointed. The War Diary gives an indication of the routine which was to be established during the voyage. Although the *Ellenga* did not leave Kiamari until 0905 hours on 26 August, the men were already being required to double around the saloon deck in groups for 15 minutes from 0700 hours in order to maintain their fitness. This was in accordance with the orders of Major General J.M.S. Brunker, GO.C. 3rd Division who, from the Officers' Mess of the Lancashire Fusiliers in Karachi on 22 September, desired that his commanders should ensure that, as far as possible, all the men should be kept hard and fit during the sea voice and constantly exercised with their boots on.[42] When the Baluchis ended their exercise session, they turned their attention to the ship and, by 0900 hours, had cleaned the decks. Two hours later they were inspected by the ship's Captain. In the afternoon machine gunners, signallers and scouts were given special instruction. Those men who had come from the Reserve and the newly attested recruits were instructed in the use of the rifle. In addition there was to be an alarm drill once a week. The British officers also did not have an easy time as it is recorded that they received their first inoculation against enteric (typhoid) fever and some undoubtedly suffered from the unpleasant side effects of the injection. It is clear that this was a wise precaution as the number of men with dysentery began to grow but it was always contained by the Medical Officer and only one soldier died in the first 15 days of the voyage.

40 The Leinster Regiment.

41 This number was made up of 18 Private followers, paid for by officers as servants, 27 Followers paid for by the battalion to whose numbers were added 4 'Supply' followers and 37 'Transport' Followers.

42 Operation Order No. 1 by Major General J.M.S. Brunker, Commanding 3rd Indian War Division. 22 August 1914.

General Sir James Willcocks, Commander of the Indian Corps, with his personal staff at his headquarters at Merville.

HMT Ellenga: The Baluchis' Transport to Europe.

The *Ellenga* had a distinguished passenger on board; the Nawab of Bhopal who was accompanying the half Battalion of 9th Bhopal infantry which had embarked on the ship.[43] This eminent officer was Colonel Ali Jah, Nawab Hafiz Sir Muhammad Nasru'llah Khan Sahib, the son of the Battalion's Colonel in Chief., described as 'an eminent lady' who, together with the Maharaja of Gwalior, had suggested the idea that the expenses of providing a hospital ship named *Loyalty* for the use of the Expeditionary Force should be shared by the various Indian Princes who were keen to show loyalty to the King Emperor.[44] The Colonel suffered from acute diabetes and it may be that life on board ships was not conducive to his condition. He was suddenly taken ill and it was clear that he could no longer continue on the voyage. Consequently after having finally joined the convoy of other transports, the *Ellenga* was forced to leave for a short while in order to land the ailing Nawab at Aden.[45] This was a sad loss to the 9th Bhopals and, as the Battalion History recorded, 'Colonel Nasrullah Khan's departure was deeply regretted and it 'wished to record their appreciation of his keen sense of loyalty and duty.'[46] Having accomplished this delicate task, the *Ellenga* re-joined the convoy and the sea voyage to Europe began

The 57th Rifle's war diarist records frustrations about the delay in the S.S. *Teesta*'s departure from the dock in India. Having boarded the four companies of the 9th Bhopals, at around 1800 hours on 26 August, the troops waited impatiently for the ship to embark. However the. *Teesta*, remained at the dockside then moved to anchor at a buoy in the harbour and, it was not until after being aboard for four days, that the 9th Bhopals and the accompanying 57th Rifles began their long journey across the Kala Pani.[47]

The 57th's War Diary presents a somewhat prosaic life on board the *Teesta* as it steamed across the Indian Ocean, There were daily exercise and parades for the men and it recorded that 'nothing of note occurred other than the death of a machine gun mule.'[48]

Both the Baluchis' and Bhopals War Diaries record few details of the voyage. The latter seems to have been written by the officers of the four Companies aboard the *Ellenga*. The ship arrived at Aden on 2 September and the officers received their

43 The remaining 419 Officers and men of the 9th Bhopals accompanied by the 57th Wilde's Rifles the embarked on the SS *Teesta*, which was also part of the convoy escorted by the RMIS *Northbrooke*.
44 *Hansard*, House of Lords Debates (09/09/14) Vol. 17, Col. 547.
45 TNA WO 95/3991: 3rd Indian (Lahore) Division, Headquarters, Branches and Services, General Staff War Diary, 31 August 1914.
46 Jackson et al, *History of the 4th Battalion 16th Punjab Regiment*, p. 38
47 Literally the 'Black Sea' Hindu Sepoys, especially those of the Brahmin Caste, saw crossing the this as a threat to their caste status. Fortunately such sensitivities did not affect those who were not Hindus but undertaking such a voyage for the peasant farmers who made up most of the Indian battalions must have been a daunting experience.
48 TNA WO 95/3923/5: 3 Indian (Lahore) Division 7 (Ferozepore) Infantry Brigade: 57th Rifles. War Diary, 24 August-5 September 1914. The mule is recorded to have died on 3 September.

S.S. Teesta: transport for the 57th (Wilde's) Rifles to Europe.

second typhoid inoculation. The 57th Rifles, on the S.S, *Teesta*, were three days behind but only remained at Aden for a little over a day. By 9 September the *Elengana* had reached Suez and the Battalions disembarked and journeyed to Cairo by train arriving on 11 September. Having been confined to the restrictions of a ship at sea for just over two weeks, the troops marched to the Racecourse at Heliopolis and pitched the tents which they had been ordered to bring from India. The Baluchi's war diarist, with one eye on the past, noted that the Battalion had marched passed the battlefield of Tel El Kebir where the Baluchis had served in 1882 under Sir Garnet Wolesley. The Battalion, on embarkation, had taken 3 weeks rations and 300 rounds per rifle and 6000 rounds per machine gun. A company of 26 Indian soldiers, under the command of a Captain, remained onboard the ship to protect the rest of the ammunition and provisions.

The *Teesta,* with the 57th Rifles and the remaining 'Bo Peeps' arrived at Suez on the afternoon of 13 September and received similar orders concerning taking three weeks

Racecourse Camp at Heliopolis.

provisions. They were also to take trains to the Racecourse Camp at Heliopolis near Cairo. Unfortunately for the 57th Rifles, the Egyptian railway system let them down because of obstructions on the line. During the time at Cairo, two Bhopal officers were able to catch up with the Battalion and the men's training continued. They practised attacking and underwent physical education drills. Machine gunners and signallers continued their specialised training and loading the transports was rehearsed.

However, it would seem that there was a sudden change of plan and the Ferozepore Division was soon on its way to re-join its various transport ships, On receiving orders to travel on to Alexandria the tents were unpitched, the supplies reorganised and on 17 September the Bhopal and Baluchi Battalions boarded trains, leaving a small number of sick behind. At Alexandria, the *Ellenga* awaited having brought the mountain artillery units which were unloaded and the horses which had been exercised, and the Baluchis re-boarded later that day. On the 19 September, the ship began the remainder of the voyage to Europe and it arrived at the French port of Marseilles on 26 September. The troops were welcomed with cries of *Vivons les Hindous* from the local populace.[49]

The 57th Rifles, having also received orders to travel to Alexandria, re-boarded their trains on 17 September, The war diarist complained that reaching the trains was a difficult task since there was a shortage of transport on which to carry the Battalion's supplies and equipment to the docks. The Battalion finally reached Alexandria and a day was spend loading stores and various items of kit onto the *Teesta* which was also loading coal. This essential activity prevented the troops from boarding until complete but, after further delays caused by the ship waiting to join the convoy and its escort, the *Teesta* had an uneventful voyage to Marseilles and the 57th Rifles also arrived at the French port on Saturday 26 September.

During the voyage from Alexandria to France a crucial change was ordered to the organisation of the Indian Battalions. Not only were they to replace their rifles, but they were also ordered to modify their Company structure. The 57th Rifles war diarist recorded that Indian battalions, which were made up of eight Companies, were ordered to reduce this number to four in order to bring them in line with the organisation of British battalions. Logical though this change was, bringing IEFA into line with the structure of the BEF battalions which had made the change in 1913, whilst the Indian's were at sea rather than on land must have caused a confusion which can only be imagined. For although some battalions, such as the 9th Bhopals, had double companies, at least half of those battalions involved had single companies in which Sepoys were familiar with their officers and NCOs, one of the key features of the Indian Army's structure. The reorganisation could have the potential to disturb the previously described important relationship with those in command and their men.[50]

49 'Long Live the Hindus' in French. The term Hindu seems to have been universally applied to the Indians no matter what their real ethnic origin.

50 BL/IOR/ L/Mil/7/120: Reorganisation, 1861-1936.

4

France

Having brought their rifles and thousands of rounds of small arms ammunition from India, the latter being left behind in Egypt, the Indian battalions were issued with the SMLE Mark III, the standard rifle of the British Army.[1] This was a sensible decision since it made life simpler for Quarter Masters who only had to deal with one type of rifle and ammunition rather than three.[2] This sudden change meant that many units went into battle without familiarising themselves with their new weapon and zeroing their back sights.. Gordon Corrigan supports General Willcocks' claim, that the sudden introduction of this new rifle significantly affected the Indian Corps' fighting capabilities at this early stage.[3] In spite of these views, it is worth noting that expertise with the rifle was very highly regarded in the Indian Army and a soldier's pay and prestige depended on his skill with his principal weapon. Similarly, the Indian Corps' Machine guns, described as an 'essential drawback' had to be rectified by cutting the front legs off their tripod even though it was not certain how this modification would work when they were fired. Entrenching tools, which were available, were inadequate but could not initially be replaced.[4]

The changing to the standard British service rifle was a break with the tradition of keeping the equipment issued to Indian battalions inferior to that of British battalions. The lack of genuine artillery amongst the Indian Army has already been discussed. In the case of artillery and the rifles this practice was for 'security reasons' since it was felt that if Sepoys were given advanced weaponry they would inevitably rise up against the British.[5] A second reason was that it was not expected that the Sepoys would have

1 The War Diary erroneously states that the new rifle was the SMLE Mark VII 9. See entry for 26 September 1914.
2 Gordon Corrigan, *Sepoys in the Trenches. The Indian Corps on the Western Front 1914- 1915* (London, Spellmount, 2006) p. 40.
3 Corrigan, *Sepoys in the Trenches,* p. 40.
4 TNA WO 95/188: War Office Report on Changes in the Indian Amy Corps, 23 October 1914.
5 Chandar S. Sundaram, 'Arriving in the Nick of Time': The Indian Corps in France, 1914-15, *Journal of Defence Studies*, Vol. 9, No. 4 October-December 2015, p. 77.

to fight a modern European army as they were required to do on the Western Front. Their usual enemy were tribesmen with very inferior rifles and no artillery.

Two French officers joined the 129th Baluchis to act as interpreters and, since the officers' horses were their own private property, a Valuation Board was held to determine their worth should they come to harm. Previous planning did not to take the European climate into account and IEFA had arrived in Marseilles wearing their light tropical uniforms.[6] Perhaps this was a further indication that a European war was still not considered as a serious possibility even as the men embarked to fight in it. It may also indicate that the original intention was for the Indian Battalions to remain in Egypt as part of the defence of the Suez Canal. However, two days after having arrived in France, the Ferozepore Brigade, were issued with warm clothing but were required to hand in any surplus kit.

Perhaps as a show of strength as well as solidarity, the Lahore Division undertook a route march through the town of Marseilles, on 29 September, and marched passed the French Commander of the District, General Armand Théodore Serviere who was accompanied by their own G.O.C., General Watkins. The Division was actually on its way to the railway station where each of the Battalions occupied its own train and undertook a journey of over 53 hours along the Mediterranean coast as far as Cette and then the train turned inland towards Toulouse and finally reached Orleans. The trains were halted at regular intervals so the men could cook their rations. The final destination was a camp at Cercottes, a very small village roughly 8 miles north of Orleans, which was reached on 2-3 October. The French populace took every opportunity to demonstrate kindness and hospitality, whenever the Indian Corps' trains stopped, and large crowds gathered and 'lavished fruit, flowers, [and] coffee on the men.'[7]

Cercottes Camp was some hundred yards from the railway line situated in a wooded area and roughly 800 yards long and roughly 200 yards wide. The eight Battalions were camped either side of a central road: four units on each side. Behind the eastern side of the Camp was the rifle range at the rear of which was a wood. The range gave some of the battalions, such as the 57th (Wilde's) Rifles, an opportunity to practise with their newly issued rifles on a morning which was described as cold and misty. The 57th Rifles War Diary concludes, somewhat guardedly, that the shooting was 'satisfactory on the whole.'[8] At the front of the camp was the Mule Corps, the 15th Cavalry, 1st Brigade of Royal Field Artillery, the Ammunition Column and 5th Field Ambulance.

Having settled into the Camp, the various Battalions went on a Route March on 4 October in order to maintain their fitness. The Connaught Rangers attended a Roman Catholic Service at which Father Peal officiated and then the Battalion practised

6 Johnson, *'I shall die arms in hand'*, p. 112.
7 Merewether and Smith, *The Indian Corps*, p. 19.
8 TNA WO 95/39243/5: 3 Indian (Lahore) Division: 57 Wilde's Rifles War Diary,10 October 1914.

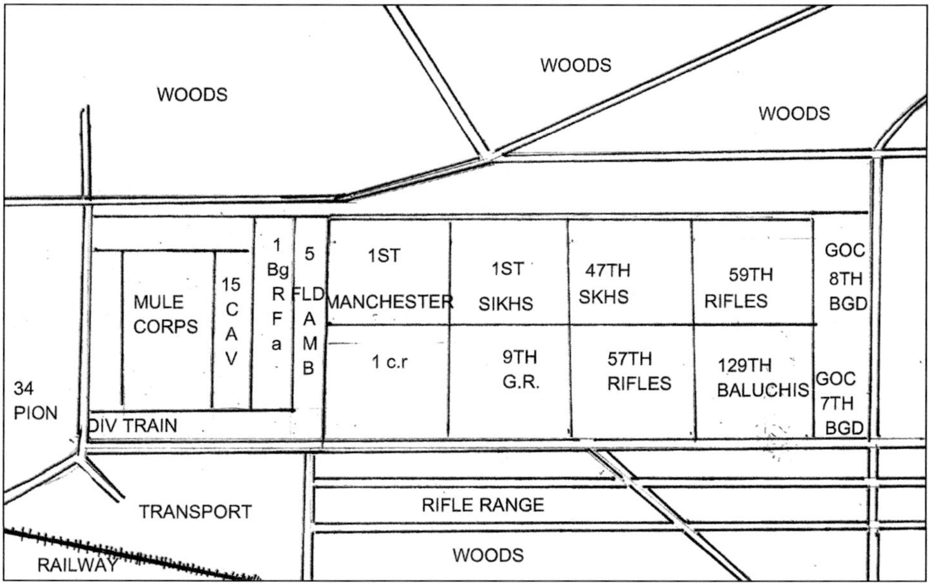

The Camp at Cercottes based on a sketch by Major E.R. Swafe, Camp Commandant.

musketry for an hour. The following day they marched passed the Commander of the Indian Corps, General Willcocks. This important recognition completed, the Quartermasters turned their attention to the more mundane needs of their men and all other ranks and as well as followers were issued with warm vests, underwear and shirts.[9] It was later found that the followers needed even warmer clothing as the weather was worsening.

Assault practice began in earnest on 7 October and, on the following day, the battalions of the Ferozepore Brigade were inspected by Prince Arthur of Connaught whom, it was noted, addressed the troops and shook hands with both British and Indian officers. It is interesting that the latter get a specific mention in the War Diary and illustrates the view that V.C.O.s were somehow inferior to those holding the King's Commission. The next few days were spent on route marches, attack practice, testing the machine guns on the adjacent range, church parades and becoming acclimatised to the French weather which was noted to be mild but cold at night.

John Boyd, the Connaught Rangers' Medical Officer, made a number of entries in the War Diary, unusually in ink rather than the ubiquitous pencil, about his Battalion's health at this time. Eight men were struck down with Malaria which they had obviously brought from India and amongst the other complaints from which soldiers

9 TNA WO 95/3924: 3 Indian (Lahore) Division, 129 (D.O.C.) Baluchis War Diary, 5 October 1914.

suffered were neuritis and sprains. There were 42 men who reported sick and were ill enough to have to be sent to hospital. The Doctor also recorded the results of a venereal inspection of the Connaught's NCOs during which 'only one case found'.[10]

Prince Arthur, Duke of Connaught.

On the 17 October the Ferozepore Brigade was ordered to board a train at Orleans Station, and then travelled to Arques, a journey to northern France of roughly 240 miles which took the Division roughly forty hours to complete. On arrival, the troops marched over 3.5 miles to billet at Wizernes in the Nord Pas De Calais. The 129th Baluchis War Diary mentions that some aeroplanes were observed which was clearly unusual enough for it to note as was the Connaught Rangers' mention that the Battalion had been issued with nine Bicycles which were almost certainly meant to improve communications. On 20 October the Connaught Rangers also observed aircraft and began to take defensive action until it was realised that they were British machines. Slowly the brigade was coming to terms with modern warfare.

The Indian Corps had arrived in the 'nick of time'. The BEF was exhausted and was hanging on having been engaged along the entire length of its sector. Seventy five of its 84 Battalions had been reduced to half strength.[11] The strategic town of Ypres was in danger of being captured by the Germans in their rush towards the Channel ports. It would have been better if the Indian Corps was given the opportunity to acclimatise, zero their rifles and then used as a new strategic force, but, as a senior British officer remarked, the 'truth was it could not wait because it had to fill up gaps … a few hundred men anywhere against us would turn the scale.'[12]

On the 21 October, with the 129th Baluchis leading, the Ferozepore Division marched to Wallon-Capel and thence to Baillieu where they paused to eat. Having marched for around six hours the men were no doubt pleased to be able to board 'omnibuses', which still had advertisements from a pre-war London on their sides and

10 TNA WO 95/39243/5: 3 Indian (Lahore) Division: 57 Wilde's Rifles, 15 October 1914. It is not surprising that the war diaries are sometimes mingled and that parts of one battalion's record was incorrectly inserted in that of another. For example, the 1st Connaught Rangers Medical officer's War Diary is inserted in the section devoted to 57th Rifles.

11 Chandar S. Sundaram, Arriving in the Nick of Time', p. 77

12 Morton-Jack, 'The Indian Army on the Western Front, 1914-1915', fn. 29, p. 339.

Contemporary postcard depicting bus transporting troops in Poperinghe.

ease their feet.[13] There can be little doubt that their boots had been well broken in during the marches of the previous few days. The Connaught Rangers were boarded on to 40 buses which, having crossed the Belgian border, proceeded to Wulverghem north west of Lille. The Connaught Rangers had left all their Battalion transport behind at Wallon-Cappel and the men were issued with an extra hundred rounds each. The Battalion had arrived at 3:30 am and the men were quickly sent to their new billets. Perhaps for the first time they were aware of artillery and rifle fire in the direction of Messines which was roughly two miles to the west.

The Connaught Rangers were ordered to occupy Messines and were the first Battalion in the Lahore Division to enter the trenches suffering their first casualty with one man wounded.

The 57th Rifles reported to Major General Gough (GOC 2nd Cavalry Division) and were ordered to support the 4th and 5th Cavalry Brigades and thus became the second Battalion in the Lahore Division to enter the trenches. Interestingly, when the war diarist described Gough's instructions, he mentions that five companies were ordered to support Brigadier General Bingham's 4th Cavalry Brigade and two Companies were to support Brigadier General Chetwoode's 5th Cavalry Brigade. The remaining two Companies were sent off to improve the trenches in the defensive line. Clearly the reorganisation of the Companies in an Indian Battalion had either not happened, or the designated war diarist failed to remember this during his narrative. On the night of the 22-23 October the 57th received its first casualties: two Sepoys severely wounded and three slightly wounded. The war diarist displayed typical sang-froid by describing the Battalion as only experiencing desultory artillery and rifle

13 A.T. Wilde, *Battalion History of the 4th Battalion 13th Frontier Force* (London: Andrews UK Limited, 2012) p. 95.

Indian bicycle troops on the Somme, 1916.

fire.[14] The 129th Baluchis quickly entered the front-line trenches and relieved three British Cavalry Battalions.[15] The Battalion came under the direction of Brigadier General John Vaughan, who had replaced Gough as commander of the 3rd Cavalry Brigade. John Vaughn had begun the War as Chief of Staff under General Allenby, Commander of the 1st Cavalry Division. The 9th Bhopals continued to march and were billeted at Voormezeele but were warned that they should hold themselves in readiness for an expected attack. The Brigade had joined the war.

14 TNA WO 95/39243/5: 3 Indian (Lahore) Division: 57 Wilde's Rifles War Diary, 22-23 October 1914.

15 16th (The Royal, Queen Elizabeth's Own Lancers), 5th (Royal Irish) Lancers & 4th (Queen's Own) Hussars.

5

Into Battle

Brigadier General Sir James Edmonds, who oversaw the production of the British Official History of Military Operations during the First World War, was awarded the Sword of Honour at the Military College, Woolwich and possessed a considerable intellect. Fluent in a number of European and Asian languages, he had entered the Staff College, Camberley in 1896 after achieving the highest score of his class in the entrance exam. His classmates included Douglas Haig, the future C-in-C of the British Expeditionary Force (BEF) from December 1915; Edmund Allenby, who led British forces in the Sinai and Palestine Campaign during 1917-18 and William Robertson, who became Chief of the Imperial General Staff in 1916. Edmonds became chief of staff of 4th (Regular) Division in the original BEF,[1] but the strain of the Retreat from Mons proved too much and he spent the rest of the war as a GHQ staff officer.

In the first volume of Edmond's Official History there is an explanation of how the IEFA came to the Western Front which, as we have seen, was because the subcontinent was the only place where regular, well trained troops could be quickly found in the Empire's time of need.[2] Volume II is more informative and in a footnote citation, Edmonds briefly explains the journey of IEFA to France and that arming them with the latest Mk III service rifles was a cause for a delay in the Indian's reaching the Front.[3] In truth, it made life easier for Quartermasters as it was the standard weapon of the British Army and therefore supplying one type of rifle ammunition was easier than supplying two. The demands of the Indian Battalions were difficult enough to satisfy as we have seen in the Meerut Division's Memorandum on the shipping of bread.

1 The 'Expeditionary Force' was renamed the 'British Expeditionary Force' on the arrival of 'Indian Expeditionary Force A' which, in turn, was renamed the 'India Corps'.
2 Edmonds, 1914, Vol. 1, p. 2.
3 Edmonds, *Military Operations France and Belgium 1914*, Vol. II (London: Macmillan, 1925), p. 92. Henceforth, Edmonds 1914, Vol. 2.

Edmonds cites other causes for the delay such as the need to employ omnibuses and tradesmen's vans, which were slower than trains, to transport the Indians to the Front and the additional need to provide them with 4.7-inch artillery from Woolwich on their arrival in France. His conclusion was that 'various causes conspired to make the force later than had been expected in its arrival at the front'.[4] This was somewhat hard on the Indians since the real delay had been in Egypt when plans as to how the Indians were to be deployed appeared to have been changed. Indeed the Sirhind Brigade was still in Egypt with orders to protect the Suez Canal when the rest of the Lahore Division was in the trenches.[5] The Sirhind Brigade which was commanded by Major General J.M.S. Brunker would not arrive in France until the end of November 1914. James Milford Sutherland Brunker was 60 years old in 1914. He had been commissioned in the Royal Artillery in 1873 and reached the rank of Major General in 1910. He had been Inspector of Artillery for Southern Indian and made Brigade Commander in December 1911. It appears that he had seen little active service before embarking for France. One could argue that the mobilisation of the Indian Brigades was extremely rapid and few of the delays which occurred could be laid at their door. Edmonds is correct, however, when he comments on the comparative under-strength of the Indian Battalions when they were compared with the manning of the British Army. He also rightly identifies the way in which numbers were enhanced by borrowing troops from linked Battalions which, to some extent, diluted the family nature of the host battalion.[6]

The Lahore Division became involved in a desperate struggle. The left flank of II Corp, commanded by General Smith-Dorrien, had been exposed when the supporting French Cavalry which was being driven out of Fromelles by German attacks. Having survived the Battle of Mons and Le Cateau, II Corps was again forced to withdraw and the depleted Lahore Division[7] was ordered to support the French Cavalry Division which were at the rear of Smith-Dorrien's left flank. This coordination of support with a French Division was an improvement on previous actions where, as Edmonds records, it was felt that the British were being left to 'do it all'.[8]

Lieutenant General Sir Horace Smith-Dorrien was one of the few British survivors of the Battle of Isandlwana during the Zulu War. Having served in Egypt, Indian, the Sudan and the Boer War, he became General officer Commander of the Aldershot Command where he was one the group senior officers who believed that Cavalry should be taught to fight on foot and be regarded as mounted infantry His

4 Edmonds, 1914, Vol. II, p. 92.
5 TNA WO 95/3928: 3 Indian (Lahore) Division (Sirhind) Infantry Brigade, Headquarters: Appendix II, 28 September 1914.
6 See Appendix ???
7 The Sirhind Brigade was still in Egypt and, as we have seen, the Ferozepore Brigade had gone north as a support of the Cavalry Brigade which meant the Jullundur Brigade under Major General P.M. Carnegy was all which was available.
8 Edmonds, 1914, Vol. 2, p. 90.

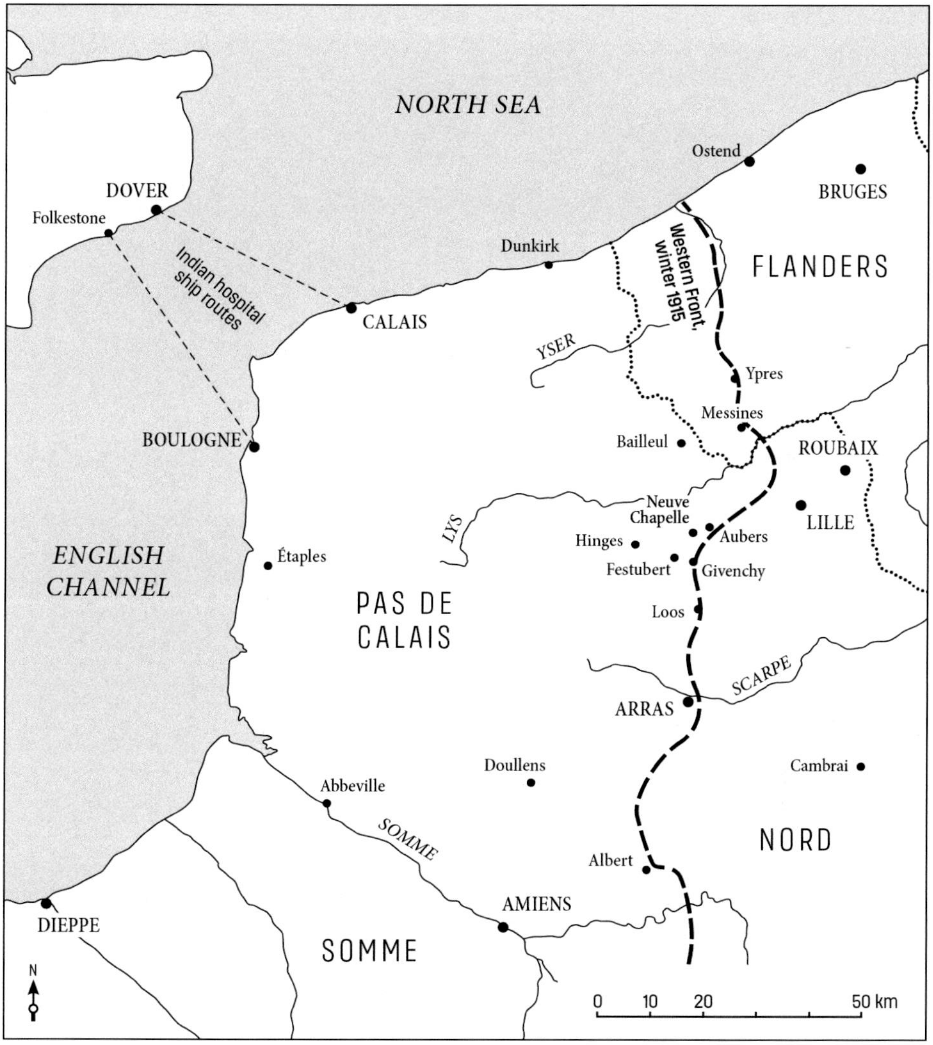

Map 1 Area fought over by the Indian Corps, 1914-1915.

General Sir Horace Smith Dorrien, the 'man who disobeyed.'

relationships with Field Marshal John French were strained, to say the least and not eased when Smith Dorrien commented that 'There were too many whores around your Headquarters Field Marshal.'[9] A difficult man to get on with, Smith Dorrien had disobeyed French's orders and had halted his retreating and exhausted Division and fought the Germans in the Battle of Mons thus delaying the enemy advance and allowing the BEF to recover.

It was at this point that the Indian Corps was thrown into battle and, in describing the actions involving the Ferozepore Brigade, Edmonds is somewhat brief, believing there was little to narrate about the fighting except that the Germans attacked day and night.[10]

The 57th (Wilde's) Rifles (FF) were on the receiving end of these attacks. The trenches which they occupied were little more than ditches and the shortage and inadequacy of entrenching tools hampered attempts to improve them. Casualty figures began to grow. On the 23 October there were nine Sepoys wounded and, on the 24 October, a further six were carefully recorded by name by the 57th Rifles' Medical Officer. The following day, the 57th suffered a further loss of 16 wounded and one killed. Amongst the wounded was their Commanding Officer, Lieutenant Colonel Gray, who received a shrapnel wound in his right shoulder whilst sitting in a room used as the Officers' Mess at Wytschaete: the German artillery having previously targeted the Battalion's billets. Whilst the majority of the wounded men were treated and remained at their posts, Gray was evacuated by the British Field Ambulance for treatment and command devolved to Major Edmund Swifte.[11]

On the afternoon of Gray's wounding (25 October) the 1st and 2nd Cavalry divisions attempted a concerted attack on enemy positions in the hopes of checking their advance. The 2nd Division, to which Wilde's Rifle, the Connaught Rangers and the 129th Baluchis were attached, was to attack positions east of Wytschaete whilst the 1st Division was to attack from the north. The Connaught Rangers had been ordered to occupy Messines but the convent which their Battalion Headquarters occupied was shelled. Consequently, the next day, headquarters moved to a nearby house. This proved to be a fortunate decision as the convent was again heavily shelled and parts of its church set ablaze. The four Companies of the Rangers took turn and turnabout in occupying the trenches and, at 1300 hours on the 26 October, they were ordered to hand over the trenches which they were occupying to cavalry during which process they lost one man killed and one wounded. The rain was heavy during the night and German sniping was a regular feature. The Ferozepore Battalions were spread very thinly but were expected to defend front lines with fewer men that their British counterparts and this made it easier for snipers to sneak close to the troops without their knowledge.

9 Richard Homes, *The Little Field Marshal: A Life of Sir John French* (London: Cassell, 2005) pp. 131-132.
10 Edmonds. 1914, Vol 2, p. 232.
11 Gray was to return to command the 57th after recovering from wounds.

British and Indian officers of the 57th (Wilde's Rifles), August 1915.

The German trenches facing the Connaught Rangers had been heavily shelled in the afternoon of the 26 October in preparation for an attack.[12] Two companies of Wilde's Rifles were to attack from the north along the 129th Baluchis' line and the Rangers were to extend the line of attack to the south. Commencing at around 1500 hours the attacking line advanced between 200 and 1500 yards towards Gapaard. The Connaught Rangers captured three German trenches and took three of their occupants prisoner, but such was the speed of their advance, they lost touch with the 57th Rifles on their left flank.[13] The 129th Baluchis suffered five men killed including Captain P.C. Hawke Vincent and 35 men were wounded with the addition of one man going missing during the attack. When darkness fell at around 1900 hours, the attack, was called off as the 57th Rifles and the 129th Baluchis had yet to reach the German front line. The troops were ordered to return to their original trenches as it was believed that the line formed by the trenches which had been captured was

12 TNA WO 95/113: 2 Cavalry Division, 4 Cavalry Brigade Headquarters War Diary, 26 October 1914.

13 See Chapter 7.

inferior to that of trenches from which they had launched the attack.[14] The 57th Rifles only suffered one casualty but thought another Sepoy had been killed or captured. However, he turned up next day having spent the night in a German trench![15]

During the preceding few days the 9th Bhopal Rifles were acting as a reserve Battalion to the 2nd Cavalry Brigade and had been preparing for attacks which had not happened. Definite orders were promised but never came. However, on the 26 October the Bhopals, who had no machine guns, were ordered to proceed by omnibus to Vielle Chapelle where they arrived at 0700 hours and immediately began to cook breakfast.[16] At 1100 hours they were ordered by a staff officer[17] to advance towards to Rouge Croix[18] and as a reserve battalion to support the Royal West Kent Battalion's attack on Neuve Chapelle. The Bhopals began to advance but found progress very difficult because of the close nature of the countryside, numerous bogs and barb wire fences which had to be traversed, to say nothing of the advancing darkness. Although they lost cohesion, they eventually all reached the West Kent's trenches.

At this point the Bhopals Battalion Diary has a series of sentences crossed out. The first erasure indicates that the West Kent's had left their trenches by the time the Bhopal Rifles arrived, the Sepoys immediately began improving the trenches but soon moved to a new position.[19] Whatever the real details of the move from the trenches, the Diary becomes clear again and records confused fighting during which 30 Germans were 'disposed' of by Captain Jones and No. 1 Company. In another display of sangfroid, the Diary says that things were critical at this point. The West Kent line was being outflanked to such an extent that the Germans were able to fire into its rear. The Bhopals were able to force this group of Germans to retreat but some of the West Kent's had been driven out of their trenches and one of the Bhopals' officers, Lieutenant Mullaly was taken prisoner. The 9th Bhopals Battalion, together with the West Kent's who had remained, began to dig trenches in a nearby orchard whilst the Germans occupied gardens close to the lane which ran through the front line. During the fighting, Lieutenant Colonel Anderson, the Bhopal Battalion's second in command who had come to see how they had been deployed was severely wounded and was reported to be lying unattended in the lane with his orderly lying dead nearby. German presence at that point made it too dangerous to attempt a rescue. Anderson is described as' a most efficient soldier,

14 Edmonds, 1914, Vol 2, p. 251.

15 TNA WO 95/39243: 3 Indian (Lahore) Division, 57th Wilde's Rifles War Diary 27 October 1914.

16 Willcocks, *With the Indians* p. 67

17 Captain Crichton of the Royal Scots, GSO3 3rd Division. The Bhopals diarist had trouble with his name and wrote Creighton. See Billy Congreve, *Armageddon Road: A VC's Diary 1914-1916* (Barnsley: Pen and Sword, 2014).

18 Describe as a 'Giant red calvary' in Herbert A. Stewart, *From Mons To Loos: The Diary of a Supply Officer* (London: W. Blackwood and Sons, 1916).

19 TNA WO 95/3923/4: 7 Indian (Lahore) Division, Ferozepore Infantry Brigade, 9 Battalion Bhopal Infantry, erased entry for 27 October 1914.

who habitually looked to the comfort of his men, as well as their training and was loved by them.'[20]

The situation continued to be a tense one. Fighting was nonstop, and the British found it impossible to dislodge the Germans. Sikh Sappers and Miners from the 20th and 21st Company, who were the field engineering Companies of the Lahore Division, were used to extend the Bhopals' left flank and link it with the neighbouring 47th Sikh Battalion. The use of such skilled troops gives one an indication as to the difficulties which the British were in at this point: they were the commanding General's last reserve.[21] Willcocks was correct when he accused Commanders of extracting 'the very marrow from a Division by using the Sappers and Miners in this way.'[22] The situation was desperate and the Sappers and Miners were almost the only reserves available. Willcocks' analysis is supported by Edmonds who claims that using Sappers and Miners as ordinary combat troops ' crippled the Lahore Division for a considerable period.[23] However, this was not the only occasion when the Sappers and Miners were used in this way and Field Marshal Sir John French, C-in-C BEF, was forced to issue a memorandum reminded commanders not to use these highly skilled specialists on tasks which should be carried out by infantry.[24]

The Sappers and Miners were the engineers of the Division. Officered by volunteers from the Royal Engineers, they were artificers, blacksmiths, builders, surveyors, road makers and trench builders; often carrying out their duties under fire. Each unit had its own signal section whose members were trained to operate the field telephone and communicate in Morse code. Although better educated than most Sepoys, few of them had much English. This strangely had the advantage of making them more reliable when acting as morse operators since they did not anticipate the contents of a message as an English speaker might be tempted to do.'[25]

It was the Sappers and Miners ability to improvise when in the field which made them so useful to the Indian Army. The experience they had gained during fighting on the North West Frontier, had, in the words of a Royal Engineer officer, ' created almost a genius for improvisation which stood the Indian Sappers in good stead, certainly during the opening stages of the War.'[26] The Indian Corps had arrived

20 James P. Cato, *Solah Punjab: The History of the 16th Punjab Battalion* (London: Gale and Polden 1967), p. 45.
21 Edmonds, 1914, Vol 2, p, 214 The GOC directing these operations was Brigadier-General McCracken commanding 7th Brigade.
22 Willcocks, *With the Indians in France*, p. 67.
23 Edmonds, 1914, Vol 2, p. 218, fn.
24 Memo from G.H.Q. to G.O.C. Indian Corps dated 13 November 1914. It also mentioned the use of Royal Engineers being used to hold a defensive line. Edmonds, 1914, Vol 2, p. 218 *fn.*
25 Trench, *The Indian Army,* pp. 29-30.
26 E.W.C. Sandes, *The Indian Sappers and Miners* (Chatham, Institute of Royal Engineers, 1948)

Reproduction Jam Tin bombs.

in France without hand grenades and mortars; vital in trench warfare. In October 1914, Indian Sappers commandeered a Belgium iron works at Béthune and used their pre-war experience of Hale's grenades to construct jam-tin bombs.[27] By November they were producing 400 bombs a day as well as several trench mortars.[28] Losing the skills of such men was a hard thing to bear and must indicate the desperate situation in which the BEF found itself in deploying these men in the front line as well as a poor appreciation of the Sappers and Miners true value.

Through the night of the 27/28 October, the Germans attacked the orchard where the Bhopals were entrenched as well as launching themselves against other British trenches. The Indian positions were swept by machine gun fire and, to make life more difficult, the area was illuminated by a searchlight situated close to Neuve Chapelle, which shone all night on the British defences. Somehow, during all this turmoil, Colonel Anderson was retrieved and taken to the Field Ambulance station but died of his wounds on 29/30 October.[29]

27 Otto Schwink, *Ypres 1914. An official account published by order of the German General staff. Translation by Graham. Chanley Wynn with introduction and notes by the Historical Section (Military Branch) Committee of Imperial Defence* (London: Constable and Company Ltd, 1919).

28 Morton-Jack, *The Indian Army,* pp. 189-190.

29 Anderson was 47 years old when he died. The 9th Bhopal Infantry War Diary states that he died on 30 October but his entry in the Dulwich College records suggests that it was actually 29 October, which is confirmed by his entry in W.T. Clutterbuck and W. T. Dooner, *The* Bond *of Sacrifice: A Biographical record of all British Officers who fell in The Great War* (London, The Anglo-African Publishing Contractors, 1918).

The fighting continued and the 9th Bhopals, having received a few picks and shovels with which to speed up their work, attempted to improve the trenches Their position in the Orchard was hampered by a nearby high hedge which allowed the enemy to sneak close to their trenches and fire from an obscured position. The Bhopals had eventually intended to cut this obstacle down and incorporate it in their defensive position as an abatis,[30] but were also hampered by the fact that the hamlet to their rear was occupied by German snipers who ' caused much annoyance ' throughout the night. In an attempt to reduce this threat, the Bhopals sent a Platoon of men to search some of the hamlet's houses but, around 1100 hours, the orchard and the Bhopals' trenches were subjected to a heavy bombardment for over fifteen minutes. This naturally caused the Indians to try to further deepen their trenches. Their war diarist conveys the confusion of the situation, for when referring to the bombardment he records that it was assumed to be friendly fire. Communications between artillery and the various units was always a precarious feature of the fog of war and there are records of many examples when soldiers were killed by their own shells.

The Germans, for their part, alleged that their troops were greatly exasperated by the treacherous methods used by Indian troops during this struggle. They were 'crouching in the hedges, and with machine guns concealed up trees, the defeated Asiatics allowed our troops to pass by them, and then got up and then stabbed them in the back with their knives'.[31] The practice described here seems to be the use of reasonable tactics on the battlefield. The account suggests that the troops involved were the 129th Baluchis, serving with the Cavalry Corps but by the dates in the account, the Baluchis had been withdrawn. The mention of 'knives' suggests, rather, that these were the Gurkhas. It is clear that the comment is racists but demonstrates the odium in German minds of employing Asian troops against Europeans.

The 9th Bhopal Infantry then received written orders to advance towards Neuve Chapelle and Major Jamieson, who seems to have taken over the Battalion as Lieutenant Colonel Anderson was wounded and Lieutenant Colonel Dobbie sick, observed the Sappers and Miners of 20 Company advancing and ordered half of his company to join them in the attack on the German trenches. The order proved to be difficult to carry out because the surrounding hedges made it very hard to move as a body but D Company was able to do so taking advantage of the only gap in the orchard hedge.[32] Advancing through Neuve Chapelle, the original groups of Bhopals almost captured a German machine gun but, during this attempt, which was described as a 'most gallant attack', one British officer was shot through the head.[33]

30 An obstacle formed of the branches laid in a row, with the sharpened tops directed outwards, towards the enemy.
31 Schwink, *Ypres 1914*, p. 84.
32 TNA WO 95/3923: 3 Indian (Lahore) Division, Ferozepore Infantry Brigade, 9th Battalion Bhopal Infantry War Diary, 27 October 1914.
33 The Diary is unclear as to who this unfortunate officer might have been. In the casualty list entry it records that two Captains were wounded, Captain L. J. Jones who was also

It is interesting that the war diary mentions that these men were members of the "Old C Company" which may indicate that the reduction to four Companies from eight had still to be fully embedded in the Battalion officers' thinking, especially since the diarist then refers to 'old E and H' Companies. It is almost certain that the Indian troops who were ordered to support their colleagues as well as the Sappers and Miners, continued to think in pre-reorganisational terms. As we have seen much was done to encourage loyalty to the Battalion and by, creating the Class companies, this loyalty extended to their fellow company members and the officers who commanded them.

Having advanced through shattered Neuve Chapelle, the Bhopals received an order from 'persons unknown' to retreat and the troops' advances went into reverse. The German machine gun was still a threat and Lieutenant Francis Poitiers Nosworthy made a further attempt to silence it, However with no additional support, this was impossible and, having lost touch with other Indian units, the men continued to retire through Neuve Chapelle whilst experiencing further rifle fire from the houses which were still occupied by the enemy. The remnants of the 9th Bhopal Infantry and the Sappers and Miners assembled at the Rouge Croix from whence they had started on the previous day. During the night, half of 3 Company under Captain Wills continued to defend the trench on the left flank of the Royal West Kent's but the Germans had driven the latter out and occupied the support and reserve trenches. By 0200 hours Wills and his men were also forced to retire. Willcocks again criticised the methods of High Command by which the Bhopals and other Indian Units were divided into companies rather than deploying them as a complete unit and maintaining cohesion and he thought that this tactic was one of the 'most senseless proceedings.[34] Merewether is perhaps a little more objective than the Commander of the Indian Corps. He argues that in the early stages of the war shortage of troops limited what could be achieved and the learning curve of defending a position which had been successfully attacked had yet to begin.[35]

The final entry in the 9th Bhopal War Diary for 27-28 October lists the casualties which the action had cost the Battalion. The Commanding Officer, Lieutenant Dobbie is listed as sick, Lieutenant Colonel Anderson, died of wounds, and four other British officers were wounded; two of whom were missing. The Indian officers had suffered equally; one Subadar[36] had been killed, two wounded, one injured and a Jemadar was missing.[37] There were 262 other ranks killed and wounded, which repre-

missing and Captain G. B. C. Irvine. A head wound is often fatal, but the diary omits the name and its reviewing officer denotes this error with three question marks. It would seem likely that The officer concerned was Captain Jones. His death is recorded on 28 October 1914.

34 TNA WO 95/3923: 3 Indian (Lahore) Division, Ferozepore Infantry Brigade, 9th Battalion Bhopal Infantry War Diary, 27 October 1914.

35 Merewether and Smith, *The Indian Corps,* p. 59.

36 VCO equivalent to Captain.

37 VCO equivalent to Lieutenant.

Lieutenant General Sir Francis Nosworthy.

sented almost a third of the Battalion's other ranks and roughly two thirds of its British Officers. The Sappers and Miners also suffered considerable loss. The 20th Company had one officer killed, four officers wounded, and 54 other ranks killed or wounded which represented a third of the Company. The 21st Company Sappers and Miners had three officers killed, one wounded and 57 other ranks killed or wounded. Field Marshal Sir John French, in his despatch of 20 November 1914, commented on the gallant conduct of the Sappers and Miners and mentions the great loss of life which this action caused.[38] Merewether and Smith also record that Sir John sent a telegram to Willcocks in which he expressed his gratitude for the gallant conduct the Indian troops had displayed. In spite of these efforts and the Indian's undoubted bravery this skirmish was not regarded as a genuine battle, perhaps because, despite Indian efforts, Neuve Chapelle was captured by the enemy.

38 John French, *The Despatches of Sir John French* (London: Chapman & Hall Ltd, 1914) Vol. 1, p. 152.

6

'I beg to submit the following brief report'

The 57th (Wilde's) Rifles War Diary reflects the confusion which the Battalion felt at this time. On 27 October it had received conflicting orders which were rarely, if ever, directed it to act as a whole unit. It was shelled and bombed by German aircraft and hid in a wood in order not to be observed by other planes. When night fell, the men marched to billets where they spent 'a peaceful night'.[1] One presumes that this was a comparative statement as Nos. 1 and 3 Companies were instructed to be in constant readiness to assist the 4th and 5th Cavalry Brigades if necessary.

During the pause on the morning of the following day, the Rifles Company Commanders had discussions with an officer of the Royal Engineers as to how they might improve the trenches which their men occupied, but new instructions were received in the early afternoon that the Battalion was to be under orders to the 4th and 5th Cavalry brigades. No. 1 Company under Major Williams together with the Machinegun Section were to occupy the trenches of the 4th Cavalry Brigade and No. 3 Company under Captain Forbes, were attached to the 5th Cavalry Brigade. Further 'penny packets' were created when the remaining two Companies were ordered to undertake a night march from Oostervarne to Messines, whilst the headquarters Section, however, was ordered to remain at Wytschaete

The Machine Gun Section of the 9th Bhopals, which had been attached to the 57th Rifles since 25 October, was ordered to march to Merville together with the Ferozepore Brigade's Headquarters section. It is interesting to speculate whether things might have turned out differently if the Machine Gun Section had been present with the Bhopals during the attack on the 27 October as they might have driven off the attacking Germans using this additional firepower,

Captain R. S. 'Jock' Gordon, a Highlander as his name suggests, commander of No. 2 Company, went to Messines in order to obtain orders from Brigadier General John Vaughan, G.O.C. 3rd Cavalry Brigade, and consequently Nos 2 and 4 Companies together with their transport, under the command of Major Barwell, marched to

1 TNA: WO95/3923 War Diary of 57th Wilde's Rifles (F.F.).

Wytschaete. It is interesting that, has previously mentioned, officers sometimes went to Headquarters in order to obtain orders. This clearly indicates the problems with communication and coordination between the Generals in charge and the units attempting to carry out their orders. That night, No. 1 Company occupied the front-line trenches and suffered casualties from shelling but No. 3 Company, in the reserve trenches, was mostly spared as it did not experience heavy fire.

At this point in its narrative, the 57th Rifles Battalion War Diary relies on a report of the actions for the 29 October to 1 November. The report was written by Major Swifte, Officer Commanding 57th Rifles, and forwarded by Major General Watkins, G.O.C., Lahore Division, to the Commander of the Cavalry Corps, Lieutenant General Edmund Allenby. Allenby was known as 'the Bull' by his subordinates because of his physique and his bad temper. He was on poor terms with some of his subordinates especially Hubert Gough, Commander of the 3rd Cavalry Brigade until September 1914, who was later to have described Allenby as a stupid man who had kept him in ignorance during the retreat from Mons.[2] One can be certain that Swifte took care when writing his report because, during the events which it described, the 57th Rifles was attached to the Cavalry Division. Swifte pointed out that this was a brief report written on 3 November 1914 'in the field', since all of his British officers had been either killed or wounded and he had not yet had the opportunity to confer with his remaining V.C.O.s.[3] In doing so Swifte reflects the common views of the superiority of British officers over their Indian counterparts since the report would incomplete without their input.

Late in the evening of the 28 October, Swifte wrote that he received orders from the Commander of the 7th (Ferozepore) Brigade, Major General Watkins, to send his remaining two Companies (No. 2 under Major Barwell and No. 4 under Captain Gordon) to Messines in order to report to the 4th Cavalry Brigade by 0500 hours on Thursday 29 October. The Headquarters Section and the Machine Gun Section were to remain at Wytschaete under the orders of the 4th Cavalry Brigade. The men detailed for Messines set off at 0300 hours and immediately on their arrival, 50 men were sent into the trenches and the remainder held in support. There was little activity that morning but, clearly suspecting an impending attack, the whole of No. 2 Company and half of No. 4 Company were sent into the trenches with the remaining few held in reserve.

At around 0700 hours on the 30 October No. 1 and No. 3 Companies which were occupying trenches in the Cavalry sectors came under a very heavy bombardment from both shrapnel and high explosive shells and, at the same time, the enemy began an infantry attack in the clear expectation that either sufficient defending troops

2 Antony Farrar-Hockley, *Goughie: The Life of General Sir Hubert Gough* (London; Granada, 1975), p. 352.

3 TNA WO 95/3923: Copy of the Memorandum No. Nil, 5 November 1914 from the General Officer Commanding 7th Indian Infantry Brigade.

would be killed, incapacitated or driven out of the trenches by the bombardment to allow their capture by the advancing German infantry. The troops defending the trenches north of the 5th Cavalry Division were eventually driven back at around 1400 hours and their trenches were occupied by the enemy. This enabled the Germans to direct enfilading fire on the 5th Cavalry Brigade's left flank. The troops in this sector, which included No. 3 Company of Wilde's Rifles, were ordered to pull back but it seems that the order did not reach Captain Forbes, the Company Commander, sufficiently quickly enough to allow him to organise a gradual withdrawal. This meant that No. 3 Company did not completely withdraw until the Germans were almost up to their trenches when the Company was under fire from both flanks as well as being targeted by enemy machine guns. During their withdrawal half of the Company, led by Lieutenant Clarke, came under 'murderous' machinegun fire. Clarke and the Company's V.C.O. Jemadar Khan Muhammad and 40 Sepoys did not return and were assumed to be either killed or captured whilst attempting their withdrawal. The survivors of No. 3 Company fell back roughly a quarter of a mile towards the village of Messines, where they occupied a previously prepared position to the front of the village's northern side.

Meanwhile, No. 1 Company did not experience quite such a heavy bombardment as had No.3 and Major Williams was able to make an organised withdrawal of both men and machine guns. They took up a position close to the road which led from Wytschaete to Messines. The bombardment of the trenches continued through the night and the Germans also targeted Wytschaete village with shrapnel and high explosives shells. At Messines, the bombardment also continued through the night whilst the Germans attacked the trenches in overwhelming numbers between 0300 and 0400 hours and, on the early morning of the 31 October, Major Barwell, who was with those remaining Sepoys from No. 4 Company providing support to those in the trenches, hearing the Sepoys' rifle fire rushed to support the front-line trench but was shot dead. The trench occupied by No. 4 Company was heavily attacked and Captain Gordon called on his Company (No. 2) to counterattack but as he stood up in his trench he too was shot and died within a few minutes. The remaining British officer, Lieutenant Molony was also shot which meant that all the officers had been ether killed or wounded.

What followed was not only a tribute to the bravery of the V.C.O.s but also an example of their ability to lead their men in the most challenging circumstances. Subadar Arsla Khan of No. 2 Company took command and succeeded in organising the orderly withdrawal of both No. 2 and No. 4 Companies into Messines village. During the withdrawal, half of No. 4 Company became almost completely surrounded before it could leave its trench and, in spite of a counterattack by No. 2 Company, led by Subadar Arsla Khan to assist their withdrawal, its Jemadar Kaipur Singh was lost; either killed or captured

Once in the village's streets, the Sepoys became disorientated and separated into small groups. Some made their way to the house in which Major Barwell had previously set up his Headquarters and came under the command of Lieutenant Reardon, who had been attached to the Battalion as its French interpreter. Others were collected together by V.C.O.s, and Indian NCOs and, still under heavy shell fire, withdrew to a reserve position.

During 1 November a few men from the two companies were ordered by an unrecognised Hindustani speaking British officer to report to the 57th's Battalion Headquarters and some Sepoys were able to do so even though the Headquarters had moved, together with the transport, two and a half miles to Kemmel in order to escape the bombardment of Wytschaete. At around 2100 hours these men were joined by some of the remaining Sepoys of No. 3 Company, led by another V.C.O., Subadar Muhammad Khan Aziz, and who had been occupying trenches to the north end of Wytschaete, but had been forced by enemy attacks to retire. During this withdrawal Captain Forbes had been wounded.[4] They had been told to report to Kemmel and it is not surprising that some on these remnants and V.C.O.s lost their way and did not reach Kemmel under the morning of 2 November.

Assaults on the trenches continued during the night of 31 October particularly against the British left flank and it became clear that these defences could no longer be defended. Major Williams, whose men had been defending a position in front of the Wytschaete to Messines Road was forced to order a withdrawal at around 0300 hours on 1 November to set up a line of defence on an artillery battery situated near a windmill south west of Wytschaete. It was during the 1 November that Havildar Ganga Singh and a small party of Sepoys were defending a trench which was attacked by a large number of the enemy. The Germans entered the trench and, in the words of Merewether and Smith, 'sanguinary hand to hand fighting took place'.[5] Most of the 57th's Sepoys were killed but the Havildar fought on until, after he had killed five Germans, his bayonet broke. Finding a sword he continued to fight but, after receiving six wounds, he collapsed and was left for dead. Fortunately, when the Indians recaptured the trench, he was found to be still alive. Merewether and Smith record that he was awarded the Indian Order of Merit (Second Class) for his courage.[6] One wonders if he had been a British Officer whether his reward would have been higher.

Later that morning, Swifte received orders from the 2nd Cavalry Division to collect the 57th's stragglers, who were congregating at Kemmel, and to report to the 4th Cavalry Brigade. There he received new instructions to take up a position on the right flank of the 3rd (the King's Own) Hussars. There, he was joined by Major Williams, and together with the surviving members of the Battalion, and they remained during a relatively quiet period. In the evening, Major Swifte was ordered to personally report to Lieutenant Colonel Southey, Commanding Officer of the 129th Baluchis

4 Forbes was to recover from his wounds and Willcocks appointed him to the Indian Corps Staff as Camp Commandant. See Willcocks, *With the Indians,* p. 37.

5 Merewether and Smith, *The Indian Corps*, pp. 35-36.

6 Merewether and Smith. *The Indian Corps*, p. 36.

at Westoutre where the transport and baggage had been positioned because Kemmel had been heavily shelled.

Willcocks comments on these actions is worth considering. In his description of the fighting he wrote:

> The movements and duties of the 57th Rifles and 129th Baluchis, during their detachment from their own Brigade, read strangely to anyone who was not in the area at the time. Here were two Indian Battalions, suddenly dumped down in a maelstrom, depending for guidance entirely on their few British officers, split up into half companies, attached to various British Corps in turn, cavalry, infantry, guns ; hurried from one trench to another, from one front to another, hardly realising the meaning or object of it all ; and then comes the hardest trial ; their gallant leaders are everywhere, encouraging and guiding with a spirit of unselfish bravery that will live for all time, when the hand of death strikes them down ; others fall sorely wounded; Indian officers share their fate; the Sepoys bewildered, but faithful, still fight.[7]

Whilst one must acknowledge that Willcocks' description is somewhat a romantic one written by a Commanding General who had great affection for his troops with whom he had served all his career, it does give something of an insight into how the V.C.O.s and Sepoys, as well to some extent, the British officers, must have felt about this type of engagement. Wilde's Rifles were part of India's Frontier Force and were used to fighting Afridi in the region of the Khyber. The Afridi, though experts in guerrilla warfare, had no artillery, somewhat inferior rifles and rarely, if ever, engaged their enemies in open battle.

The summary of the results of the actions from to 1 November was clearly set out in the War Diary entry for 2 November which records a fully named casualty list of a total of 314 Officers and men. Perhaps the most striking figure are those reported as missing: 101. Although some of these would return to the Battalion in the next few days, such a high number indicates that with the proximity of the enemy, some of the missing must have been taken prisoner. It also suggests, as has been noted, the chaotic nature of the 57th Rifle's fighting during which small numbers of Sepoys were separated from their companies but slowly returned to the Battalion by various routes at a later date.

7 Willcocks, *With the Indians*, p. 35.

7

'There should be a gap of eight to ten yards between each man'

Chapter 5 left the Connaught Rangers, having been in the front line for two days. handing over their trenches at Messines to the Cavalry on 26 October. They were relieved by the 5th (Princess Charlotte of Wales) Dragoon Guards and marched to Wytschaete. In the afternoon, the Connaughts advanced to attack Gapaard some 1 3/4 miles from Wytschaete, believing that the 57th (Wilde's) Rifles were on the left and the 9th Bhopal Infantry on their right. C Company of the Connaughts drifted too far to the left in an attempt to link up with the 57th and lost touch with the rest of their Battalion. The attack was called off and the bulk of the Connaughts, minus the missing Company, withdrew to the village of Wulverghem, where they arrived in the early hours of the 27 October. Later that morning, the missing Company caught up with the Battalion having occupied three enemy trenches and bringing with them three German prisoners including one officer. Although the Company had lost touched with the main group of Connaughts, it was regarded as a fortunate accident and this action was reported as 'smart work' by the Lahore Brigade when describing the taking of prisoners to Divisional Headquarters.[1] The Connaught Rangers returned to Messines and reoccupied the trenches which they have left the previous morning. During the next three days the Connaughts moved from Messines via Wulverghem and Estaires to the Rouge Croix area where they were billeted close to trenches which they then occupied. Orders were sent from Lieutenant General Watkins, GOC Lahore Division, which instructed Major General Carnegy of the Jullundur Brigade, that he was being sent two Battalions, the 1st Battalion Manchester Regiment and the 1st Battalion Connaught Rangers to relieve two of the Division's Battalions which had been defending Fauquissart and needed relief and rest. Watkins left Carnegy, the man on the spot, to decide which of these Battalions required the respite the most. Once chosen, Carnegy could then decide to where the relieved Battalions could be moved in order that they could get the most rest. However, Carnegy was urged by

1 TNA WO 95/3923: Appendix 10 I, Copy No. BM 16d y 28/20/14 from 7th Indian Infantry to Lahore Division.

Watkins not to put the whole of the relieving Battalions in the front line. The trenches should only be thinly occupied in order to protect the men from the German barrage which always preceded an attack. There should be a gap of between eight to ten yards between each man in the front trench to minimise casualties from these artillery bombardments. The Battalion should have developed a strong line of communication with its support Companies so that they could be ready to enter the front trenches once an infantry attack had begun. These supporting Companies were not, in reality, reserves at all, just men kept back from the firing line until an attack began. They were, however, an extremely important part of Watkins' plans to defend the front line and every Battalion was required to have such a group, no matter how small, since their purpose was to launch a counterattack 'with the bayonet' if the enemy had broken into the front line.

Trenches needed to provide their defenders with a clear field of fire of between two hundred and three hundred yards in length but the troops were told not open fire until the enemy was within that range. In order to prevent German snipers from approaching close to the front-line trenches, the British Battalions were told they should play them at their own game by sending out their own snipers into No Man's Land. This would also prevent the Germans from moving machine guns forward to within two hundred yards of the front trench during the hours of darkness. The Brigade's machineguns should be placed on the flanks of the front line in order to deliver enfilading fire on advancing enemy, but guns should be well hidden and protected. There should also be a system of piquet's and night patrols to prevent the Germans surprising the defenders.

Carnegy was also directed to attempt to collect a genuine local reserve of half a Battalion strength and hold it close to the Brigade Headquarters in order that it could be quickly deployed where needed.

This set of instructions or orders explain much as to why the previous actions were conducted as they were. The manning of trenches with one company whilst keeping another in reserve was clearly an attempt to follow Watkins' instructions not to overman a trench. But it does not explain why 57th Rifles and the 9th Bhopals were split into two and sent to support different Cavalry Brigades. These decisions were clearly based on the lack of manpower and the plan to reduce gaps in the line with penny packets.

On 1 November the Connaughts moved to the forward trenches replacing the Royal Scots Fusiliers. Compared with the two Indian Battalions in the Brigade the Connaught Rangers had a relatively easy time of it during this period; suffering only 16 casualties which may explain why a private soldier, who had badly cut hand caused from handling a rusty piece of old tin, was worthy of mention in the medical officer's diary.[2]

2 WO95/3923: Connaught Rangers Medical Officer Diary, 26 October 1914.

8

'The doings of my Battalion'

During the last week in October 1914, the experiences of the 129th Baluchis were similar to those of the 9th Bhopals. The Baluchis were also attached to the British Cavalry under the orders of the 3rd Cavalry Brigade of the 2nd Division and, having been taken by omnibus from Baillieu to Eloi, they occupied the support trenches on the early morning of the 23 October. Shortly afterwards they took over the defence of the village of Hollebeke by occupying the front-line trenches as relief for three British Cavalry battalions; 16th (The Queen's) Lancers, 5th (Royal Irish) Lancers, 4th (The Queens Own) Hussars[1] The Baluchis faced the advancing Germans under extreme conditions; they were standing in water-logged trenches,[2] with insufficient hand grenades and barbed wire as well as gaps in the line due to a shortage of soldiers. In fact, the Baluchis were outnumbered by the Germans five to one.[3]

The 16th Lancers had been stationed at the Curragh in Ireland and its officers were involved in the Curragh Incident which almost denuded the British Army of many of its leading officers. It had been rumoured that they would resign if the Irish Home Rule Bill was passed and they were asked to put down a Protestant uprising in Ulster, Even Hubert Gough, Commander of the 3rd Cavalry Brigade threatened to do so, The problem was solved when Asquith's Government backed down and exempted Ulster from the legislation. The 16th Lancers had landed in France on 18 August 1914 and fought at Le Cateau on 26 August where its Commanding Officer, Lieutenant Colonel E M. L MacEwen was wounded. Compared with many Cavalry Battalions, the 16th Lancers was to have a quiet war but did occupy the trenches from time to

1 16th (The Queens) Lancers, 5th (Irish) Lancers, 4th (the Queens Own) Hussars
2 At Festubert, two Gurkhas drowned in their 'miniature canals'. Rob Johnson, 'I Shall Die Alms in Hand Wearing the Warriors' Clothes': Mobilisation and Initial Operations of the Indian Army in France and Flanders. Alan Jeffreys (ed.) *The Indian Army in the First World War* (Solihull: Helion & Co., 2018), p. 46
3 Foreign and Commonwealth Office. Case study: WW1 Pakistani VC recipient Khudadad Khan <https://www.gov.uk/government/case-studies/ww1-pakistani-vc-recipient-khudadad- khan> (accessed 18 June 2020).

time. By the time of its relief by the Baluchis, the Lancers had spent several days in the front line and were due for a rest.

The 5th (Royal Irish) Lancers had been stationed at Dublin for four years at the time of the outbreak of the First World War and landed in France on 17 August. It also took part in the battle of Le Cateau but then seemed to have spent a great deal of time marching to and thro and only occasionally occupying the trenches. They were being kept for an anticipated break through when it was hoped that a retreating German Army could be pursued once the infantry had broken through their defensive trench. Such was Haig's belief that this was an opportunity to use cavalry in this way that when the Indian Infantry left the Western Front the Indian Cavalry remained. Bushman argues that this is not surprising as cavalry provided Haig with the only flexible, mobile force for most of the war and one should not be surprised he would wish to retain it and use it decisively whenever the opportunity should present itself. It is to the credit of those British, Indian and Canadian cavalry forces on the Western Front, that they unfailingly and bravely responded to the challenge.[4]

The 4th (The Queen's Own) Hussars were also relieved by the Baluchis but left a number of troopers and its Machine Gun Section behind to support them in the trenches. Cavalry numbers were low, and several Battalions sent troopers to form a 'composite' Battalion in order to join in an attack with I Corps, but this amalgam of troops was, in the end, not employed.[5] The gradual stagnation of the mobile war caused by the increasing number of trenches was beginning to make the cavalry somewhat out of place. The War Diaries of these cavalry Battalions describe how they entered the trenches and were relieved by the 129th Baluchis over a period of about twenty-four hours during the last week of October.

The summary report for this period of action by the Baluchis, written by their Commanding. Officer. Lieutenant Colonel Southey mentioned that the 23 October was the first time the Sepoys had experienced heavy shelling. They were described as standing up to it well.[6] Three of the four companies occupied the trenches whilst the fourth was held in reserve together with 90 men from the 4th Hussars. The Germans constantly sniped the Baluchis' trenches and caused casualties of two men killed and two wounded. The heavy shelling continued the next day and one signaller in the Headquarters Section was 'blown to bits!'[7] On the 25 October the cavalry troopers in support were withdrawn except for its Machine Gun Section. The Baluchis sent out a patrol of twenty men to reconnoitre the enemy position in a nearby farm. On

4 Bob Bushaway, Haig and the Cavalry, *Journal of the Centre for World War Studies* (accessed 20 December 2021).

5 TNA WO 95/1134: War Diary of the 4th (Queen's Own) Hussars War Diary, 24 October 1914.

6 TNA WO 95/3924: 3 Indian (Ferozepore) Division, Infantry Brigade 129 (D.C.O.). Baluchis. Summary Report to Brigade Major, 3rd Cavalry Brigade.; 2 November 1914

7 TNA WO 95/3924: 3 Indian (Ferozepore) Division, Infantry Brigade 129 (D.C.O.) Baluchis. Summary Report to Brigade Major, 3rd Cavalry Brigade.; 2 November 1914.

Monday 26 October the Germans shelled Hollebeke heavily and set the church alight. In response the Baluchis, attacked the enemy's position losing one British Officer and six Sepoys killed and forty wounded. One section had got within 300 yards of the German trenches but were forced to retire in the face of four cleverly placed machine guns.

The Baluchis were later withdrawn from the firing line but on the 28 October, they were back in the trenches which protected the village Chateau. The following day, two of the Baluchis' companies were sent to the bridge over the canal north west of Hollebeke as a support to the Cavalry in the village, Later the Baluchis marched to Kleine Zillebeke to become part of the reserve for I Corps. The 30 October began quietly for the Baluchis. As usual, early in the day, part of the Battalion was relieved by the Cavalry Battalions during which the Germans launched a heavy artillery barrage which lasted all morning. The enemy then delivered a skilful attack, possibly knowing that the line would be disorganised as one unit was relieving another which was not a rapid process.[8] One company of Baluchis had been in the trenches and then relieved by the 16th Lancers. Southey found them using a wood as shelter whilst gathering together before returning to the billets. He was shocked to hear that one of his most experienced officers, Major George Geoffrey. Prendergast Humphreys, who had been in command of 2nd Company, which was in the support trenches, had been wounded by shrapnel. Humphreys was later to die of his wounds on 30 October. Major Humphreys had been born in Ireland and commissioned in the Welch Battalion in 1892 and later transferred to the Indian Army taking part in the Uganda Campaign of 1897 and the China Field Force in 1901. Humphreys had been attached to the 129th Baluchis from his own Battalion, the 127th Baluchis when, as the link Battalion, it provided a double company to make up the 129th's numbers. He is said to have commanded his Company with great coolness and judgement. He is buried in Kemmel churchyard.

Chaos began to develop, and Southey's frustration is apparent when he reported that Companies appeared to become separated from their officers. Number 3 Company had been ordered to form up, march to the Chateau where they were to wait further orders from the G.O.C. 3rd Cavalry. One platoon had done so but the remaining three platoons had not arrived. Lieutenant Colonel Southey found Captain Maclean and his V.C.O., Subadar Ahmed Din at the Chateau but without their men. One can imagine Southey's mood when he ordered the two to return and bring their men back. At this point Southey was ordered to reinforce the trenches with all the men he had available and he took No. 1 Platoon from No. 3 Company together with his 4th Company to the firing line, which was just behind the Field Hospital, an indication of the proximity of the German advance. Southey also sent men under Major Henry William Ross Potter to hold the nearby wood which was on the line's right flank whilst Major Hannyngton went to look for the missing platoons from No. 3 Company

8 Merewether & Smith, *The Indian Corps,* p. 32

whilst Southey 'rallied' the men from No. 1 Platoon. On the arrival of Lieutenant Lewis and Subadar Adam Khan, Southey handed these men over to these officers and the two were able to successfully maintain the defence of the position until the order to retire was given.

Southey was no doubt embarrassed to receive an order from Brigadier General Vaughan, G.O.C. 3rd Cavalry Brigade, informing him that ' there were a lot of (his) men straggling and he wanted (Southey) to reform them ' and then get them to return to the trenches at the Chateau.[9] Southey went to discuss the problem with Vaughan who provided additional information that the stragglers had been taken back by Major Stewart assisted by some Lancers. Southey was later to discover that most of these men were from No. 3 Company who were without officers 'and were consequently out of hand.'[10] It was this sort of incident which confirmed the unreliability of Indian troops in the eyes of some. However, as has been argued, they were not encouraged to show initiative, they were fighting in an alien fashion and may have considered themselves abandoned by their British officer and V.C.O. Southey showed some sympathy for their plight for he pointed out the Company was made up of young Sepoys of less than three years' service; many with only one year, and Southey had not been surprised that, under the circumstances, they had broken.[11]

Captain Maclean was not available to give his Colonel an explanation as to why he had left his men as he had become a casualty. Southey was told that the order to retire in twos and threes when they could, had been given to the Sepoys during heavy shelling. The German's advance towards the Indian firing line gradually moved forward and forced the 129th slowly backwards but the Indians' rifle fire was able to delay the enemy's advance. The 129th Baluchis' retirement was assisted when an additional company took up a forward position on the 129th's right flank and was able to check the Germans' advance with enfilading fire. At 1600 hours Southey was ordered to withdraw his men to the trenches north of the Chateau. Demonstrating his experience in battle, Southey made sure that this message had been passed on to the 16th Lancers which were on the 129th Baluchi's right flank and the Royal Horse Artillery who were in his rear. When the guns had limbered up and retreated, Southey finally gave the order to withdraw.

The action had cost the 129th (D.O.C) Baluchis dear and Merewether and Smith provided a more accurate butcher's bill than that contained in Southey's report which was written in haste. Major Humphreys, Captains Adair and Hampe-Vincent were killed, Captains Maclean, Dill and Lieutenant Lewis were wounded. Three of the V.C.O.s had been killed and two wounded. The rank and file had also suffered

9 Merewether and Smith, *The Indian Corps,* p. 32
10 Merewether and Smith, *The Indian Corps,* p. 32
11 The Baluchis as the 29th Baluchis had last seen action in 1890 when they were part of the Zhob Valley Punitive Expedition. It is, therefore, unlikely that any of the 129th had actually experienced combat.

greatly: 164 had been killed or wounded and 64 were missing, the majority of whom, Merewether assumed, were probably killed.[12]

Merewether and Smith, writing in retrospect, were able to provide details of the fate of the 129th British officer casualties which had not been included in Southey's early report on the action. Captain Adair is described as a most gallant leader, who was mortally wounded and when his Indian Havildar (Sergeant), Zauf Khan, and two others of Adair's Company attempted to extricate him under heavy fire, he refused to let them to put their lives at risk as he knew his wounds were mortal.

Captain Robert Foster Dill, the son of the Very Rev. Marcus Dill, D.D., a former Moderator of the Church of Scotland, commanded the Machinegun Section and when one of his machineguns was put out of action, he ordered his men to retire but continued to fire his remaining weapon until he was severely wounded in the head by a shell splinter. He was awarded the D.S.O. for his gallantry.[13] His men did not withdraw but continued to fight until overwhelmed by the enemy and all but one, Sepoy Khudadad Khan, were killed.

Twenty-six-year-old Khan had been born of a Muslim family in the Punjab. On the 31 October he was part of Dill's two machine guns team which had had been in action all day and had prevented the Germans from making a break in the defensive line. One machinegun was disabled which gave the enemy an opportunity to rush the section. All of the machinegun team were shot or bayoneted to death but Khudadad Khan continued to work his gun. Eventually he was badly wounded and left for dead but during the night he was able to crawl back to his Battalion in spite of his wounds.

For his conspicuous bravery, Sepoy Khudadad Kan was awarded the Victoria Cross;[14] the first soldier in the Indian Army to be so recognised.[15] The bravery of Khudadad Khan, his fellow Baluchis and the other Battalions at Hollebeke delayed the German advance sufficiently to allow enough time for reinforcements to arrive and

12 Merewether and Smith, *The Indian Corps*, p. 39.

13 Dill was educated at Marlborough College and the RMC Sandhurst he obtained a commission in the Indian Army in 1904 and was gazetted to his Captaincy in 1912. He was killed in action on 15 April 1915. His younger brother, Lieutenant John Rowe Dill, of 69th Baluchis was subsequently killed in action on 6 June 1915 at the age of 26. Dill's other two brothers qualified as doctors and served in the RAMC.

14 *The London Gazette (Supplement)*. No. 28999. 7 December 1914. p. 10425.

15 Khudadad Khan was presented with his V.C. by George V on 26 January 1915 the place where this presentation was made is uncertain. The Foreign and Commonwealth Office suggests it was at Buckingham Place. The Comprehensive Guide to Victoria and George Cross suggests that it was at the Indian Convalescent Home in New Milton Hampshire as he was too ill to attend a ceremony elsewhere. The Guide suggests that Darwan Singh Negi of the 1/39th Garhwal Rifles was the first Indian to be actually presented with the V.C. on 5 December 1914. This award was for action on 23-24 November over three weeks after that of Khudadad Khan when meant that Darwan Singh Negi was the second Indian to be awarded the VC. See *VCs Online* <http://vconline.org.uk/khudadad-khan-vc/4587318329> (accessed 18 June 2020).

deny the Germans reaching the Channel Ports which would have cut off the BEF. It marked the end of the First Battle of Ypres.

Khudadad Khan survived the War and returned to India to serve on the Northwest Frontier; in 1929 he was promoted Subadar. Other members of Khudadad Khan's section were also recognised for their gallantry and, somewhat unusually, are named by Merewether and Smith as Havildar Ghulam Mahomed who was awarded the Indian Order of Merit and Sepoys Lai Sher, Said Ahmed, Kassib Khan and Lafar Khan, who were awarded the Indian Distinguished Service Medal.[16]

Lieutenant General Allenby, GOC of the recently formed Cavalry Corps, was full of praise for the actions of the Indian Corps who had supported his troopers. Brigadier General George Barrow, on Allenby's staff, also wrote a complimentary note to Watkins saying the two battalions which the Lahore Division had loaned the Cavalry Corps had fought splendidly and somewhat ghoulishly observed that he was returning 'what was left of them'.[17]

16 It has been suggested that Darwan Singh Negi of the 1/39th Garhwal Rifles was the first Indian to be actually presented with the V.C. on 5 December 1914. This award was for actions on 23-24 November over three weeks after that of Khudadad Khan when meant that Darwan Singh Negi was the second Indian to be awarded the VC.

17 TNA WO 95/3922: Ferozepore Infantry Brigade Headquarters, Appendix 1, 3 November 1914. Barrow had been first commissioned in the Connaught Rangers in 1884 before transferring to the 35th Scinde Horse.

9

'And show HIM what British Soldiers can do'

For the Connaught Rangers, the first week in November proved to be very draining. The weather was extremely wet and the trenches which they occupied were very muddy and, in some cases, partially flooded. It was difficult for the men to keep the mud out of their rifles and their bolts and ammunition became clogged with the mud which caused the rifles to jam.[1] This was particularly serious when two platoons from A Company, having driven Germans from a forward trench, were meant to cover another party from C Company which was sent to fill in the trench, and the A Company platoons found that, after a short period of firing, they were unable to reply to the enemy's fire because of mud-clogged rifles. Both parties were helpless and forced to retire. The battalion war diarist, clearly dismayed by the situation, concluded that the task of taking the trench and filling it in would only be possible if the enemy's forward trench had also been completely captured. Taking that trench was 'much beyond the powers of two platoons.'[2] Perhaps an implied criticism of the original orders especially since a diversionary action meant to distract the Germans from A Company's actions had 'apparently completely failed.' In that early morning action the Connaught Rangers lost four officers and four other ranks killed and thirty wounded. Three of the officers were buried in the nearby orchard of a farm in the village of Laventie, but the fourth, Captain C. Haik's body was missing and could not be found. At the beginning of November the Connaughts mustered 25 officers and 774 other ranks. By 6 November the numbers had fallen to 17 officers and 689 men. The cause of 28 of these casualties were the orders for A Company to relieve D Company of the Connaughts and C Company to relieve a company of the Duke of Cornwall's Light Infantry [DCLI] which was on the left flank of D Company. C Company successfully relieved the DCLI but as soon as A Company left the communication trench it came under heavy artillery fire as well as being targeted by substantial machine gun and rifle fire. Captain Callaghan of D Company and six of his men were successfully

1 TNA WO 95/3923: Connaught Rangers War Diary, 5 November 1914.
2 TNA WO 95/3923: Connaught Rangers War Diary, 5 November 1914.

relieved but such was the intensity of the enemy fire that the rest of his company had to return to their original trench and assist A Company in repelling an attack by the Germans opposite. The battalion war diarist observed that the casualties were slight since many of the men of D Company had reached the communication trench before the enemy fire had reached its peak. At 0300 hours, the men of D Company were able to retire to their billets. The Connaughts were sandwiched between the Duke of Cornwall's Light Infantry on the left and the 9th Bhopals on their right.

The Ranger's strength was increased slightly on the 7 November when 12 men re-joined the Battalion from hospital but, by the end of the next day, the number of other ranks was reduced to 673; 14 of whose wounds were serious enough to be taken to hospital rather than a casualty clearing station. Captain Boyd, the Connaughts' Medical Officer, recorded that the First Aid Post was hit by a piece of shell but is full of praise for 'most' of the stretcher bearers whose work was excellent.[3] Boyd's work must have increased considerably since, on the previous day, his assistant Lieutenant Kidson had been sent to join the Casualty Clearing Station at Baillieu and was consequently removed from the Connaught Rangers' roll.

Fighting continued and, on 9 November, A Company was issued with rifle grenades which enabled them to attack the German firing line with great success. However, the Germans returned the compliment and seven of A Company troops were wounded by German grenades. The Connaughts had now been reduced to 661 men.

On the early morning of 11 November, the Connaughts were ordered to engage in slow fire in order to cover an attack by the Meerut Division which was on the Connaught's right flank. However, the rate of fire in the Connaught's front line was too heavy for such a form of distraction but the Battalion Headquarters could not communicate with the firing line as either the telephone wire was too thin and poorly insulated for the wet conditions, or the telephones themselves had been affected by the damp. Some of the wire was found to be actually under water.

It appeared that the Germans, using the darkness and the rainstorm on the previous night as cover, had dug a new forward trench some 25 yards closer to A Company's trench. An attempt was made to rush this new trench, but the corporal and eight men designated to do so were forced to return having found it too strongly held by an alert enemy.

On the 13 November, the Connaughts prepared to send a stronger attacking party but, before they could do so, the Germans launched an offensive of their own on A Company's firing line with a party of 100 men. There followed hand to hand fighting in which one officer was wounded by a bayonet thrust. The attacking Germans were reported to have lost 25 men killed. The new forward trench clearly posed a threat to the Connaughts' firing line and Brigadier General Egerton arrived to discuss the possibility of launching a heavy attack upon it. After consulting his subordinate officers, Egerton decided not to attempt to take the trench as it would require a force

3 TNA WO 95/393: Connaught Rangers Medical Officer's War Diary, 5 November 1914.

of greater strength than the Connaughts could muster. The unfortunate A Company were forced to remain in the firing-line as it was very late in the evening. One of the Connaughts' sergeants, L.C. Badham was promoted to Lieutenant which brought the officer strength to 16.

The constant shelling and defending the trenches were beginning to take their toll on the Connaughts. On 14 November they were subjected to shelling by a mortar which fired high explosive and shrapnel shells causing damage to part of the front-line trench which consequently collapsed and buried two men. The Diary, somewhat desperately, noted that number of cases of sickness were rising, and that relief was now a necessity.[4]

The Connaught Ranger's Medical Officer's Diary provides a more detailed explanation for the cause of the increased sickness. Twenty-one men had been sent to the field hospital and most of these were from A Company. These men had been in the trenches almost continuously for fifteen days and the previous three days had been very challenging. The trench they occupied was only 25 yards from the firing line of the enemy and it needed to be very deep in order to protect the men from enemy fire but they also had constantly to be on the look-out for enemy activity. The conditions in the trench meant that its bottom was very damp, and the Company had little straw to place in the lowest part of the trench in order to absorb the water. Many of the troops were suffering from 'Trench Foot' and frost bite.[5] The Battalion M.O. wrote to the Officer Commanding who should remind the men that the treatment for frost bite was contained in *The Soldiers' Pocket Book for Field Service* to which they should refer.[6]

Early in the morning of 15 November a party of 60 Connaughts from A and D Companies attacked a German trench but found it contained only 7 to 10 snipers; of whom 6 were 'accounted for'. The Rangers returned to their own forward trench, but, whilst doing so, four men were wounded by Germans who had returned to their front trench and fired at the retreating Connaughts. The Battalion was relieved during the night of 15/16 November by The Sherwood Foresters and East Lancashire Regiment and then marched to billets at La Gorgue. After 24 hours, they moved again to fresh billets at Zelobes, where on 18 November, D Company and the Headquarters section were inspected by Sir James Willcocks, Commander of the Indian Corps. The War Diary records that ordered to mobilise, the Connaughts' muster now consisted of 15 officers and 513 other ranks. A Company of the Battalion participated in a parade that was inspected by the Prince of Wales whilst others collected brushwood or dug trenches.

The 9th Bhopals had begun November as the general reserve and were based in the vicinity of Laventie. On 1 November they received news that the German Emperor,

4 TNA WO 95/3923: Connaught Rangers War Diary, 14 November 1914.
5 The conditions in the trenches during this wet and cold period prevented the Sepoys from keeping their feet dry. They found it difficult to obtain dry socks and prolonged periods in the trenches produced blistering, blotchy skin on their some on which was dead and falling off.
6 TNA WO 95/3923: Connaught Rangers Medical Officer's War Diary, 21 November 1914.

Kaiser Wilhelm II, had arrived to conduct the enemy's operations. Such a claim was far from the truth, as the Kaiser was increasingly in the grip of his Generals and his visit was probably merely to encourage his troops. On the same day they saw an aeroplane overhead and shortly afterwards were shelled. Clearly this was a German spotter plane acting as a forward artillery observer and in communication with the neighbouring guns. The Indian troops sheltered under the hedges until the barrage was over. They were subsequently ordered to be in constant readiness since, even this early in the war, artillery bombardments were often the precursor of an infantry attack. They spent the night in the grounds of a Chateau on the Rue de Paradis; hardly a paradise, which was west of Laventie.

Sleep must have been at a premium for, at 0430 hours on the following day, the Battalion began to dig trenches and sat in them to shelter from shrapnel. Shortly afterwards, the 9th Bhopals received orders to relieve an Indian Infantry Brigade but this order was cancelled and they were ordered to advance to the Rouge Croix, where they had been at the end of October, in order to act as reserve to the 8th British Infantry Brigade. Again the order was changed to the Bhopals acting as support to the Meerut Division. The Battalion billeted at Rouge Croix but were kept in constant readiness. The constant changing of orders must have been frustrating for officers and Sepoys alike. One suspects that this confusion was also created by what seems to have been the reluctance of High Command to use the Bhopals as a front-line Battalion but to keep them always as a Reserve.

On 3 November the 9th Bhopal Infantry were ordered to return to the trenches close to the Chateau at Rue de Paradis to act as a reserve Battalion for the Manchester Regiment. Under the cover of darkness this manoeuvre was completed and the Bhopals remained in the trenches during the night. At around 2330 hours, there was an attack with much firing and the Battalion 'stood to arms.' Back to the Chateau the next morning and then back in the trenches on evening of 4 November which was to prove to be a quiet night. On the following evening they returned to the trenches as relief for the Royal Scots Fusiliers. Again it proved a quiet day but there was a bombardment which did not cause casualties.

It was a lull before a storm and on the 7 November the left-hand section of the Bhopals front trench experienced a very heavy bombardment at 1630 hours which caused 55 casualties. At 2300, another enemy bombardment caused a further 15 casualties from the same section which was under the command of Captain Gaskell. On the 8 November, although there were no signs of the enemy, the Battalion was subjected to what was described as 'promiscuous sniping' and suffered a further ten casualties. The bombardments increased in intensity towards the end of the day when the Bhopals were being relieved by the Connaught Rangers. The Germans often used this tactic at such a time in order to take advantage of troops being disorganised and unintentionally exposed themselves. The section which had occupied the front line had lost 1 Indian Officer, and 75 other ranks killed or wounded. The Battalion war diarist made critical observations about the Bhopals' experiences in the trenches as his unit's learning curve of Western Front combat increased. His advice was:

1. Trenches should be lightly manned during the day and the remaining Sepoys should be in the support trenches which must be made splinter proof and be at a distance from the front-line trenches. This advice was to prevent heavy casualties when the front-line trenches were shelled.
2. The front line or fire trenches should be very narrow and under cut at the bottom to enable Sepoys to shelter during a bombardment.
3. The Sepoys in the front-line trenches should not engage in 'promiscuous' firing at night but only shoot when the enemy was seen.[7]

The diarist's advice was sensible since it was designed to prevent needless casualties from enemy fire and avoid both wasting ammunition and the identification of the disposition of troops in the front line. It had been, however, an expensive lesson for the Bhopals to learn.

Having rested for a short time, a company of 100 were sent to clear the enemy from a village in the proximity of Rouge Croix. Again changing orders were to prove frustrating. The Bhopals were informed at 1600 hours on 9 November that they would be relieved at 17:30 hours by an Indian Cavalry Battalion and would march to Estaires where they would have a few days' rest. They left their billets as instructed but had only marched around a mile before they received fresh orders to return to their original billets where they were told to be held in constant readiness.

Verbal orders were then received from an unidentified Staff Officer that they should, after all, march to Estaires which the Bhopals began to do on 10 November. On arrival, Lieutenant General Willcocks, Commander of the Indian Corps, spoke to the British and Indian Officers informing them he had recalled the Battalion for a rest, and he was very appreciative of the work they had done. The Bhopals finally were able to begin the rest and clean their clothes and equipment. On 12 November some of the Bhopals were drafted to be inspected by 'Bobs', Field Marshal Earl Roberts, once Commander in Chief of both the British and the Indian Armies. The Bhopals were joined by Major Carlton and Captain Apthorpe, of the 90th Punjabis, who had arrived from India, and were to make up for Bhopal Officers who had been killed or wounded. Again on 14 November the 9th Bhopals received orders to move but these are cancelled. The 15 November was a day of sleet and rain and the Battalion moved to fresh billets in two farms in the hamlet of Beaupre which was close to the village of La Gorgue where the Ferozepore Brigade was said to be assembling. These orders were again cancelled and the Bhopals endured further cancellations in the next two days during which they received a further British officer reinforcement, Lieutenant Balfour from the 98th Infantry Battalion.[8]

7 TNA WO 95/3923: 9th Battalion Bhopal Infantry War Diary, 9 November 1914.

8 The arrival of these three British Officers, direct from India, was evidence of the weakness of the Indian Army' special requirements for its British Officers which has already been described. Unlike British battalions which could recruit from the Home Country or the

57th (Wilde's) Rifles resting by the side of the Estaires – La Bassée Road.

On 17 November, the Battalion moved from La Gourge to Zelobes; a distance of approximately three and a half miles. Here they were joined by another British officer, Lieutenant Fletcher from the 97th Deccan Infantry. Perhaps more importantly, Jamadar Nazim Khan arrived with the Bhopal Battalion's first batch of 26 reinforcements since they had arrived in France. It is hard to imagine the impression which these newly arrived Sepoys had of the battlefield which they had just arrived. Their coming also demonstrated another weakness of the Indian Army when fighting in Europe. Their base was thousands of miles away and sending newly trained soldiers required considerable time and effort and it would be obvious that the 26 newcomers were insufficient to fill the gaps in the Bhopal Battalion's ranks which the recent fighting had made.

The Bhopals now moved to the nearby village of Les Lobes where, on the 18 November, Lieutenant General James Willcocks visited their billets and inspected their rifles and accoutrements. On the following day the Battalion constructed a

military colleges, Indian battalions required commissioned officers who understood the peculiarities of the regimental system and could at the least speak Urdu.

second line of trenches close to Béthune. It started to snow and one wonders for how many this type of weather was a new experience. It was probable that the snow was the reason why they were engaged in running drill in order that to keep them warm especially as the weather became even colder. One of the Companies was inspected by the Prince of Wales, who was serving in the British Army. The less fortunate were used for fatigues and collecting brushwood presumably for fires to alleviate the very cold weather.

This period of peace and quiet could not last long and on the 22 November the Bhopals were ordered forward to La Plantin, which was near the town of Festubert. Captain Gaskell took the right half of the Battalion into the firing line while the left half remained in La Plantin in support. No. 1 Company were ordered to occupy a support trench to the east of La Plantin and at 0932 hours on 23 November it was commanded to advance in order to assist the 34th Sikh Pioneers Battalion which was in the firing line.[9] The Pioneers were subject to a bombardment from German hand grenades from a Sap which was within five yards of their front line.[10] The German grenades pushed the right half of No. 4 Company of the Pioneers backwards onto the Connaught Rangers who were to their left and the right half of No. 4 Company was pushed onto their own No. 3 Company. Consequently the Germans were able to enter the Pioneers' front trench almost unopposed. Anxious to recapture their front line, the Pioneers No. 1 Company was ordered to advance towards it and reached a ditch which was 15 yards from the trench. Before they could launch an assault, however, the were subjected to enfilading fire from a German 'maxim'. Both Nos. 1 and No. 3 Companies were forced to pull back as were the Bhopals under Captain Gaskell. At this point the telephone ceased to work and a runner was sent forward to ascertain Gaskell's situation. After 90 minutes the runner returned. He had been unable to reach Gaskell because the enemy were attacking his troops from the rear and the runner couldn't bypass them. A few stragglers appeared and confirmed that Gaskell and his men were surrounded.

At this point the G.O.C. of the Brigade, Major General Watkins, arrived at what was a tense moment for his command, and ordered a counterattack. This took place at around 1630 hours and involved a Company of Bhopals, three hundred Connaughts and six of their officers, the 6th Jat Light Infantry and the 2/8th Gurkhas, the latter two Battalions from the Meerut Division.[11]

This combined attack successfully recaptured the trenches in which were found bodies of some of Gaskell's men and of the enemy. The defence and recapture had cost the Bhopals 2 officers wounded, 3 officers including Gaskell missing, 3 Indian

9 The 34th Sikh Pioneers was also part of the Lahore Division and were another specialist battalion being led as ordinary infantry.

10 TNA WO 95/3914: 34 Sikh Pioneers War Diary, November 1914. A Sap was a trench dug towards the enemy's front-line trench under cover without having to 'go over the top'.

11 The 6th Jats were part of the Meerut Brigade, Dehra Dun Division and the 2/8th Ghurkhas were part of the Bareilly Brigade.

Officers killed and 2 missing, 6 other ranks killed and 43 wounded with 165 missing: a total of 224 killed wounded or missing. On the 22 November the Connaughts were deployed to the right section of the firing line where it was intended that they should relieve the Royal Highlanders (Black Watch). Before this could happened, however, the ever-busy D section was ordered to support the troops in the centre of the firing line who were under considerable pressure.

9th Bhopal Infantry losses recorded on the Menin Gate.

On the 23 November the Connaughts were ordered to march to Gorre, described as a 'a somewhat squalid village' two miles behind the Givenchy-Festubert Sector, which was held by the Meerut Division, and report to the Brigadier General Egerton, the Brigade Commander.[12] Reaching Gorre at 1430 hours, the Connaughts were immediately ordered to provide a detachment of 6 officers and 300 men which represented more than half of the remaining Connaughts, to support the 2/8th Gurkhas who were about to attack the centre section of the line which had been captured by the enemy.

The Connaughts did not make sufficient progress to reach the trenches and, such was the fog of war, believed that the 'native troops' had also failed in their assault. This was not completely correct as the 6th Jat Light Infantry was able to capture part of the lost trench but at the cost of 20 Killed, 110 wounded and 27 missing The Connaught Rangers confusion can be excused when it is realised that the three Connaught Companies involved had literally fought themselves to a standstill and were unable to make any further progress. By the end of the action the Battalion was now reduced to a total of 8 Officers and 393 other ranks.[13] For the next four days the

12 H. W. R. Hamilton, 'The 20th (Field) Company, Royal Bombay Sappers and Miners, 1914-18' in *The Royal Engineers Journal*, Vol.XL, No. 4, December 1926, p. 546.

13 Six Killed, 53 Wounded and 54 Missing. See TNA WO 95/3923: Connaught Rangers War Diary, 23 November 1914.

much-depleted Connaughts occupied the trenches and relieved small parties from one day to another. By the end of the month they were reduced to 349 other ranks and 'all ranks very fatigued through want of relief'.[14]

For the next four days, the 9th Bhopals were kept in 'constant readiness'. Parties of the Sepoys were designated to dig a communication trench from the support trench to the firing-line to enable troops to move forwards and backwards without exposing themselves to enemy fire. They also sent out patrols to see if any of the in habitants of the village of Festubert were still in their homes. Unexpectedly one man died, and four others became seriously ill from carbon monoxide poisoning caused by sitting close to a charcoal fire in an enclosed room. On the 23 November the body of Captain Mortimer, one of the officers who went missing during the earlier fighting, was found. Like so many reported missing after fighting in the trenches, Mortimer had been killed and, in the chaos of attack and retreat, his body had been overlooked. Many bodies were never found, and their names appear on monuments such as the Menin Gate.

14 TNA WO 95/3923: Connaught Rangers War Diary, 30 November 1914.

10

'Having rendered services of such high praise'

The 129th Baluchis received a message at 0100 hours on the 1 November from the 3rd Cavalry Brigade warning them that the farm in Major Potter's section of the line had been captured by the enemy and the GOC wished to have further information. The Battalion itself had not received any report to this effect and so Lieutenant Lewis was sent to find out the situation. On Lewis' return at 0200 hours he confirmed that the information was correct, and the Germans were in the farm. Ten minutes later GOC 3rd Cavalry Brigade, Brigadier General John Vaughan, ordered that the farm should be recaptured. At 0400 hours the Baluchis successfully assaulted the farm and it was recaptured; ten Germans were killed, and 14 prisoners were detained during the assault.

At 0500 hours the Baluchis handed over their trenches to French cavalry and marched under heavy artillery fire to Voormezeele. It took two hours for the Baluchis to reach the town and they were immediately ordered to march to Kemmel; a distance of roughly four miles. It was now 0815 hours and the men were probably relieved to be allowed to halt and cook their food and rest for four hours. They were then ordered to march to Westoutre, a distance of four and a half miles and finally reached their billets at 1430 hours. During the day only one Sepoy was wounded.

The rest at Westoutre provided the Battalion time to reflect on their losses in their various actions whilst attached to 2nd Cavalry Division. The toll on British officers was already a feature during the whole of the Indian Corps' three months spent on the Western Front and the 129th Baluchis' experience was no exception. Their War Diary records that on 2 November, there were only six effective British officers with the Battalion. The rest had been either killed or wounded. Perhaps the compliments which the GOC 2nd Cavalry Brigade paid to the Battalion as it marched through Westoutre may have provided some small compensation to the Baluchis. They were then moved to fresh billets in Strazeele; a distance of roughly ten and a half miles. On 4 November the Baluchis finally left the 2nd Cavalry Brigade and together with the 57th Wilde's Rifles re-joined the Ferozepore Brigade.

Wilde's Rifles had also been decimated during the last weeks in October. By 2 November they reported 2 British Officers killed, 3 wounded and 1 missing. One

Indian Officer had been killed 2 wounded and one missing with a total of 304 casualties amongst the Sepoys which included 95 missing and 24 sick. Such was the diligence of the war diarist that every Sepoy is named in the casualty list. Perhaps this was a confirmation of the family character of this Battalion and other Indian Battalions. The number of missing was reduced slightly when on 2 November, a few stragglers were able to re-join the 57th which was now under the orders of Colonel Southey, the Commander of the 129th Baluchis. The two Battalions, much reduced in number, were combined to form a composite Battalion and after marching some 17 miles between 3 and 4 November and having reached Estaires, they were allowed to rest.

Wilde's Rifle was so reduced in strength that it was modified into two, rather than the normal four Companies. The new No. 1 Company, commanded by Major T.J. Williams, was made up of two Indian Officers and 173 Sikh and Dogra other ranks and No. 2 Company under the Command of the Adjutant, Captain W. S. Trail, had eight Indian Officers and 224 Punjabi Mussalman and Afridi other ranks. Such an arrangement would obviously damage the familiarity which men had with their Class comrades and must have been psychologically damaging but was the only way in which Wilde's Rifle could organise itself after such extensive numbers of casualties. The War Diary points out that these numbers include all the various Classes of Sepoys which were still attached to the Battalion, and included the cooks, baggage guards and the Headquarters Section.

On 5th November, the 57th Wilde's Rifles entered the trenches again at Pont du Hem where they experienced frequent daylight and night-time attacks together with heavy shelling for the next four days. Roughly a third of the Sepoys were kept in reserve to repel possible attacks or replace casualties. There is something stoical about the Wilde's Diary's entry in recording that the casualties during these four days, 10 wounded and one killed, as being light 'considering the amount of shell and rifle fire that went on.'[1] Fortunately the 57th received reinforcements during this period. Captain C. A. Milward from the 53rd Sikhs, which was also part of the Frontier Force, joined the Battalion as did 48 Sepoys who had arrived from Marseilles and this enabled half of the men in the trenches to be relieved and stand down. It is possible that the choice of Milward's as a replacement was based on the fact that he too was from a Frontier Force which gave him a link with the Rifles, The 57th also received congratulatory messages on 9 November from Major General Allenby of the Cavalry Corps and Lieutenant General James Willcocks, GOC Indian Corps, for their gallant performance alongside the cavalry.[2]

The newly constituted Companies of the 57th were again in the trenches whilst the British artillery fired through the night. By the morning of the 11 November the Diary records it as desultory firing and the Sepoys had to endured heavy rain and high winds which would have made their life in the trenches very difficult. The following

1 TNA WO 95/3923: 57 (Wilde's) Rifles War Diary, 10 November 1914.
2 TNA WO 95/3923: 57 (Wilde's) Rifles 9 November 1914.

day the Germans returned the artillery barrage and attempted to drive a Sap towards the firing line, but they did not press hard enough for this to be considered to be a genuine attack. Officer replacements again arrived to make up the gaps which still existed. Captain G. A. G. Shepherd, a Wilde's officer, and Captain Douglas Harry Acworth of the 55th (Coke's) Rifles, two of the British Indian Officers who were on leave in England at the outbreak of the war where they had been detained in order to train the New Army, joined the Battalion.[3] The casualty list continued to grow, and, on the 11 November, 5 Sepoys were wounded and on the following day 13 were wounded. By the 13 November the 57th had moved into trenches at Laventie.

There followed a two-day artillery duel during which each side attempted to silence one another's guns. The 57th Rifles continued to man the trenches using the usual turn and turn about method as each Company or Section replaced another in the firing trench at regular intervals. The weather continued to be cold, wet and windy. Hope seemed to be on the horizon, however, when orders came that the Ferozepore Brigade was going to be relieved and its Battalions should return to their billets that evening. However, as often happened, the orders were cancelled. In those three days, the 57th Wilde's Rifles had lost Sepoys the number of which was the equivalent to half of that of the recently arrived replacements.

On Sunday 15 November, the Battalion again received orders that it was to be relieved and together with the rest of the Brigade was to proceed to billets in La Gorgue. The Diary complains that the relief took nine hours to complete because the relieving Battalion wasted time and the Battalion on the 57th's right flank continued to fire throughout the night which attracted German counter fire making the leaving the trenches very hazardous. By 0530 hours the relief had been completed and the 57th arrived in La Gorgue at around 0800 hours. That evening two new officers were entered on the Wilde's strength, both from the 55th (Coke's) Rifles. The Battalion, after roughly two days' rest, marched to Zelobes on a cold wet day and entered the billets there. Three more officers joined the Rifles from various Punjabi Battalions which meant that only around half the British officers remained from the Rifles' original muster.

During the two day's rest in the billets of Zelobes, the Battalion took the opportunity to check their rifles and other kit, attempting to replace any which proved to be defective. The 57th Rifle's War Diary observes that replacement was particularly difficult with regards to the rifles as they were in very short supply. The weather remained very cold and the snow began to settle. The respite was to be short lived as the Ferozepore Brigade received a warning that sometime in the next two days it was to relieve the Bareilly Brigade, which was in the front line. At least one Sepoy enjoyed the day, however, as Havildar Gian Sing was promoted Jemadar to replace Kapur Sing who had been killed on the 31 October.

3 55th (Coke's) Rifles, Frontier Force, were meant to remain on the Northwest Frontier and They were not part of the original IEFA but individual members of the 55th like Acworth were to be used as reinforcement for Indian Battalions serving on the Western Front.

The Battalion supplied a working party on the 20 November which was required to construct reserve trenches. It is possible that this backbreaking work helped the Sepoys keep warm as the weather continued to be very cold with occasional falls of snow. In spite of the Battalion's refit being incomplete, the 57th Rifles were ordered to relieve part of the Bareilly Brigade on the 22 November. The war diarist complained that there was very little ordnance stocks available to replace defective rifles.[4] Nevertheless, the Battalion marched to Festubert and, together with the 129th Baluchis, took over the left section of the line, thus relieving the Bareilly Brigade. Both the Divisional and Battalion Headquarters were established in houses in Festubert.

In early November the Ferozepore Brigade Headquarters had issued a reminder to the Brigade that no 'ammunition manufactured in Dum Dum or the wrappers of such ammunition ' must be in the possession of troops since, if found by the enemy, it would provide them with an excuse to shoot prisoners.[5]

The front line was about one mile from the village of Festubert with the support and reserve trenches in its rear. about 100 yards apart. The night was extremely cold but made considerably worse by constant sniping and enemy bombing attacks. In the early morning of 23 November the Germans launched a determined attack on the front-line trench to the right of the 57th Rifles forcing the occupants back. The Germans were able to occupy the trench and, in spite of a counterattack by three British Battalions, the enemy could not be dislodged. In the afternoon, the Germans began a heavy bombardment of the village of Festubert and absolutely 'wrecked' the Dressing Station. Captain Kanwar Indarjit Singh,[6] Surgeon Assistant Hakim Rai, both of the Indian Medical Service, were killed. Ward Orderly Zaman Khan and Sepoy Akbar Shah, who was Captain Singh's orderly and Surgeon Major Ratal (IMS), Medical Officer of the 129th Baluchis, were also killed. Three other Sepoys, who were part of the Battalion's Headquarters Section, were badly wounded. The Dressing Station caught fire and it took the combined efforts of Sepoys from the 57th Wilde's Rifles, 129th Baluchis and 107th Pioneers and 32nd Company, Sappers and Miners, to put out the blaze and who, in spite of continued shelling, rescued the dead bodies with the exception of that of Captain Singh's. The rescuers

4 The Indian Corps what not the only unit to suffer these types of shortages. Edmonds points out that by mid-December 1914 only 240,000 rifles of the 400,000 needed had been delivered. See Edmonds, 1914, Vol. II. p. 12.

5 TNA WO 95/3924: 129 (D.C.O.) Baluchis, Message from Brigade HQ, 9 November 1914.The Arsenal in the town of Dum Dum was the centre of ammunition manufacturing. In 1896 Lieutenant Colonel Neville Sneyd Bertie-Clay invented an expanding bullet which had more stopping power that the standard Lee-Metford Mk II bullet.The Dum Dum caused massive wounds and its use was banned by the Hague Convention in 1899. However the arsenal continued to manufacture some ammunition of the unconventional type.

6 Captain Singh had been trained at Kings College Hospital in London and was one of the first recipients of the newly created Military Cross for 'distinguished and meritorious service.' See *The London Gazette,* 1 January 1915, p. 8.

also recovered a large amount of ammunition which was buried in the ruins. Juman, Captain Singh's private follower servant, was pulled from the wreckage 'in a critical state'.[7] The building was burned to the ground and undiscovered ammunition continued to explode. In a further act of heroism, Sepoy Mian Singh rescued the Battalion's Yakdan which contained the Battalion's documents and its Treasure Chest which contained a large amount of money.[8] So determined was Miam Singh to rescue anything of value, he continued to search the ruins even though the area was subjected to further heavy shelling and only stopped his search when an officer gave him a direct order to do so. Amongst the documents rescued was the Battalion Diary in which there is a large hole made by a shell fragment which was attached to the cover of the original diary.

The 57th Rifle's line was re-enforced by men from the 2/39th Garwhal Rifles and the newcomers attacked the adjacent trench, which was still occupied by the enemy. Captain Acworth and eight Afridis also joined this attack together with an officer from the Sappers and Miners, Lieutenant R. G. G. Robson RE, who threw bombs into the occupied trench.[9] The trench was eventually retaken and then occupied by the Garwhalis who captured prisoners, three machine guns and a mortar. The 57th Rifle's Afridis returned with four Mauser rifles. a bayonet and some ammunition. They also brought back two German pickelhaubes, probably as souvenirs. The unfortunate Captain Acworth was wounded in the face during the action as when jumping into the trench, he had landed on the bayonet of one of the Garwahlis.

Although no citation exists, Acworth was also one of the first recipients of the newly instituted Military Cross almost certainly for his part this action.[10] The use of the bombs was Robson's idea who had demonstrated the technique to be used by clearing a group of Germans out of a nearby house.[11]

The method of taking the trench with little loss was considered to be an exemplar for other officers to follow. Brigadier General Havelock Hudson of the Indian General Staff was so impressed with the action that he issued a note regarding its success. The description was as follows:

7 TNA W O95/3923: 57 (Wilde's) Rifles War Diary, 24 November 1914.

8 The Yakdan was a large chest which contained much of the Battalion's records and other important paperwork.

9 Ralph George Griffiths Robson was an innovator and a pioneer in the use of 'jam-tin bombs '. Promoted Captain, on 18 December, he was killed in action on 23 December 1914. See *Indian Army List, 1915.* p. 2203 Ian Cardozo, *The Indian Army in World War I, 1914-1918* (London: Routledge, 2019) p. 51.

10 *London Gazette*, 1 January 1915 p. 8. Douglas Acworth was 29 years of age when he took part in this daring action. Educated at Winchester College, he joined the Indian Army in 1906 and was promoted Captain on 5 August 1914. An officer in the 55th (Coke's) Rifles had had been on leave on declaration of war and was retained to train the new Army. In 1915 he was promoted to the Staff but was severely wounded in the forearm and thigh by shrapnel during the battle,

11 J Willcocks, *With The Indians,* p. 130.

> Having entered the zig zagged trench three or four Sepoys advanced along it with fixed bayonets. Immediately behind two officers threw hand grenades over the traverse which was between them and the enemy. The party immediately rushed around the traverse into the next section and dealt with any surviving Germans. The process was then repeated, and, in this way, 500 yards of trench was cleared of the enemy and recaptured. Grenades had to be only thrown a short distance and so were very effective, The assaulting party was followed up by a Battalion.

Willcocks is said to believe that this method should be brought to the attention of others and demonstrates what a well-planned, cool headed attack can achieve rather than a much more costly frontal assault might do.[12] It was Captain Acworth and Robson of the Sapper and Miners and the seven Afridis from the 57th Rifles with one seconded from the 55th (Coke's) Rifles who made up this assault party. During the assault, the 57th had another two Sepoys killed and 14 wounded.

The 57th Rifle's Battalion Office, having been partially destroyed, was transferred to a farm and re-established. The weather thawed a little and the trenches were very cold but slushy. The 57th remained in the trenches and the weather conditions made things worse with some of the communication trenches full of mud which came up to the Sepoys' knees. There was no specific attack by the Germans, but they continued to Sap the firing line and two other Sepoys were wounded. Life in the trenches was very unpleasant and the was a constant drain on numbers through wounding.

It was with considerable pride that the Battalion diary recorded that one of the 57th Wilde's Rifles, Havildar Ganga Singh, a well- known gymnast, had been awarded the Victoria Cross for his efforts in the fight on 31 October.[13] It seems that this award for Ganga Singh's bravery, which was not previously mentioned in the diary, came of something of surprise for the officers of 57th Rifles as they first learned of the award from French Newspapers; an event which was later confirmed in British Newspapers.

In Chapter Six it was recorded that he was actually awarded the Indian order of Merit (Second Class). Ganga Singh had been evacuated to the Indian Hospital in Brighton. Corrigan reports that the *Brighton Herald and Hove Chronicle* carried regular accounts of his recovery and reported that he had been awarded the Victoria Cross but later corrected its error whilst insisting that he should have been. Corrigan confirms that Ganga Singh was awarded the Indian Order of Merit.[14] The error was compounded and Ganga Singh's 'award' was commemorated by the cigarette manufacturer W.H.O Wills which issued a set of 25 cigarette cards of VC winners and which included Ganga Singh. He is also recorded as a Victoria Cross winner in the

12 Indian Army Headquarters, Note dated 27 November 1914, signed Brigadier General H. Hudson, General Staff.

13 See Chapter 6.

14 Corrigan, *With the Sepoys*, p. 342

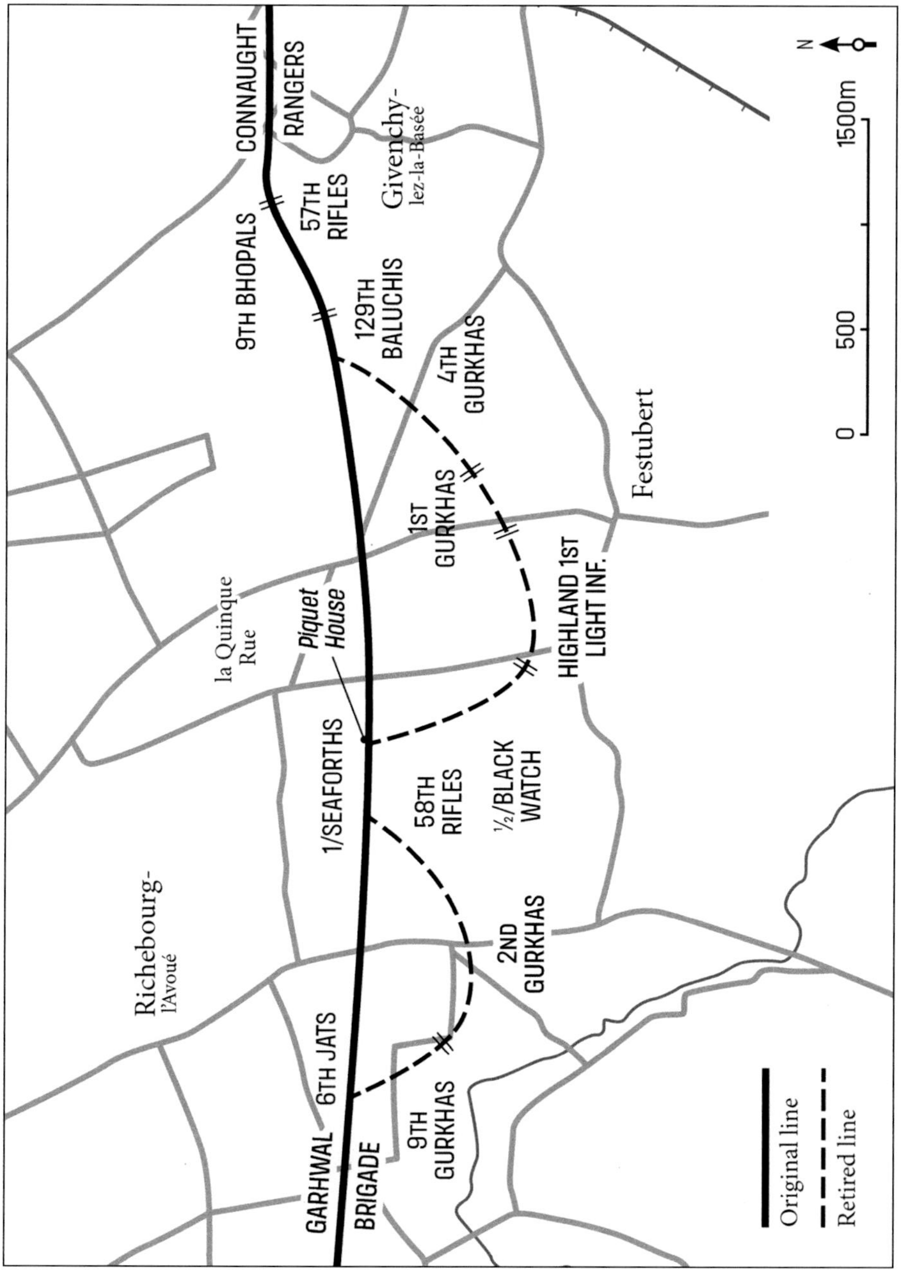

Map 2 Defence of Festubert; 23–24 November 1914.

Medical staff of the General Hospital for Indian troops, Brighton.

Indian Biographical Dictionary of 1915.[15] Even today it is possible to find his name amongst other Victoria Cross winners.[16] It is expected that the 57th Wilde's Rifles war diarist was very surprised by the news since a recommendation for such an award would have initially been made by the commanding officer.[17]

15 C. Hayavadana Rao (ed.), *Indian Biographical Dictionary* (Berkley, California: University of California Libraries reprint of 1915 edition).

16 *Chattri* <http://www.chattri.org/briefHistory/bh1.aspx?sectionID=h1&mv=0&p=> (accessed 17 July 2020).

17 Gagna was an expert with the sword and the bayonet and gained a very high place in the opening rounds of the all-India bayonet and sabre competitions which were held during George V visit to Delhi for his coronation as King-Emperor in 1911. He received his Indian Order of Merit from the King whilst recovering from his wounds at the Brighton Hospital.

11

'The most serious engagement of the Indian Corps to date'

The previous two chapters have recounted individual battalion experiences in attempting to regain the trenches near Festubert. This was an action, as has been shown, which involved a number of other Indian Corps formations/units as well as British formations/units. As with many battle descriptions, each account provides only part of what actually happened as the individual soldier's account of a battle, centres on his own experience. The war diaries of the four Ferozepore Brigade battalions concentrated to a large extent on their individual participation in the Festubert defence of front-line trenches and their subsequent recapture. We are fortunate that an officer attached the headquarters of the Indian Corps, Major Richard Alexander Steel p.s.c, provided a 10-page summary of the action dated 12 December 1914.[1] In addition there is an account by Captain Acworth, whose bravery and methods of clearing the German from the trenches was previously recorded by Brigadier General Hudson.

Steel's account describes the activities of the Indian Corps up to November 1914. The Corps is described as continuing to hold the trenches which it had occupied from the beginning of the month of November 'with little variation'.[2] As has been shown, it would be wrong to assume that in holding these trenches the various Battalions led a static life but, as their individual accounts have shown, they constantly were marched from one billet and one set of trenches to another. Major Steel is correct when he records

1 Major Steel was 31 years old and had been commissioned in the 7th Dragoon Guards in 1892. He joined the Royal Irish Fusiliers in the following year and in 1898 entered the Indian Staff College at Quetta. Subsequently he had had a distinguished career on the staff serving as A.D.C. to the G.O.C. China Relief Expedition 1900-1901 for which he had been mentioned in Despatches and Military Attaché to Tehran before joining the Indian Corps. In January 1918 Steel was promoted to full Colonel and he was made a Commander of St Michael and St George and became a Companion of the Order of the Indian Empire.

2 R.A. Steel, The Action for the recovery of trenches near Festuburt [sic], November 23- 24, 1914, 12 December 1914. A Copy of Steel's report can be found in TNA WO 95/3923: Connaught Rangers War Diary 1-3 December 1914..

that the Germans had not been able to break through the line but had only captured part of the front-line trenches for short periods before being thrown out by counter attacks. Again, this belies the efforts of the various Battalions in the Ferozepore Brigade which were recorded in their War Diaries In this case Steel's overall picture undersells the contribution which the Brigade had made during October and November and the number of casualties which they had suffered as a result. Steel correctly conjectures that the Germans had yet to make a determined effort to attack the British front-line but, the fact that they were keen to move so closely to it through Sapping, did indicate that there would be a concerted attempt to capture the whole line in the coming days. Such an attempt would be more likely to succeed if the attacking troops had the shortest possible distance between their own and the British trenches to cover. Similarly, the closer the German Sap moved towards the British front-line the less likely British Artillery could be called upon to shell the enemy for fear of hitting their own troops.

A successful attack on the British front-line would also need large numbers of troops to be in reserve in order to occupy the captured trenches quickly and with sufficient numbers to defend it against counterattacks. The slow advance made by the German digging the trenches would allow these reserve troops to gradually move forward unobserved and provide distribution in depth. This was particularly significant as the British Battalions involved had been greatly weakened by a high casualty rate. The Ferozepore Brigade, for example, had been reduced to close to half its normal strength by the end of November.

Steel observes that this method of preparing an attack was possible because of the terrain; it was flat, close and intersected by a variety of obstacles, as has been described, and this forced the British to defend orchards and sunken lanes which crisscrossed the battlefield and would otherwise provide the Germans with defensive positions.

Before preparing for a concerted assault, the German trenches were originally three to four hundred yards from the British front-line.[3] By using the tactic of zig zag Saps from different points of their firing line, the Germans slowly advanced towards the British trenches. At the 'elbow' of a Sap a loop holed trench was constructed which would permit the German supporting troops to fire from cover in order to assist those comrades who were advancing.[4] After a number of these Saps had been constructed, they could then be joined together to make a new firing line which was closer to the British forward trench, thus reducing the distance which had to be covered. This process would then be repeated until the German front line was only 50 yards from that of the British. Finally a further series of Saps were constructed which were only a few yards from the British trench into which the attacking force could move almost completely unseen. Once this advanced trench was complete, large numbers of troops could make their way through the Saps to the new front line protected from the British artillery fire since it feared hitting its own men. Further 'elbows' were created in this final line which

3 TNA WO 95/3923: Steel, The Action for the recovery of trenches, p. 2.
4 The 'elbow' the point at which a Sap turned to form the next part of a zigzag.

give the Germans the opportunity to throw bombs into the nearby British trenches. These bombs/grenades would not only kill British troops but also collapse part of their trenches which would prevent British reinforcing troops from moving up and down the line. It would create a series of shortened trenches with obstructions caused by the front part of the trench collapsing as a result of a bomb blast at each end which would assist with their defence once taken. Steel speculates, somewhat waspishly, that the German assault was launched because the German Officer in charge was seeking a higher decoration than the one he already possessed. The German troops involved in this process were the 4th Baden Infantry Battalion, Prince Wilhelm No. 112 which was part of the 58th Infantry Brigade.[5] The commander in question was Oberstleutnant Konrad Neubauer. So far, suggested Steel, the Germans had only been pushing 'lightly' at the British defenders presumably whilst they were preparing their Saps.

The attacking Germans threw bombs into the British front-line trenches making them undefendable and, by collapsing the trench walls, divided the defenders from one another. As Steel remarks such techniques for taking front line trenches were a 'very efficient strategy' when artillery was not available or could not safely be used.[6]

It was this method of attack which enabled the Germans to assault the centre of the British line on the morning of the 23 November. This section of the line was occupied by the 34th Royal Sikh Pioneers, who were part of the Lahore Division, centre left and the 9th Bhopals at the centre right, The Germans began their bombing attacks at around 0800 hours and such was the intensity of the attack that by 1100 hours the two Battalions, who had no bombs themselves, were forced out of their trenches. This withdrawal forced a company of Connaught Rangers, whose right flank was now exposed to the German attackers, to move towards their left and take cover in trenches occupied by the 57th Wilde's Rifles. Working together. the Connaughts and the 57th constructed a barricade of sandbags across the communication trench between the now vacated trench and that occupied by the 57th Rifles. Lieutenant Robson assisted Captain Acworth's men by bringing a supply of bombs with which they could defend the barricade.

The Germans continued to press their advantage and the 58th Vaughan's Rifles, who were on the 9th Bhopals' right flank, were also forced to withdraw. With four Battalions either retreating or displaced it seemed as if the centre section of the British line was about to be lost. The German attack, conjectures Major Steel, was aided by the fact that the Sikh Pioneers and the Bhopals were in the process of being relieved and, at this crucial moment, were somewhat disorganised.[7] However, this disadvantage was to be reversed as, since the relief had not been completed, extra troops were in the area

5 4. Badisches Infanterie-Regiment Prinz Wilhelm Nr. 112. When mobilised in August 1914 the Regiment had a compliment of 66 officers and 3159 men.

6 TNA WO 95/3923: Steel, The Action for the recovery of trenches, p. 3.

7 If this is the case the German knowledge must have been based on observation rather than intelligence. Germans did not have the ability to intercept Allied communications until June 1915.

and their numbers were to aid the eventual recovery of the trenches. The British far-left flank of the centre section was held by the 129th Baluchis and a party of Connaught Rangers who prevented the Germans moving further down their right flank of the firing trench and the far-right flank of the British line was held by a composite group of 58th Rifles and some soldiers of the Black Watch. This prevented the Germans from moving down the trench to their left. The 6th Jats and 2/8th Gurkhas, meant to be the relieving troops, occupied the communication trenches and the 107th Pioneers were ordered to remain in their trenches rather than march to their billets.

The 34th Sikh Pioneers attempted to retake the trenches they had lost but this failed as did a similar attempt by the 9th Jats. At this point Brigadier General Egerton, G.O.C. Ferozepore Brigade, arrived having been ordered by Indian Corps Headquarters to take over the situation. Egerton had been expecting to take over command of this section of trench which was to be occupied troops from the Lahore Brigade. Egerton's task was to drive the Germans out of the firing line trenches which they now firmly held. The occupied section of the trench was bounded by the 129th Baluchis and Connaught Rangers barricade on the British left and 58th Rifles and some soldiers of the Black Watch on the right.[8] Egerton's force was quite considerable, and amounted to five different Battalions, some of which, like that of the Connaught Rangers were incomplete or composite Battalions such as one from the Secunderabad Cavalry Brigade. The problem which faced Egerton, therefore, was not lack of troops but the need for them to advance over 'some hundred yards of coverless ground' swept by German machine guns and mortars. 'An advance in the daylight,' argued Steel, unsupported by artillery, appeared impossible.'[9] Lieutenant Colonel Southey, Commanding Officer of the 129th Baluchis, had already asked for the assistance from the 28th Battery, Royal Field Artillery, in shelling the line of trenches vacated by the 34th Pioneers and, according to Steel, the battery had targeted these trenches 'well, as far as could be ascertained.'[10]

Egerton ordered that all available guns should shell the occupied trenches for three quarters of an hour until the launch of the fresh British counterattack at 1645 hours and, once this attack had begun, to deliver a creeping barrage to cover the area in front of the trenches to prevent the Germans, once driven out, returning before the British had completely secured their objective. The artillery fire was very accurate and not only killed and wounded a number of the enemy but also damaged the trenches themselves, which, as been explained would make them more difficult to defend; this time by the Germans.

8 It is interesting that Steel omits to mention the presence of the 129th Baluchis with the Connaughts behind the barricade. This in keeping with his concluding comments of how the British and Indian soldiers were comrades in arms, but Steel professes that 'the value of the British soldiers [sic] example cannot be exaggerated.' See TNA WO 95/3923: Steel, The Action for the recovery of trenches, p. 9. In fairness Steel was recounting the extreme bravery of four members of the Black Watch but devotes more space to their exploits than he does to the Indian VC winner Darwan Singh Negi.

9 TNA WO 95/3923: Steel, The Action for the recovery of trenches. p. 5.

10 TNA WO 95/3923: Steel, The Action for the recovery of trenches, p. 5.

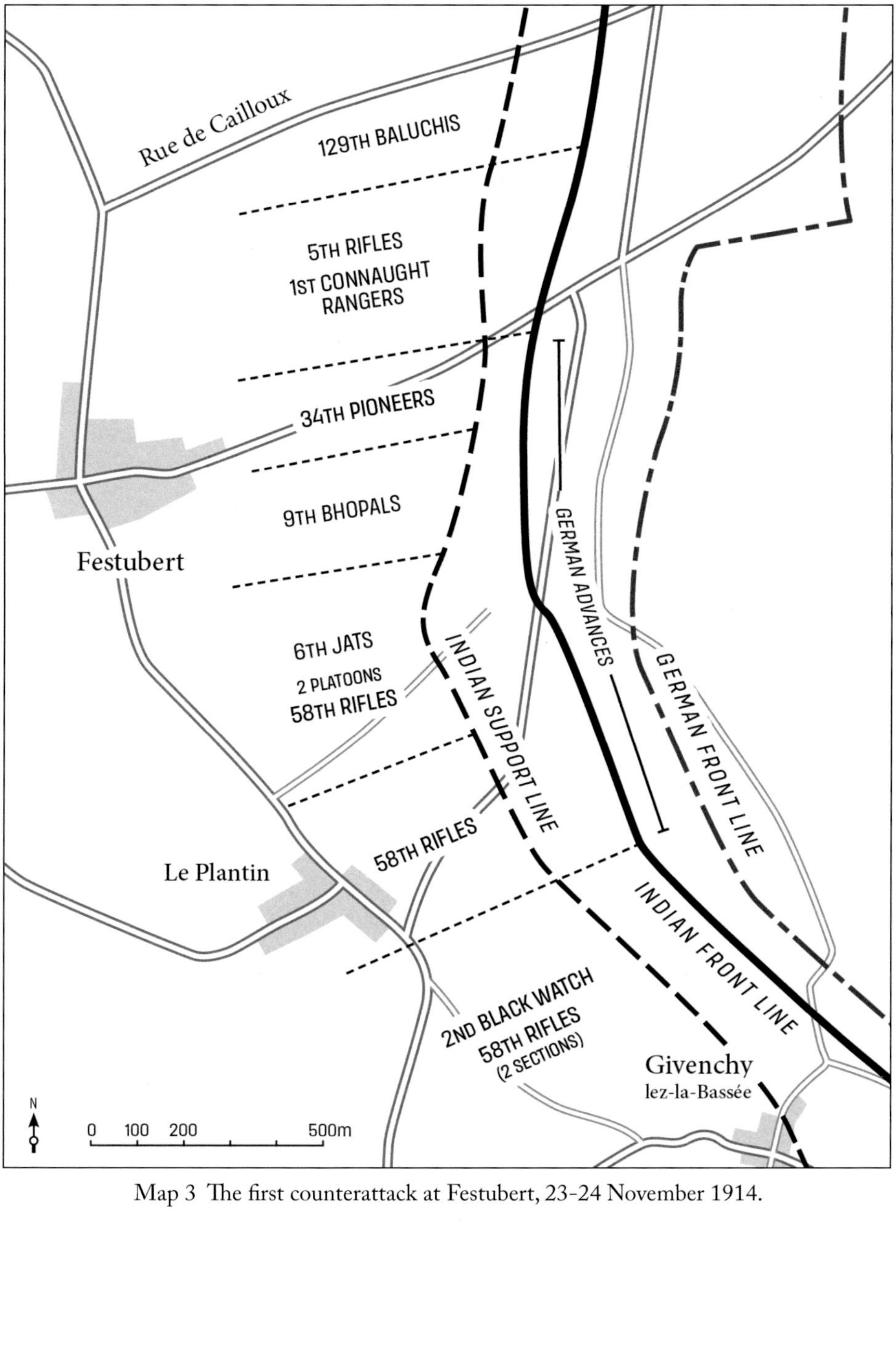

Map 3 The first counterattack at Festubert, 23-24 November 1914.

The main counterattack was launched by the 2/8th Gurkhas, the 6th Jats and a detachment of the 34th Pioneers but they were also joined by soldiers from other Battalions who had been taking cover in support trenches and ditches between the start line and the enemy. In addition the three companies of Connaught Rangers supported the right of the attack and the gap left by the advancing units was filled by the 107th Pioneers. The ground was covered in snow and, even in the failing light, the advancing troops were easily seen by the German defenders and therefore made easy targets. The Gurkhas, in spite of facing heavy machinegun and rifle fire, were able to retake the right section of the captured trench and with the support of some Sepoys from the 6th Jats and 9th Bhopals were able to hold the trench until morning when the British firing line was restored. The 58th Rifles also pushed forward and retook their original trenches but progress on the British left flank was halted because of heavy German fire. The 107th Pioneers, who were sent to support the right flank were also in difficulty in spite of being assisted by the Gurkhas because of heavy German resistance, especially from bombs which the Pioneers, who were without these vital pieces of equipment, could not reply.

The 2/3rd Gurkhas arrived as reinforcements and were placed in reserve. It was 2000 hours and, in spite of strenuous efforts to evict them, the Germans still occupied part of the line they had captured earlier that day. The British were desperate to retake the trenches as their line was in danger of being permanently breached which would enable the Germans to sweep through. Meanwhile, the Leicester Regiment arrived and it was ordered that the trenches be recovered before dawn at all costs and the troops were to be informed that the Corps Commander, Lieutenant General Willcocks, expected them to do so.'[11] The counterattack was continued with the Garwhalis attacking the left of the centre section and the 107th Pioneers attacking the right but they were again checked by the heavy fire of the Germans. The Leicester's were able to capture a small section of the right of the centre section. A second reinforcement, in the form of the 1/39th Gurkhas arrived, after being delayed by unfamiliarity with the ground and the failing light. They realised that a frontal attack on the trenches would fail and so they attempted to attack down the trench from the left flank and recapture its section by section. It was at this point that Major Steel paid tribute to Robson's and Acworth's ingenuity as well as the performance of 1/39th Garwhalis under their Commanding Officer, Colonel Ernest Swiney.[12]

Acworth's report briefly explains the situation during the morning of the 23 November and the construction of the barricade in his trench. He describes how Lieutenant Robson RE had crawled alone some 40 yards down the communication trench and launched a number of bombs into a German working party who were in

11 TNA WO 95/3923: Steel, The Action for the recovery of trenches, p. 7.

12 Colonel Ernest Robert Rainier Swiney had been born in India in 1863. Whilst returning to India in on SS *Persia* in November 1915, the ship was torpedoed by a German U-boat near Crete.

the captured centre trench. It was a 'very gallant performance.'[13] The 57th Wilde's Rifles' bombs were almost all used up when at 22:30 hours Robson returned with a fresh load of 'efficient' bombs[14] and Acworth then went on to describe the method they used to retake the trenches. The Garwhalis, as has been previously described, charged into each section which had been bombed to deal with any remaining Germans who had survived the bombs. The Sepoys progressed down the right section of the trench whilst Acworth and Robson went along the left section throwing bombs to prevent the Germans attacking the Garwhalis' flank or rear, Having dealt with this threat the two British officers attempted to get to the front of the Garwhalis' column but could not do so as their trench was 'utterly blocked with prisoners'.[15] Although Acworth does not mention his face wound or the Afridis who accompanied him and Robson, Steel does refer to this 'gallant little band' of six [sic] Afridis accompanying Acworth and Robson.[16] The War Diary of the 57th Rifles goes so far as to proudly name these Sepoys as:

Naik Yakub Khan	Alyas Khan
Lance Naik Said Akbar	Lalak
Mir Badshah	Mir Baz
Daulat Khan	Mir Babshah[17]

The counterattack continued through most of the night and the complete trench was not recaptured until just after daylight of the 24 November. Steel remarks that, although the action resulted in many casualties, it was absolutely necessary. In addition, four German officers and 100 other ranks were captured as were two mortars and three machine guns and together with 100 rifles. The German casualties found in the trenches and supposedly cause by the heavy artillery fire from the creeping barrage beyond the trenches were surmised to have been not 'less than 500 and they may well have been much heavier'.[18] Steel concludes with an extensive tribute to the four members of the Black Watch who defended their trench throughout the action and also mention the bravery of 'Darwan Sing [sic] Nagi' and his award of the VC.[19]

Nagi's was not the only VC awarded for Bravery during the Festubert action. Lieutenant Frank Alexander de Pass, of the 34th Poona Horse, was killed in action

13 D.H. Acworth, Report on activities 23/24 November 1914, p. 1. The word 'alone' is underlined in this document.
14 It was not unusual for 'bombs' failing to explode
15 Acworth, Report on activities 23/24 November 1914, p. 3.
16 TNA WO 95/3923: Steel, The Action for the recovery of trenches, p. 8.
17 Mir Babshah was member of 55th (Coke's) Rifles as was Robson and probably accompanied him as a batman.
18 TNA WO 95/3923: Steel, The Action for the recovery of trenches, p. 9.
19 The Black Watch war diary has little or nothing to say about Festubert.

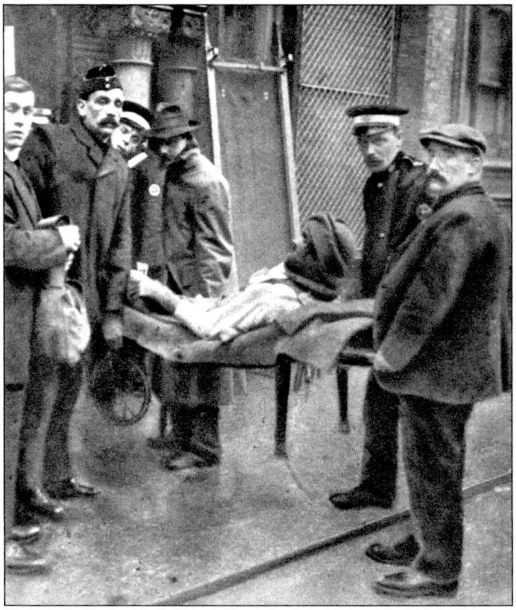

Darwan Singh Negi being carried into the Indian Hospital in Brighton (*Illustrated War News*, 23 December 1914)

Lieutenant Frank Alexander de Pass VC.

near Festubert on 25 November but his VC was awarded for his bravery for actions during the preceding two days. He entered the enemy sap accompanied by two Sowars and, despite of being under heavy fire, destroyed sufficient of its traverse to expose it to British rifle fire and thus prevent the Germans throwing bombs for the whole of the 24 November. Later that day, together with a trooper of the 7th Dragoon Guards, de Pass recued a Sepoy of the 58th Rifles who was lying exposed to enemy fire. On the 25 November de Pass again approach a Sap in order to improve its defences against enemy bomb throwing which had begun again and, whilst attempting to eliminate a sniper, was himself shot through the head.[20] Steel ends his account with the sobering conclusion that the action of 23/24 November 1914 may add a page to the glorious history of British and Indian arms but it is 'dwarfed by the magnitude of the struggle in which [they] were engaged.'[21]

20 TNA: WO95/1187, 2 Indian Cavalry Division, Secunderabad Brigade, 34th (Prince Albert Victor's Own) Poona Horse; Report by Captain Roland William Wrigley Grimshaw, Commander of D Squadron, 34th Poona Horse to Lieutenant Colonel W. G Cooper, CO 34th Poona Horse. dated 28 November 1914. Roly (Roland) Grimshaw kept a diary of his experiences in France: R. W. W. Grimshaw, et al., *Diary of an Indian Cavalry Officer 1914-1915* (Tunbridge Wells: D J Costello, 1986).

21 Steel, *The Action for the recovery of trenches*, p. 10.

12

Morale, Medicine and Desertion

Although this account concentrates on the experiences of the Ferozepore Brigade it is impossible not to reflect on Indian Corps as a whole during the first months of its time in France. It was in November 1914 that the headquarters diary of the Lahore Division first mentioned the spate of self-inflicted wounds amongst Sepoys.[1] The diary, in an Appendix from the Assistant Adjutant General, was very clear that self-wounding was, without doubt, occurring and steps should be taken to inform all Sepoys that any of their number who was reported by a Medical Officer for wounding themselves would be immediately tried by courts marshal. The Appendix, which was circulated throughout the Indian Corps not just the Indian Battalions, pointed out that that Medical Officers were reporting that many hand wounds had been self-inflicted. Major General Watkins, GOC Lahore Division, is said to have found this claim hard to believe but directed his subordinates to immediately warn their men that such cowardly behaviour would receive a death sentence. Although the allegation of self-inflicted wounds is only alleged to involve Indian troops, Watkins also wished this threat of punishment to be communicated to British troops under his command. Whether this was because there was similar evidence about their behaviour or, as is more likely, it was done in order not to undermine the confidence of British troops about the bravery of their Sepoy colleagues, is uncertain.

There were many claims that the reason there were large numbers of self-inflicted wounds amongst the Indian soldiers was because they hoped that they would be returned to India. It was of such concerned that the Deputy Director of Indian Medical Services Indian Corps, (DDMS), Colonel Francis Trehern, ensured that the statistics of such wounds were carefully monitored.[2] On 2 November 1914, the DDMS' Diary recorded

1 TNA WO95/3911.3: Indian (Lahore)Division, Headquarters, Branches and General Services General Staff War Diary, Appendix 1 (5), 1 November 1914.

2 TNA WO 95/1093: Indian Corps, Deputy Director of Medical Services War Diary, 1 November 1914. Sir Francis Trehern, KCMG, FRC (Ed) was later to become Medical Director of the 3rd Army and later served in Mesopotamia. One of his sons, a captain in the RAMC, was killed in the war.

that six Sepoys were court martialled for having self-inflicted wounds to their left hand. DDMS' Diary records that fifty-seven percent of the wounded Sepoys, who were treated from the beginning of their time in the trenches until the end of 3 November, had hand wounds. In the Lahore Division it was almost sixty-two percent.[3] Trehern's calculations carried much weight during the War and have been subsequently repeated by some modern historians. Greenhut, for example, claimed that self-inflicted wounds accounted for fifty percent of Indian wounds suffered during the first month of the War. [4] Gardner's estimate was sixty-five percent and also suggested that this phenomenon was not found in British battalions.[5] E.B. Howell, who was the head of Indian Mail Censor Office (IMCO) wrote that amongst the Sepoys there was a belief that ' he who had been into the trenches and there been wounded (has) very amply discharged his duty ' and ' the prospect of a return to the firing line appears to be regarded with something approaching dismay.'[6] Howell's conclusion is supported in the letters which wounded Sepoys sent home. A wounded Sikh, convalescing in New Milton Hospital, Hampshire, in January 1915 wrote to his brother in the Amritsar District:

> I pray the Guru that I may return home. I do not know for certain but I expect so. For I was hit on my trigger finger and the third part of it is cut off.[7]

Willcocks was so concerned about self-wounding and the apparent fragility of his men under fire that that he informed Sir John French, Commander of the BEF, that his men 'might go at any moment' and requested the addition of two additional British brigades to the Indian Corps. He appears to have got short shrift from the peppery Field Marshal.[8] Unsurprisingly, the Indiophile, Willocks, failed to mention this in his account of his time commanding the Indian Corps but, shortly after this interview with Field Marshal French, Willcocks issued an order that anyone suffering from hand wounds would be returned to active service when fit.

On 14 November, the DDMS[9] Diary recorded that two Sepoys were court martialled for having self-inflicted hand wounds but had been acquitted.[10] By 15

3 TNA WO 95/1093: Indian Corps, Deputy Director of Medical Services War Diary, 4 November 1914.
4 John. Greenhut, 'The Imperial Reserve', pp. 57, 59-60 and D. Omissi, *The Sepoy and the Raj: The Indian Army 1860-1940* (London, Palgrave Macmillan, 1998) p. 38.
5 Nikolas Gardner, *Trial by Fire: Command and the British Expeditionary Force in 1914.* (London: Greenwood Publishing Group 2003), pp. 195-197.
6 BL: IOR, L/MIL/5/825: Reports of the Chief Censor, E.B. Barrow to General Sir Edmund Barrow, 15 February 1915.
7 Omissi, *Indian Voices,* p. 31, suggests that this injury may have been self-inflicted.
8 Imperial War Museum, Private Papers of Field Marshal Sir Henry Wilson, 2 November 1914 correspondence.
9 Deputy Director of Medical Services.
10 TNA WO 95/1093: Indian Corps Deputy Director of Medical Services War Diary, 14 November 1914.

Field Marshal Sir John French Commander of the BEF, photographed in France by H.R. Birdwood.

November the number of hand wounds for the whole of the Indian Corps had fallen to fifteen percent.[11] There are no further mentions of hand wounds in the Diary for the month of November 1914 which may suggest that Willcocks' orders about punishing offenders had been effective. Self-harming does not appear again in the DDMS Diary until 13 June 1915 when it records that the Indian Corps is to be asked to speed up the Courts of Enquiry into suspicious wounds as sufferers are being retained in the Field Ambulances,[12] presumably taking up much needed space, until a decision was made about how they might have acquired their wound.[13] The entry for 27 June records that there was an increase in self-inflicted bullet wounds but notes that a Medical Officer could only give an opinion as to the range from which a bullet was fired. The solution to this increase, it argued, was greater Battalion

11 TNA WO 95/1093: Indian, Deputy Director of Medical Services War Diary, 15 November 1914.

12 These were front line medical units not vehicles.

13 TNA WO95/1093: Indian Corps, Deputy Director of Medical Services War Diary, 13 June 1915.

discipline.[14] It seems that the monitoring the possibility of self-wounding continued throughout the year since the DDMS, now Colonel R. Kirkpatrick who had been transferred from the South African Command, noted a change in the method of monitoring men who have wounds 'below the elbow'[15]

Sir Bruce Seton,[16] of the Kitchener Indian Hospital, Brighton, studied a series of 1000 wounds with special reference to the theory of the prevalence of self-infliction.'[17] His examination of wounded soldiers revealed only 6 cases where the cause of the injury could 'possibly' be self-inflicted.[18] His conclusion was that 'there was no evidence of the self-infliction of wounds which could be supported by statistical examination.'[19] Seton suggested that the 'Indian Army should look elsewhere for some other explanation'.[20] Although Seton does not suggest where 'elsewhere' might be, his analysis might result from the suggestion that many wounds to the hand were caused by injuries received because Sepoys, a lot of of whom were shorter than British soldiers, were forced to hold their rifles over the top of a trench exposing their left hand. It was felt that head wounds received in a similar manner were unlikely to be self-inflicted because of the obvious risks they incurred.

Support for Seton's 'elsewhere theory' can be found in Frederic Coleman's personal account of his experiences on the Western Front. Coleman was an American member of the Royal Automobile Club who, with 24 fellow members, had taken their cars to France 'to drive officers of the General Headquarters Staff to the front.' Coleman recounts that on 30 October, during the First Battle of Messines, whilst attached to the 1st Cavalry Division, he observed 'a score of wounded Wild's (sic) Rifles, who, almost to a man 'had been shot in the left hand or arm.' One of their officers told (him) that this was due to 'the peculiar way the Indians shield their head with the left arm while firing.'[21]

The War Diary of the 15th Ludhiana Sikhs also throws some light on the possible cause of wounds which have been previously thought to be self-inflicted. The Sikhs

14 TNA WO 95/1093: Indian Corps, Deputy Director of Medical Services War Diary, 27 June 1915.
15 TNA WO 95/1093: Indian Corps, Deputy Director of Medical Services War Diary, 1 October 1915.
16 Brevet Colonel Sir Bruce Gordon Seton (1868-1932), C.B., 9th Baronet of Abercorn, entered the Indian Medical Service as a Surgeon Lieutenant in 1892. He served on the North-West Frontier in the Waziristan Campaign of 1894-95 where he was severely wounded. He also received a medal in the Tochi campaign of 1897-98. During the War Seton served as the commanding officer in charge of the Kitchener Indian Hospital at Brighton.
17 BL IOR/L/ML/17/5/2402 Bruce Seton, An analysis of 1000 wounds and injuries received in action, with special reference to the theory of the prevalence of self-infliction.
18 Seton, An Analysis, p. 8.
19 Seton, An Analysis, p. 8.
20 Seton, An Analysis, p. 8.
21 Frederic Coleman, *From Mons to Ypres with French: A Personal Narrative* (London: Sampson Low, 1916) p. 230.

"Gentlemen of India marching to chasten German Hooligans": 15th Ludhiana Sikhs matching through Marseilles.

entered the fighting at Fauquissart, near Laventie, on 24 October 1914 as part of the Lahore Division's Sirhind Infantry Brigade. On the following day they were ordered to occupy trenches which had recently been evacuated by French cavalry. The trenches had been partly filled in by the enemy bombing and were subjected to enfiladed fire and had to be re-dug at night in close proximity to the enemy. The Sikhs were subjected not only to heavy artillery fire but also to accurate sniping. Their CO, Lieutenant Colonel J L R Gordon, was wounded in the thigh although some distance from the firing line. The War Diary complained that the Sikhs, who were totally unused to trench warfare, mistakenly thought that if they couldn't see the enemy, they were safe and 'the Germans picked off any man showing himself above the parapet.'[22] The Diary reports that the Battalion had experienced 58 casualties, many of whom were wounded in the arm or left hand. These injuries were 'caused by the men being slow in coming up to fire and getting under cover again.'[23]

Doherty and Donovan argue that the continued effectiveness of the Indian Corps would be difficult to understand if it was socially acceptable to self-wound since this would encourage many more to indulge in this method of avoiding the War. If unacceptable, it was difficult to explain why so many apparently got away with it in the face of peer pressure, individual and Battalion *Izzat* as well as the fear of punishment.[24]

Such was Willcocks concern for his Corps' reputation, however, that he executed five Indian troops for self-inflicted wounds as an example to their comrades.[25]

22 TNA WO 95/3929: 3 Indian (Lahore) Division, 9th (Sirhind) Infantry Brigade, 15 (Ludhiana) Sikhs War Diary, 25 October 1914.
23 TNA WO 95/3929: 3 Indian (Lahore) Division, 9 (Sirhind) Infantry Brigade, 15 (Ludhiana) Sikhs War Diary, 28 October 1914.
24 Simon Doherty and Tom Donovan, *The Indian Corps on the Western Front* (Brighton: Tom Donovan, Editions, 2014) p. 45. *Izzat* refers the unwritten contract between Sepoys and the British.
25 Returns showing court martial convictions in Indian Corps, October 1914 to February 1915. No British servicemen convicted of self-inflicted wounding were executed.

These punishments seemed to have deterred Sepoys from self-mutilation but there were occasions such as in May 1915 when these incidents increased again. Morton-Jack suggests this occurred amongst newly arrived Sepoys who had yet to learn the consequences of this behaviour and were shocked by the conditions in which they were expected to fight.[26] This conclusion could also be applied to the hundreds of British BEF troops who also wounded themselves and, as Asquith wrote, such behaviour demonstrated 'what a shattering thing the trenches must be'.[27] Asquith's assessment is confirmed, for example, by the fact that at Second Ypres, French, African, Canadian and British troops fled from shellfire and poison gas; and by 1918 every army on the Western Front had experienced routs of a greater or lesser degree.[28]

Such was the contradictory nature of Seton's conclusions to popular belief about the Sepoys' strength of character that it was marked 'top secret' and never published during wartime. Hilary Buxton suggests that this may because the India Office was worried that if the existence of such a report became known to the Sepoys there would be considerable discontent since the premise of the inquiry was that they were in some way untrustworthy. Alternatively the Report might have been kept under wraps through a reluctance to absolve Indian soldiers of shirking their duty which could have been thought to encourage them to do so.[29]

Perhaps because of the secret nature of Seton's Report, the belief that Sepoys were prone to faking injury continued to have wide circulation. Sir Robert John Collie, who held several senior medical posts including that of Director of Medical Services for the Ministry of Pensions, was a strong advocate of malingering amongst the Sepoys. He was author of the revised *Malingering and Feigned Sickness, with Notes on the Workmen's Compensation Act 1906 and compensation for injury, including the leading cases thereon.* One of the examples described by Collie was that of a malingering Sepoy who had faked a hand injury by constantly sitting on it. This was easy for the Sepoy to accomplish, claimed Collie, as squatting was the Sepoys' normal behaviour.[30] A somewhat circumstantial conclusion to say the least! There is evidence that some Indians did consider self-wounding to be appropriate action. Mohammad Rafi Khan, a Sowar

26 Morton-Jack, *The Indian Army on the Western Front,* p. 341.
27 Michael Brock and Eleanor Brock (eds.), *H.H. Asquith: Letters to Venetia Stanley, Letter no.234 (December 1914)* (Oxford: OUP, 1985).
28 Daya Ram Thapar, *Morale Builders: Forty Years with the Medical Services of India* (London, Asia Publishing House, 1965), p. 23.
29 Hilary Buxton, Imperial Amnesia: Race, Trauma and Indian Troops in the First World War, *Past & Present,* Vol. 241, Issue 1, November 2018. pp. 232-233 Gary Sheffield and John Bourne (eds.), *Douglas Haig. War Diaries and Letter* (London, Weidenfeld and Nicolson, 2005), entry for Saturday 7 November 1914, p. 78, describes British troops abandoning trenches 'on account of little shellfire'.
30 Robert John Collie, Malingering *and Feigned Sickness, with Notes on the Workmen's. Compensation Act 1906 and Compensation for Injury, including the Leading Cases Thereon, 2nd ed, revised and enlarged* (London: Edward Arnold, 1917), pp. 1-2.

in the 30th Lancers serving in France, received a letter from home which described several ways in which the Sowar might make himself temporary *hors de combat*. The letter described how to produce inflamed skin, reddened eyes or cutting the foot and inserting a piece of copper; all methods which were designed to get the participant into hospital.[31] There is no evidence that the Sowar acted on this advice and it is unlikely that it passed the Censor.

Indians were not unique in attempting this method of escaping the War. Arthur Butler, the Official Australian Historian, wrote that, 'from fear, many men, not depraved or psychopathic, fled into disease, into wounds, even into death itself.'[32] There were similar examples in the Canadian Expeditionary Force as Mark Humphries described.[33] Almost 3,900 British soldiers were convicted of self-wounding during the First World War: self-wounding was clearly not just an Indian Corps phenomenon. Morton-Jack, correctly points out that, although self-mutilation did concern Willcocks, the Commander of the Indian Corps,' it may not be used as evidence that, collectively, the Sepoys were especially poor in battle.'[34]

Sepoys in the Kitchener Indian Hospital Brighton also felt that some of their injuries were considered to be faked and this resulted in harsh treatment from the medical staff and being sent back to the Front when they should not have been. 'They even punish a man for going lame.'[35] As an officer from the Garhwal Brigade observed, 'of course, evil is to be found in every army and every nationality'.[36]

Gary Sheffield remarks, 'Morale, one of the most common terms in modern military lexicon, is an imprecise term'. He defined the morale of an army as a whole as depending upon that of its individual units, which in turn depended upon the morale of individual soldiers.[37] The morale of individuals can depend on a number of ordinary factors such as the weather or the shortage of food.[38] Contemporary studies were made regarding the morale of Indian troops on the Western Front. The first of these was carried out by the Army Mail Censors (IMCO) who, from as early as December 1914, monitored the letters which Sepoys sent home. Similar detailed censorship of British

31 Mohammad Gaki Khan of the United provinces to Mohammad Rafi Khan, 6 June 1915 in Omissi, *Indian Voices of the Great War*, p. 67.
32 Arthur Graham Butler, *Official History of the Australian Army Medical Services, 1914- 1918: Volume* III – *Special Problems and Services* (Canberra: Australian War Memorial, 1943), p. 92.
33 Mark Humphries, Wilfully and With Intent: Self-Inflicted Wounds and the Negotiation of Power in the Trenches, *Histoire sociale/Social History*, Vol. 97, Issue 47 June 2014, pp. 369-397.
34 George Morton-Jack, The Indian Army on the Western Front, 1914-1915: A Portrait of Collaboration, *War in History* (Vol. 13, Issue 3, 2006) p. 341.
35 B. Ram Singh (47th Sikhs) to Jam Dhola Singh, 21 October 1915.
36 Imperial War Museum, Henderson Papers, p. 121.
37 Sheffield, Command *and Morale,* p. 154
38 Imperial War Museum Private Papers of R. Crude. p. 52 A. Smith, *Four Years on the Western Front* (London, London Stamp Exchange 1987 reprint of 1921 edition), p. 100.

soldiers did not begin until 1918 when lower standards of recruits, poor morale and general war disaffection at home and in the trenches were having impact.

Although many Sepoys were illiterate,[39] there were a large number of letters sent to family and friends in India which were written on behalf of these men by literate comrades, followers or orderlies These letters were initially censored by Battalion officers who removed sensitive information such as geographical details. The IMCO then removed any anti-British or subversive content from the letters. The IMCO was headed by Evelyn Berkeley Howell and based at Rouen. Howell had served for 15 Years on the North West Frontier and was fluent in Urdu and Pashtu. He had risen rapidly from being a 2nd Lieutenant serving as interpreter for an Indian Cavalry Battalion in 1914 to the rank of Major and was made a Companion of the Order of the Indian Empire in January 1916. Howell, though energetic in his role, was something of a reluctant censor. The tenure of increasing number of letters as the War progressed was not necessarily anti-British but displayed a fatal resignation to the dangers of the War which suggested that the Sepoys were beginning to suffer from the mental strain of combat. Howell's staff found it difficult to easily translate the meaning of many of the letters since they were obtuse and, even if translated correctly, frequently had a hidden meaning which European officers found it hard to decipher.[40] However, Howell, as we have seen, was clear that the mental condition of Sepoys was affected by being in the trenches.[41] In February 1915, The India Office found these comments on the mental condition of the Sepoys so concerning that it asked Howell and his team to provide an analysis of those Classes and battalions which were showing marked despondency. In making a request of this nature, the Indian Office was adhering to the Martial Race Theory which has already been discussed. It believed that all were aware of the 'great differences which existed between the various classes not only to courage which was mostly common to all, but in grit and endurance which 'have been severely tested by this present war'.[42] Following his instructions, Howell carefully classified the letters he censored according to the Martial Race Theory as to which class was the most prone to 'despair' as evidenced by their letters. In the last week of January 1915, his Report indicated that there was not one Class which was particularly susceptible but the Pathans were less likely to experience despondency. As Howell compiled more reports, it was clear that the level of despondency varied from ethnic group to ethnic group which may have had something to do with their changing experiences as the war progressed. A significant weakness in Howell's analysis was that it did not drill down to individual battalions but generalised the different classes which Hilary

39 The Superintendent, *Census of India, 1911*, Vol. I (Calcutta, Government Press, 1913), pp. 294-295

40 Gajendra Singh, *The Testimonies of Indian Soldiers and the Two World Wars: Between Self and Sepoy* (London: A & C Black, 2014), p. 66.

41 BL IOR L/MIL/5/826/6: Censor Report, 16 September 1916. BL IOR L/MIL/5/826/7: Censor Report, 11 March 1916: BL IOR L/MIL/5/826/2.

42 BL IOR, L/MIL/5/825/1: India Office to Evelyn Berkeley Howell, 15 February 1915.

Buxton has criticised as a typical 'colonial approach'. Buxton correctly points out that, if a similar study was being undertaken on British battalions, assumptions would not be based on which county or city from which they came. Not to analyse morale by individual battalions which had had different experiences was to assume that every member of a particular class had a similar mental constitution.[43]

This attitude was similar in many ways to the British authorities who were reluctant to acknowledge the existence of conditions such as shell shock, a definition which first appeared in an article in the Lancet in February 1915. The use of the umbrella term 'shell shock' fell out of favour in military medical circles by 1917 and was qualified by terms such as 'shellshock (wound)' or 'shell shock (sick)' but was still often regarded as a physical rather than a mental condition. It was acknowledged that some soldiers who displayed shaking, tinnitus, poor concentration or loss of memory, to name but a few of the symptoms, suffered from a condition diagnosed as 'neurasthenia', or weakness of the nerves.[44] Walter Lawrence, the Commissioner of Indian Hospitals in a letter to Lord Kitchener thought that it was unfortunate that this concept of the Sepoy should be so prevalent that people would jump to the conclusion that self-infliction of wounds 'was common practice' and he was aware that knowledge of this belief damaged the Sepoys' morale.[45]

Lawrence, an old Indian hand, also drew Kitchener's attention to the theory which was prevalent amongst many Indian soldiers that the British were prepared to use up 'black pepper' before they used up the red. This was a refence to the Sepoys' belief that they were being placed in greater danger and more were being killed than were British soldiers which was seen a clear breach of *Izzat*.[46] Lawrence believed that it would help disperse this myth if a comparison of the casualties of British and Indian troops caused during the battle of Neuve Chapelle was available. Unfortunately if this comparison was given in percentage terms it was unlikely to solve Lawrence's problem since there were so fewer Indians than British involved in the battle. However, Lawrence's claim is hard to justify by examining the experiences of the Indian Corps. It was also claimed that the Indian Corps had a higher sickness rates than units in the BEF.

The belief of troops in their medical arrangements is often cited as an important contribution to morale.[47] It has been claimed that medical services on the Western Front 'reached a level of efficiency and sophistication unprecedented in British military history'.[48] At the beginning of their arrival on the Western Front, the Indian Medical Services were greatly inferior to those in the BEF and even that of the French Colonial

43 Hilary Buxton, *Imperial Amnesia*, pp. 230-231.
44 Caroline Alexander, The Shock of War, *Smithsonian Magazine*, September 2010.
45 TNA WO 32/5110: Sir Walter Lawrence to Lord Kitchener, 27 December 1915.
46 TNA WO 32/5110: Sir Walter Lawrence to Lord Kitchener, 27 December 1915.
47 Karen F. Vogt, 'Origins of Military Medical Care as an Essential Source of Morale', *Military Medicine*, Vol. 180, Issue 6, June 2015 p. 604
48 Mark Harrison, *The Medical War' British Military Medicine in the First World War* (Oxford, OUP, 2010) p. 171.

soldiers who also fought in France.[49] The Diary of the DDMS has a number of references to diseases which were prevalent amongst the Indian Corps such as mumps and measles. It also refers to the conditions under which the Indians were forced to live which included extreme cold and wet, as well as occupying insanitary billets and suffering outbreaks of food poisoning.[50] So poor were the provisions for Sepoys' medical care in the Winter of 1914-15 that there was a crisis of morale and a public scandal. Sepoys had come to expect that medical care was part of *Izzat* and the paternalistic duty of the Raj. This duty was clearly under threat when Indian Stretcher bearers, whom we have seen, displayed great bravery, had to struggle though snow and mud with only the Chappals in which they have arrived from India and so incurred cases of frostbite in their feet.[51] There is certainly evidence to suggest that the conditions in France did cause discontent amongst the Indians and they regarded this as a betrayal; 'All men will be finished here!'[52]

As with each Indian Division, the Lahore Division had five Field Ambulance Units. Since the Indian Corps was a mixed force of British and Indian Battalions, Ambulance Units and hospitals were divided along ethnic lines. Therefore the Lahore Division arrived with Nos. 7 and 8 British Field Ambulance and Nos. 111, 112 and 113 Indian Field Ambulances. These latter units were organised in a different manner from British Field Ambulances; the former had four sections each of designed to be ready to accommodate 25 patients, whilst the Indian Field Ambulance was organised in to 3 sections each with space for 50 patients. This may appear to be an imbalance in favour of the BEF but in fact, since each British Division had only two Field Ambulance Units capable of treating a total of 300 patients, an Indian Division could cater for 450. A closer examination however reveals that the Sepoys and Sowars were greatly disadvantaged since their numbers considerably exceeded the British troops within an Indian Corps division by roughly 3 to 1. In reality, however, neither the BEF nor the Indian Corps was geared to cope with the number of casualties which were to occur.

The next level of medical care in the Lahore Division was the Clearing Hospital which, as its name suggests decided what type of treatment was required for each of the wounded soldiers. Again, organised on ethnic grounds, with one section for British casualties and three sections for Indian wounded. These small units had four surgeons and eight assistant surgeons together with twenty-five members of the Indian Bearer Corps and eight ward orderlies. However, the normal establishment for a division was twice that actually sent to France which again suggests the effects on both the strain on the IEF's resources and the underestimation of the likely casualty rate on the Western Front.

49 Mark Harrison, Disease, Discipline and Dissent: The Indian Army in France and England 1914-15 in Roger Cooter, Mark Harrison, Steve Sturdy (eds.), *Medicine and Modern Warfare* (London: Wellcome Trust, 1999), p. 185.
50 TNA WO 95/1093: Indian Corps, Deputy Director of Medical Services War Diary.
51 Chappals: Sandals: Abantika Gosh (ed.), *History of the Armed Forces Medical Services* (Hyderabad, Orient Langman, 1988), p. 106.
52 BL IOR/L/5/825/Vol 1: Censor of Indian Mails, Letter No. 3, 15 January 1915.

Sepoys needing further medical care were sent to the Divisional Stationary Hospital which could cater for 200 wounded. Further care was provided by the General Hospital and the Lahore Division had both a British and an Indian establishment. The British General Hospital was organised for 200 casualties whilst the Indian could accommodate 1,000. One advantage which the Indian Medical Corps medical services had over its British equivalent was the X Ray Section which was attached to the General Hospital. Normally designed for hill warfare it was relatively easily transported by mule and was in charge of an officer of the IMS. The Lahore Division also had and Advanced Depot of Medical Stores for supplying medical and surgical equipment to troops and hospitals. It was in the charge of a senior assistant surgeon assisted by five Followers employed on tasks such as for carpentry, packing and water carrying. Strangely the Indian Corps was not accompanied by a Sanitary Section on its arrival in France.

The high rate of casualties was undoubtedly unexpected and provision for treating the Indians away from the front line had not been properly thought out by the time of their arrival at Marseilles. The idea of the Nawab of Bhopal and the Maharaja of Gwalior that the Indian princes should provide a hospital ship, *Loyalty,* has already been mentioned. This ship was the renamed *Empress of India* in March 1915. However, the initial plans for treating severely wounded Sepoys were to transport them to Marseilles by rail and then by sea in Hospital Ships like *Loyalty* or *Takada* to Egypt and Bombay. However, the difficulties of using railways to transport the wounded to Marseilles were such, that this plan was soon abandoned which meant that hospital beds had to be found elsewhere and, whilst this was being considered, the two Indian Hospital Ships were used to treat the wounded.

The Indian war plan did allow for personnel to be allocated for the Hospital Ships and ambulance trains, but no such personnel accompanied the IEFA to France. Similarly there were no Ambulance Trains allocated for the Indian Corps and places had to be reserved for Indian wounded on British Ambulance Trains. The sudden rise in Indian casualties in November 1914 found that the preparations for their treatment, care and evacuation from Boulogne, the centre of chief hospital centre, was not yet complete, especially in assembling the necessary Indian personnel. In addition, when it was decided that the Indian wounded would be evacuated to England, the War Office's order decreed that they should be accompanied by Indian personnel which was a complete impossibility since none had been allocated for such duty and that evidence of the true situation regarding Indian Medical Services had not been fully appreciated.[53] Such accompanying personnel had to be found from within the Indian Hospitals described above in spite of the fact that they were already understaffed. In fact the IMS, which was designed for coping with casualties in Frontier warfare, could hardly cope with the numbers

53 W.G. Macpherson, *Medical Services General History: The Medical Services on the Western Front, and during the Operations in France and Belgium in 1914 and 1915* (London: HMSO, 1928), p. 123.

suffering from the sickness which began to occur soon after the Corps arrival in France, let alone the large numbers of wounded. Of particular concern was how the Bearers, a vital element in the IMS, would cope when faced with conditions at the Front. They were completely untrained and ignorant of the necessary stretcher work. Such was the concern that Surgeon (Major) General Sir William Grant MacPherson, who had experience of Medical Services in India, was appointed to improve the organisation of the IMS and make it fit for purpose in France. MacPherson had previously examined the Medical Services in use during the Boer War to see what lessons could be learned.

Macpherson realised that there was an immediate need to increase the number of followers attached to the IMS. The duties of such men has already been explained as had the type of services which they supplied which would not be done by Sepoys and Sowars. There was also a need for ward and nursing orderlies to be transferred from the Royal Army Medical Corps or from the Voluntary Aid detachments to assist with the nursing of the wounded. He criticised that the Field Ambulance Units each had six horsed ambulances which was unsatisfactory, given the nature of fighting on the Western Front with its risk to the horses, and he recommended that there was a need for motorised ambulances. This did not happen until 1915 since such vehicles were initially in short supply even though each Divisional ADMS had been provided with three motor ambulance cars at the beginning of the Corps' arrival in France. Indian Cavalry was much better equipped with seven motorised ambulances on their arrival.

Macpherson's account of the IMS is one of improvisation, ingenuity and afterthought. Hospitals were initially set up in tented areas and inadequate buildings were improved. The dietary and religious needs of the individual Classes, such as the need for Hindus to be cremated close to water, complicated matters. Unsurprisingly, the Indian Corps had left India ill prepared in many respects for what it would encounter in France and Flanders, but conditions gradually improved over time and, by 1915, Sepoys and Sowars could expect care of a similar standard to their British comrades. Accusations of excessive Sepoy ill health failed to consider the numbers of cases of mumps and measles which occurred and had been incubated during the Corps' long sea voyage on its way to France.

The Medical Situation of the Lahore Division at the at the end of 1914 was as follows:

- The Lahore British General Hospital and the Lahore Indian Stationary Hospital at Orleans (Advanced Base).
- One section of the Lahore Indian General Hospital, and the Lahore Advanced Depot of Medical Stores.at Rouen (Base Depot)
- The Lahore Indian General Hospital (less one section at Orleans), and the Lahore X-ray Section. at Hardelot (Hospital Base)
- The Lahore Clearing Hospital and the Lahore Advanced Depot of Medical Stores at Lillers[54]

54 Macpherson, *Medical Services General History*, pp. 133-134.

Another method of assessing an Army's morale is by examining its desertion rate. All armies suffer from desertion and the Indian Corps was no exception. During the period between August 1914 and March 1920 more than 20,000 servicemen were convicted by courts-martial of offences which carried the death sentence. Of these 80% were convicted of desertion. Only 3,000 of men who were court marshalled were sentenced to be put to death and of those, just over 10% were executed. These numbers are extremely small when one considers the total number of British and Empire troops who were involved in the First World War. In the winter of 1914-1915 the Germans attempted to stir up subversion amongst the Indian troops by airdropping thousands of leaflets printed in Hindi which encouraged them to mutiny. On other occasions, messages were left in bottles which suggested that the Indians should kill their British officers and Muslim deserters would to be taken the Middle East where they could take part in the *Jihad* (Holy War) which was being waged by the Turks against the Allies and receive grants of land as a reward.[55] The Indian treated these attempts with distain.[56] Such was the failure of German attempts to create unrest amongst the Indian Corps that by January 1915, they had given up trying.[57]

Unlike the British deserter who could, to some extent, melt into the French background, the Indian who deserted would find it hard to be inconspicuous. However, it was

Surgeon (Major) General Sir William Grant MacPherson, Deputy Director General Medical Services.

Jemadar Mir Dast V.C. (Gallagher, *The Great War: Victoria Cross Heroes, 1915-16*)

55 TNA WO 157/597: 'Intelligence Summary on Indian Corps Headquarters, November 1914, Secret reports on captured German soldiers and documents.

56 David Omissi, *The Sepoy and the Raj,* pp. 110-111.

57 Merewether and Smith, *The Indian Corps,* p. 330.

the innate loyalty which the vast majority of Sepoys and Sowars had to the King Emperor, their Battalion, Company and its officers which maintained their desire to be' true to their salt'. In this respect, the traditions of creating a 'family' loyalty amongst Indian Battalions was an advantage. There were well known desertions such as that of Jemadar Mir Mast, 54th Vaughan's Rifles, brother of Mir Dast VC, who defected to the Germans. This was not a case of cowardice since Mir Mast was considered to be politically aware and it is not certain that he, or the 15 Afridis who accompanied him across No Mans' Land, were motivated by personal or political grievances or whether Turkey's entry into the War was the deciding factor. Being Afridi they were from the Northwest Frontier and technically subjects of the Emir of Afghanistan and therefore might have expected to go unpunished for deserting. Mir Mast was later falsely, rumoured to have been decorated with the Iron Cross. In fact, he was awarded the Order of the Red Eagle for diplomatic services to Imperial Germany when attempting, unsuccessfully as it transpired, to obtain the Emir of Afghanistan's support for the Ottomans. Perhaps the Iron Cross tale was a direct contrast to support for his religion and the loyalty demonstrated by his brother's devotion to the Empire.[58]

58 According to Manimugdha S. Sharma, Sepoys who served during 1914-18 underwent a university-like experience. See *The Times of India,* 10 November 2018.

13

'I have been hit in the head but not enough, I hope, to prevent me carrying on'

On 22 November Field Marshal Sir John French issued a 'Special Order of the Day' in which he gave a somewhat one-sided picture of the situation on the Western Front and the state of German morale. Germany was fighting on two major fronts: in the West against the combined armies of France, Britain and Belgium and the East against the numerically strong Russian Army. The fighting in France and Flanders had caused many German casualties and sections of the German High Command, headed by Field Marshal Paul Von Hindenburg, Commander of the German Eighth Army and his Chief of Staff, General Erich Ludendorff, had begun to argue that the War must be won in the East. General Erich von Falkenhayn, Chief of the German General Staff, believed that this was something of a pipe dream and that victory must come in the West. Germany's ally, the Austro-Hungarian Empire, had had a disastrous 1914 in military terms by the end of which it had lost 1,250,000 men killed and wounded. This destroyed their Army as the number of casualties was greater than the total number of their professional soldiers and trained reservists at the beginning of the War. Falkenhayn was therefore forced to agree to send seven Divisions from Flanders to the Eastern Front to bolster the tottering Austro-Hungarians or face the possibility that they might drop out of the War and expose Germany's 'back door' to Russia.

Aware of the struggles the enemy faced in the East, French argued that with the withdrawal some of German troops in the West, *we must follow them up and harass their retreat to the utmost of our power.* 'French's hope was that the combined Allied Forces would be able to push the Germans further away from the Channel. Kitchener's instructions were clear: 'The special motive of the Force under your control is to support and cooperate with the French Army against our common enemies.'[1]

At the beginning of December 1914, the BEF was deployed along a 21-mile front from La Bassee to Wytschaete with French troops on either flank. The Indian Corps was deployed at the far right of the British Line, defending a two mile front. To its

1 Edmonds, 1914, Vol I, Appendix 8, p. 409.

left was IV Corps under Henry Rawlinson. Sir John French was constantly under pressure from the French High Command to take the offensive and was also aware that the French people believed that the BEF was not making every effort.[2] It was clear that in order to satisfy these demands the BEF could not just remain on the defensive until Kitchener's New Army was ready. Consequently, the Indian Corps, along with IV Corps, was instructed to take part in 'local operations' to inhibit the enemy's activities.[3]

In the first two days of December 1914, the Connaught Rangers were in the trenches at Le Plantin, with a strength of eight officers and 343 men. They were relieved on 2 December by the Seaforth Highlanders and returned to billets in Gorre having had five more men wounded. On 3 December they arrived at Le Touret where they received a draft of four officers and 130 men and the interestingly named Lieutenant Frederick Lewis von Stieglitz returned from hospital.[4] During that day the 440-man strong 2nd Battalion Connaught Ranger arrived at Le Touret from Gorre, and the two Battalions amalgamated in ordered to increase their effectiveness.

Their total strength was now 19 Officers which included Captain Boyd RAMC and Lieutenant J. Hornswell of the Royal Irish Fusiliers, and 913 other ranks.[5] In a similar fashion much of the BEF was reinforced by Reservists and Battalions made up of men who had previously been serving overseas. Supplies of all types were extremely short and the Indian Corps continued to rely on the ingenuity of its Sappers and Miners for hand grenades. They were also perfecting catapults designed to launch grenades up to a distance of 300 yards and creating searchlights from automobile headlights.[6]

The numbers of Connaughts again began to dwindle as men became sick and by 15 December there were 867 other ranks. On the same day, four of the Connaughts' Lieutenants were promoted to the rank of temporary Captain in recognition of the need for Company Commanders.

Meantime, on 16th December, the 129th Baluchis and the 57th (Wilde's) Rifles had been selected to attack and capture two German Saps which were in front of the 15th Sikhs north of Givenchy and then take as much of the German main trench as

2 J. E. Edmonds, *Military Operations, France and Belgium, 1915, Vol. I* (London, Macmillan, 1927) (Henceforth, Edmonds, 1915, Vol. 1) p. 2.

3 Edmunds, 1915, Vol I, *Instructions for Operations Commencing 14 December,* Appendix 7, p. 379.

4 Von Strieglitz was later to join the Royal Flying Corps as a balloon officer. *London Gazette,* September 1917 p. 9540

5 The 2nd Battalion landed at Boulogne on 14 August as part of the 5th Brigade in the 2nd Division with the British Expeditionary Force for service on the Western Front. Its strength on 14 August, was 30 Officers and 936 men half of whom were Reservists. Its CO. Lieutenant Colonel Alexander Abercrombie, a Bengal Solicitor, was captured during the action at La Grande Fayt, escaped but was killed on 5 November 1915. On 7 December the Sirhind Brigade, under Major General Brunker, arrived from Egypt completing the Lahore Division.

6 Merewether and Smith, *The Indian Corps,* p. 139.

possible.[7] The Connaughts were ordered to march to Givenchy in order support them and 142nd French Territorial Battalion was to be held in reserve. The Baluchis and the 57th Rifles carried 200 rounds per man with seven picks and fourteen shovels per Company to improve and extend the trenches. The attack, which had been scheduled for 0800 hours, was made earlier in the morning at around 0630 hours and, in order to maintain the element of surprise, was unsupported by artillery. The 15th Sikhs were supposed to have dug a communication trench to the German Saps, one to the Sikh's right and one to their left, during the hours of darkness but had been unable to complete the work because of heavy resistance from the enemy. This meant that the Baluchis had to advance across open ground with good visibility in the face of intense enemy fire. Consequently, they lost 'a good deal of men' in the process.[8] Two Companies of the Baluchis and the 57th Wilde's Rifles, who were in their rear, were unable to leave the Sikh's trench because of the German rifle and Maxim fire. However, Major Potter's Company of Baluchis dashed across the 25 yards between the Sikh's trench to the German left-hand Sap and a second Company, under Major Buist of the Guides, attacked the right-hand Sap which was about 50 yards away. The Sikhs in their own trenches continued to dig to extend the communication trench in anticipation that it would reach the German left-hand Sap by night fall.[9] However, as the 129th Baluchis were unable to get their two remaining Companies out of the trenches, the 57th Wilde's Rifles took no part in the attack other than returning German fire, and the Sikh's stopped digging.

The attacking Companies of the Baluchis were able to enter the two German Saps but then disappeared from view. Only the dead and injured, who had been hit in the initial rush were visible. It appeared that the attack on the right-hand Sap had failed. The Germans were putting up a heavy resistance and sniping or bombing those Baluchis who were at the Sap head. Many attempted to climb back over the Sap's sides but were picked off. Given this apparent failure it seemed sensible to get Major Potter's Company to withdraw but since it was out of sight there was a problem of communication with them. Eventually this was solved by attaching a message to a weight and throwing into the Sap.

The Company in the right-hand Sap had actually been successful and had almost reached the German front line trench but it was impossible to support them because the other two Companies of Baluchis could not leave the Sikh's trench in the face of heavy enemy fire,. The Germans regrouped and gradually pushed the Baluchis backwards in both Saps to the Sap heads. Help for the Baluchis came in an unusual form,

7 Merewether and Smith, *The Indian Corps,* p. 141.

8 Message from Major Buist to Major Hannyngton 129th Baluchis, 7:30 am 16 December 1914.

9 Merewether and Smith, *The Indian Corps,* p. 143 suggests the digging was from the Sap to the Sikh trenches. The 15th Sikhs' War Diary indicates that it was from their trench to the sap. See TNA WO 95/3927: 3 (Lahore) Division, 9 (Sirhind) Brigade, 15 (Ludhiana) Sikhs war diary entry for 16 December 1914. Either there was digging at both ends, which appears unlikely, or the 15th Sikh diary entry is correct.

Sir John Smyth in later life.

Two Sikh British officers, Lieutenant Arthur Barstow, and 2nd Lieutenant John Smyth, each, from different points on the Sikh firing line, had the unusual sight of Germans showing themselves in the trenches adjacent to the Saps.[10] Both officers together with two Indian V.C.O.s were able to kill a number of Germans with well-placed rifle fire. So effective was their response that the Germans stopped exposing themselves when firing into the Sap head but continued to throw bombs from cover. The struggle went on until early evening when the Communication trench eventually reached Major Potter's men in the left-hand Sap and they were able to return to the Sikh trenches and were replaced in the Communication trench. The men in the left hand trench under Major Buist waited until dark and then crawled back to the Sikhs. During the day the Sikhs had had 6 killed and 14 wounded, whilst the Baluchis had 114 casualties.

The Connaughts were not used in this attack and returned to Béthune where they were joined by an additional Officer, Lieutenant Ivan de la Bere of the Dorset Battalion.[11] The Connaughts then entered the trenches south of the La Bassee Canal

10 Arthur Edward Barstow, known as 'Bustling Bill', was to continue his military career after the First World War and command the 9th Indian Division in the Battle for Malaya and was killed fighting the Japanese in January 1942. John Smyth was awarded the VC for conspicuous bravery in May 1915. He went on to have a controversial career and while commanding the 17th Indian Division during its retreat in Burma, was sacked by the C in C India, General Wavell, for failing to expedite a strong bridgehead on the enemy side of the Sittang River and was forced to blow the bridge to halt the Japanese whilst two thirds of his Division was on the enemy side. This led to the loss of Rangoon and Lower Burma. Smyth was later exonerated as it appears, he wished to retreat across the Sittang 10 days previously and defend the opposite bank but his request to General Hutton, G.O.C, Burma Command, was refused. Smyth later became an M.P. and was knighted.

11 de La Bere was to have an interesting career. Whilst on attachment to the Connaughts he was wounded and on recovery he was seconded to the Royal Flying Corps. He then became a conducting officer escorting official visitors to the Western Front and was the Assistant Press Officer to the British Army on the Rhine. By 1939, he was the CO of the 1st Battalion Dorset Regiment and was involved in the Siege of Malta. Retiring as a Brigadier after the Second World War, de la Bere was appointed Secretary-General of the

relieving the 1st Battalion Manchester Regiment and the Irishmen were deployed amongst the brick stacks and railway embankment in the immediate vicinity.

On the 17 December the Indian Corps were instructed to join with the 3rd, 4th and 5th Corps to attack all along the front. In the late evening they received a second order which confused matters by instructing the Indian Corps to demonstrate along the whole front and seize any opportunity to capture enemy trenches.[12] An indignant Merewether points out that a demonstration is quite a different thing from an attack and is almost apoplectic when the second order was modified to demonstrate along their whole font and capture enemy trenches when the opportunity arose. Douglas Haig, Commander of I Corps, was also frustrated by the contradictory order and questioned both French's Chief of the General Staff, Major General Archibald Murray, and French himself. Haig agreed with Murray that 'no definite results could be expected from such ambiguous orders of this nature'.[13]

Sir John French's Sixth Dispatch of 2 February 1915 further confuses the situation by stating that Willcocks believed this was a favourable moment to launch an attack.[14] Again, Merewether looks elsewhere for enlightenment regarding the situation and, having drawn his reader's attention to the confused set of orders already mentioned, he then points out that both Willcocks and French accepted that the Indian Corps was exhausted and needed rest. Rather than being an error of judgement on Willcocks part, it was rather his desire to obey orders however vague, which brought about the heavy casualties which occurred during the demonstration / attack. French's approval of Willcocks' decision was subsequently shown by orders issued in the evening of 19 December which stated that some of the action taken was marked with success; 'the balance of advantage rest with us and promises well for further progress'.[15] Field Marshal French's retrospective comments, argued Merewether and Smith, indicated that the action which Willcocks took was therefore reasonable.

The attack by the Ferozepore Brigade on the 18-19 December was made in combination with the Sirhind Brigade on a 300-yard front at the point the two Brigades conjoined. They were to be supported by Sappers and Pioneers whose job it was to strengthen the enemy trenches which it was expected would be captured. The 47th Sikhs. which had been detached from the Indian Corps reserve was to be ready to follow up on the attack's success. The assault was to be preceded by a heavy, four-minute, artillery barrage.[16] Although this short barrage might be useful to surprise the

Central Chancery of the Orders of Knighthood, an office within the Royal Household at St James's Palace responsible for administering a large part of the British Honours system.

12 Merewether and Smith, *Indian Corps,* p. 45.

13 Sheffield and Bourne (eds.), *Douglas Haig,* diary entry for 18 December 1914, p. 85.

14 My emphasis.

15 Merewether and Smith, *The Indian Corps,* p. 146.

16 Willcocks. *With the Indians, p. 154.* Willcocks reminds his readers that the barrage was short because of the lack of ammunition.

General Sir James Willcocks] talking to Indian officers at an inspection parade near Merville, (H.D. Girdwood. Open Source)

Germans, the real reason was the shell shortage as only 40 rounds had been allocated to each 18 pdr. and 25 rounds per 4,5-inch mortar.[17]

The night was cold, wet, and windy and the Lahore Division's objective was a 300-yard line of enemy trenches in front of and northwest of Givenchy. The original plan was to involve the 129th Baluchis, who were occupying trenches at the juncture of the Ferozepore Brigade and the Sirhind Brigade and for them to advance on a frontage of roughly 150 yards over ground with which they were already familiar from their attacks on 16 December. However, because of the losses the Baluchis had suffered during these attacks, it was decided that their place should be taken by the 59th (Scinde) Rifles of the Jullundur Brigade and the Baluchis were to act in support. The 59th (Scinde) Rifles' war diarist is somewhat scathing about the idea of small, local attacks:

The C.O. of the Baluchis and the G.O.C. of the Ferozepore Brigade both realised the futility of these local attacks, they cost a lot of men and, even if they are successful, no good whatsoever is obtained by gaining 150 yards of German trench …

17 Edmonds 1915, Vol I.

He also suggested that the attack was at Willcocks' insistence as the French had made an extensive advance on the right of the Indian Corp's line but the Indians 'had done nothing.'[18] Gathering a further head of steam, he complains that the Battalion is unfamiliar with the ground over which they must advance and it would have been wiser if the attack were to take place a day later to allow the Company Commanders a night during which to reconnoiter.

The 59th (Scinde) Rifles war diarist described the attack as 'bald headed'. It needed the 129th Baluchis to evacuate 200 yards of trench in order for the 59th Rifles to occupy the space which this created, prior to beginning the attack. This evacuation was carried out in darkness and the front line was occupied by two companies of the 59th Rifles with the remaining two companies in the support trench. The time taken to affect this move was longer than expected and the Scinde Rifles had hardly occupied the trenches when the order to attack was given. The officers of 59th had no time to confer with the officers of the attacking party from the Sirhind Brigade with whom the 59th were meant to keep in touch. The reason for the haste was undoubtedly an attempt to surprise the German defenders and to take maximum advantage which the artillery barrage provided the attackers. Further delay was caused by the overcrowding in the trenches which were very deep and hard to climb out from, and the variety of angles into which the front trench was divided meant that some men, in the confusion, were unsure as to the actual direction of the enemy which they were supposed to be attacking. These factors obviously reduced the momentum of the attack.

The 59th Rifles' attack resulted in mixed results. One platoon captured part of a German Sap and held it for the whole day until the Sappers and Miners were able to dig a communicating trench from the British front line. Another platoon got to within 30 yards of the enemy but were repulsed with considerable loss. The third attack was described by a V.C.O., Havildar Dost Mohamed whose platoon, in the confusion, joined that led by the 24-year-old Lieutenant William Arthur McCrae Bruce. Bruce was the first man to get into the enemy trench and the occupying Germans surrendered and handed over the rifles to the Indians who were lying close to the edge of the trench. However, the Indians who put their heads over the trench were shot at and some killed. Eventually the attackers were able to enter the trench which they were to hold all day having fortified it against counterattack. Bruce was shot in the neck but continued to walk up and down the trench encouraging his men, but he was eventually killed. The two platoons fought hard, but their rifle bolts became clogged with mud and they were unable to fire them without continual cleaning. Eventually the Germans brought up a mortar and the platoon's situation was untenable. Havildar Dost Mohamed ordered the Sepoys to retreat but they refused arguing that Bruce had ordered them to defend the trench and that is what they would do. Most were killed as a result. Was this a case of loyalty or loss of a British officer? One suspects the former.

18 TNA WO 95/3927: 3 Indian (Lahore) Division, 8th (Jullundur) Infantry Brigade, 59th (Scinde) Rifles War Diary, 18 December 1914.

William Arthur McCrae Bruce VC.

Dost Mohamed and another wounded Sepoy tried to move up a Sap but were warned by a British officer that they were moving towards the Germans. The two moved onto open ground but found themselves in front of a German trench and had to use the direction of hostile shelling to find their way to their own lines. In the confusion, Dost Mohamed was fired at by his own side but was able to convince a British sergeant that he was an Indian and not a German. Dost Mohamed wanted to go back to rescue his wounded colleague, but the sergeant prevented him from doing so.[19]

The attacks by the other platoons continued with mixed success and the day was regarded as miserable failure; the worst day the 59th (Scinde) Rifles had ever experienced. The Battalion lost four British officers killed and one wounded, four V.C.O.s wounded and missing, and twenty-nine other ranks wounded with fifty-seven missing. Most of the latter were believed to be dead. [20] For his gallantry Lieutenant Bruce was awarded a posthumous Victoria Cross. [21] Dost Mohamed was awarded the Indian Order of Merit, Second Class.

Bruce' citation read:

> For most conspicuous bravery and devotion to duty. On the 19th December 1914, near Givenchy, during a night attack Lieutenant Bruce was in command of a small party which captured one of the enemy's trenches. In spite of being severely wounded in the neck, he walked up and down the trench, encouraging his men to hold on against several counterattacks for some hours until killed. The fire from rifles and bombs was very heavy all day, and it was due to the skilful disposition made and the example and encouragement shown by Lieutenant Bruce that his men were able to hold out until dusk, when the trench was finally captured by the enemy.[22]

19 The war diary indicates that this needed to be confirmed.

20 Merewether and Smith recorded that they were all wounded and only one was missing. See Willocks, *The Indian Corps,* p. 167.

21 *London Gazette,* Fourth Supplement, 2 September 1919. 4. 11206. Bruce's VC was bought by his old school, Victoria College and along with those of other VC's winners, his citation is read on Remembrance Day.

22 Fourth Supplement to *The London Gazette of 2 September 1919*, 4 September 1919, No. 31536, p. 112

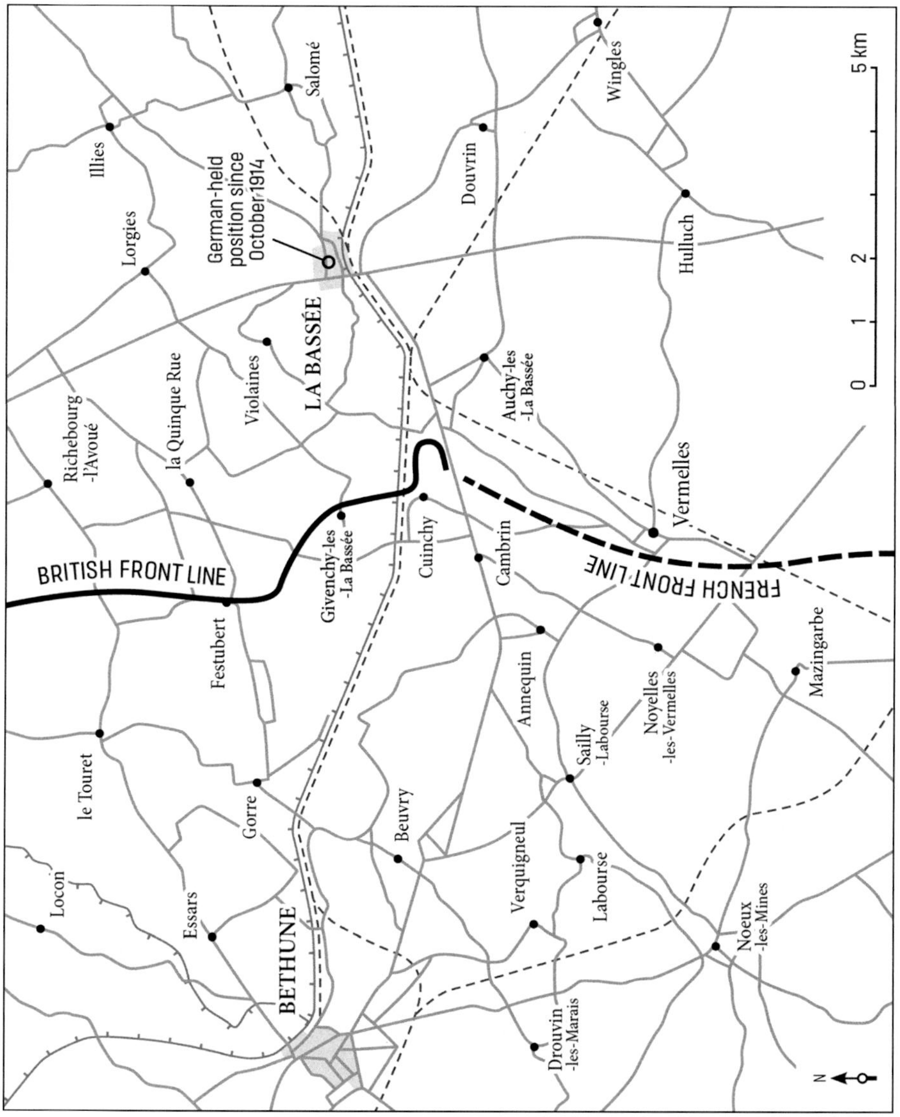

Map 4 Givenchy and vicinity.

The Scinde's Diary criticises 129th Baluchis for their lack of support. After all the 59th Rifles had done work which the Baluchis were not considered to be up to carrying out. The orders which the 129th received were very clear; they were to be ready to assist the 59th Rifles in any way possible. It was the Baluchis who finally relieved the 59th Rifles at the end of the fighting but, in some cases, the Rifles were forced to evacuate the trenches they had captured at such great cost. The 59th's war diarist is particularly scathing about the loss of men in the attack since nothing tangible was gained. He also hoped that the generals far behind the line would recognise what folly these local attacks were.[23] Willcocks, perhaps in support of this remark, argued that 'All one can do is to endeavour by every means in one's power to carry out the Commander-in-Chief's plans.'[24]

On the 20 December, the Connaughts were aware of the 'vigorous' shelling of Givenchy and the trenches to the east.[25] Later that day, rumours circulated of a serious German attack on the Sirhind Brigade which also involved the 129th Baluchis and these proved to be which true as has been explained. Major Hannyngton described the situation as being extremely tense. The Baluchis had rushed a German Sap which the 59th Rifles had 'apparently missed'. The German attacks have been fierce and he feared that, if the enemy made a further concerted effort, the Baluchis would be unable to hold their own because of the rifles being jammed with mud and the bomb fuses being damp. There was also a need for rope with which to get the bombs across from one trench to another. The men were 'all in' and needed support; 'it (was) no good sending indifferent troops' as reinforcements, since the enemy were quite active.[26] The most that Hannyngton could hope for was to being able consolidate the position and a further advance by his men was out of the question.

Even in this very difficult situation, the Major sympathetically reports the capture of a badly wounded German officer who could not be evacuated until the trenches had been deepened to protect the men carrying his stretcher. Hannyngton also wonders about the whereabouts of the 59th Rifles. The messages which the Major sent back from these occupied trenches clearly indicate the difficulties under which he and his men were attempting to do their best to prevent the Germans recapturing the trenches and also show the problems of communications in the battlefields since they were all carried by runner rather than sent by telephone.

It was during the 20 December that the Germans succeeded in undermining the Sirhind Brigade's trench parapet and set off a series of ten 110-pound mines. As Willcocks records, the Indian Corps had yet to acquire the ability to detect such

23 TNA WO 95/3927: 3 Indian (Lahore) Division, 8 (Jullundur) Infantry Brigade, 5 (Scinde) Rifles War Diary, 19 December 1914.
24 Willcocks, *With the Indians*, p. 158.
25 TNA WO 95/3923: War Diary of Connaught Rangers War Diary, 20 December 1914.
26 TNA WO 95/3924: War Diary of 129th Baluchis letter from Major Hannyngton to O.C. 129th Baluchis, 20 December 1914 carried by Lieutenant J.P. Drew, Engineering Officer.

Indian reinforcements who fought at Givenchy.

mining operations nor to counter 'this underground warfare'.[27] Many men were blown up or buried. The Germans made a determined advance and some of the Sirhind Brigade were forced to abandon their trenches to the enemy. This was not a rout of the Indian Corps, but they were forced to retire in the face of determined and fierce opposition. The 57th (Wilde's) Rifles, again under the command of the recovered Lieutenant Colonel Gray, found themselves enfiladed and fell back in an orderly fashioned with Sepoys turning and firing at their attackers from behind defensive positions as the Battalion withdrew. On the 21 December it was confirmed that the Germans had occupied the left section of trenches and the 57th Rifles doggedly defended a barricade within te rest of the trench against frequent enemy attacks. These trenches were knee deep in liquid mud and the Reserves were constantly employed moving up and down the communication trenches, which was long and very narrow, to bring ammunition and supplies to the barricade but were thus unable to assist in its actual defence. The pressure on the 57th Rifles increased when around 1500 hours the 1st Battalion Manchester Regiment halted their attack on the village of Givenchy having found that the Germans occupied several of its houses and were putting up strong resistance. The pressure was eased when the Manchester's were reinforced and recommenced their attack.[28] The British 1st Division, 1st Brigade established communications with the 57th Rifles but the Germans continued to attack the 57th's trenches with

27 Willcocks, *With the Indians,* p. 161.

28 The 1st Manchester's lost 2 Officers and 64 men killed with 3 officers and 123 men wounded. 46 men were missing after the action. See TNA WO 95/3927: 3 Indian (Lahore Brigade, 8 (Jullundur) Infantry Division, 1 Manchester Regiment War Diary, 21 December 1914.

determination and were successfully repulsed by dogged Sepoys under the leadership of Subadar Arsla Khan, who had committed many risky operations during this action.[29] Reinforcing troops from the 59th (Scinde) Rifles arrived which eased the pressure somewhat allowing sick men to be sent back to receive treatment. Such was the intensity of the action that this had not been possible until the relief arrived. The 57th Rifles were relieved over a 10-hour period on the night of the 22/23 December by the South Staffordshire Regiment. The 57th had been in combat for three days and had extremely wet feet for the whole of that time[30] and the march to billets at Béthune took a considerable effort as many men were suffering from frost bite and badly swollen feet.[31]

On Christmas Day, Christmas cards from King George V and Queen Mary were distributed and each man received a present, of a tin containing an ounce of tobacco, 20 cigarettes, or a pipe a, a tinder lighter together with a picture of Princess Mary, the daughter of the King and Queen, from the Sailors' and Soldiers' Christmas Gift Fund who was the founder of the fund. Ever sensitive to religious differences the Sikhs received a bag of raisons and other spices instead of the tobacco.[32]

The 9th Bhopals had been involved in the fighting alongside the 57th Rifles and eventually successfully held their trenches until relieved by the South Staffordshire Regiment, and like the 57th Rifles marched to billets in Béthune having sustained 2 British officers, 3 Indian officers and 1 Sepoy killed and 31 wounded with 75 missing. The 129th Baluchis also marched back to Béthune and were billeted at Lapugnoy.

During this period The Connaughts defended the area of Pont Fixe and the railway embankment until they were relieved by the King's Royal Rifle Corps battalion on the evening of 22 December and then marched to billets the Caserne Chambord, an army barracks, at Béthune.

On the 23 December they marched to La Beauvière where they were to spend the week of Christmas, by the end of these actions the Connaughts had been reduced to 19 Officers and 769 men.[33]

29 Subadar Arsla Khan was described by Merewether and Smith as 'one of the finest specimens of the Indian officer imaginable.' He was awarded the Military Cross for his bravery during the second battle of Ypres in 1915., *The Indian Corps*, pp. 197-198.

30 TNA WO 95/3923: 57th (Wilde's) Rifles, Report on the part taken by the 57th Riles in action on 21, and 22 December: dated 24 December 1914.

31 TNA WO 95/3923: 57th (Wilde's) Rifles War Diary, 23 December 1914.

32 TNA WO 95/3923: 57th (Wilde's) Rifles War Diary, 25 December 1914.

33 During this period 29 men had been sent to hospital. The original number of officers was 18 but this was increased when Company Sergeant Major W J O'Brien was promoted to Lieutenant. O'Brien was promoted Captain in 1922, *London Gazette* 5 January 1923, after the Connaughts had returned to India, O'Brien was to act as President of a Court of Enquiry into the deaths of two Connaught Privates soldiers who mutinied in protest of alleged atrocities by the Black and Tans in Ireland. Their 'leader', Private James Daly, was executed whilst the others were sentenced to penal servitude.

There were several cases of influenza, myalgia, coughs and colds and six cases of venereal disease. All told 146 Connaughts were sent to hospital and yet the health of the Battalion was described as fair.[34]

The accusation by the Writer of 59th (Scinde) Rifles war diary that the local attacks were foolish deserves some close examination.[35] It could be argued that there was a shifting of blame for these actions as Willcocks suggests that he was forced to obey orders. This might indicate that he also thought the idea was a folly. Field Marshal French, on the other hand, having given the unclear orders already described further confused the issue as to where the responsibility lay for the attacks by suggesting that Willcocks thought this was a favourable moment to launch an attack.[36] Merewether and Smith look elsewhere regarding Willocks' decision and, having drawn their reader's attention to the confused set of orders already mentioned, they then point out that both Willcocks and French accepted that the Indian Corps was exhausted and needed rest. Rather than being an error of judgement on Willcocks part, it was rather his desire to obey orders, however vague, which brought about the heavy casualties which subsequently had occurred. That French did approve of Willcocks' decision as is shown by subsequent orders issued in the evening of 19 December which stated that some of the actions taken were marked with success; and as a result, 'the balance of advantage rest with us and promises well for further progress.'[37] Field Marshal French's retrospective comments, argued Merewether and Smith, indicated that the action which Willcocks took was therefore reasonable. It is likely that both of the senior officers felt it was necessary to take the offensive if at all possible. Willcocks was being urged to do so and French was under pressure from Kitchener who was conscious of criticism of inactivity by the French High Command. To do nothing would bring accusations of poor commitment all along the chain of command.

Christmas was a week of scrutiny for the Ferozepore Brigade. On the 24 December, the 129th Baluchis were inspected by the Brigade Commander, Brigadier General Egerton. On the 26 December the whole Ferozepore Brigade was inspected by its commander, Major General Watkins and on 28 December a further inspection was carried out by the Corps Commander, Lieutenant General Willcocks accompanied by Major General Sir Edmund Barrow, Military Secretary to the India Office. It was on 28 December that the award of the Military Cross was instituted for Officers of the rank of captain and below and Warrant officers. The first awards appeared in the *London Gazette* of 1 January 1915 and included 11 Officers of the Indian Corps including Captains Acworth and Kanwar Indarjit Singh.[38]

34 TNA WO 95/3923: 1st Connaught Rangers, Medical Officer's War Diary, 31 December 1914.
35 See page 133.
36 My emphasis.
37 Merewether and Smith, *The Indian Corps*, p. 146.
38 See Chapter 8.. The MC was not awarded posthumously until 1979 but could be awarded, as In Darjit Singh's case, to men whose deeds had occurred before they died.

Major General Edmund Barrow photographed in 1916.

As Merewether and Smith comment, 'After two months of constant combat with the enemy and the elements, the troops were greatly in need of a rest.'[39] The Indian Corps had lost at total 1,397 killed, 5,880 wounded and 2,322 were missing. The comparatively quiet at the end of December enabled the Corps to be reinforced and overhaul its equipment. Reinforcements of both officers and Sepoys arrived from India. Many were from other battalions rather than fresh recruits and gradually the Ferozepore Brigade regained its manpower.

Willocks was pleased to note that both Field Marshal French, General Luis de Maud'huy, commander of the French Tenth Army and General Paul Maistre, commander of the French XXI Corps, all communicated their congratulations on the performance of the Indian Corps during this difficult period. Somewhat ironically, in light of subsequent events, Willcocks quotes from French's Book, *1914* in which the Field Marshal pays a personal tribute to his ' 'valuable assistance' rendered in difficult conditions during the First battle of Ypres and especially the support of the Lahore Division under Lieutenant General Watkins.[40] The respect between Willocks and Field Marshal French seems to have been mutual but it is probable that French's praise was a softener to Watkins and Willcocks for what had subsequently happened to them

39 Merewether and Smith, *The Indian Corps*, p. 199.
40 Willcocks, *With the Indians*, pp. 176-177. Sir John French, *1914* (London: Constable, 1919), p. 196.

General Luis de Maud'huy, commander of the French Tenth Army.

General Paul Maistre, Commander of the French XXI Corps.

However, Edmonds is a little more detached when reviewing the Indian Corps performance and their inability to hold the line to which they had been allocated. He suggests the reasons for this failure were as follows:

- General ignorance of trench warfare and bombing. Shortage of technical troops owing to a weak establishment
- Heavy casualties
- Lack of engineer stores
- Too many troops exposed to shelling in the front trenches

In mitigation, Edmonds reminds his readers that the climate in Flanders, insufficient warm clothing and appropriate rations had adverse effects on Sepoys who were used to hot climates.[41]

It is true that the Indian Corps had little or no knowledge of trench warfare and, in this respect, were in a greater state of ignorance than the BEF who had experienced of defending trenches, such as those at Mafeking, during the Boer War of 1899-1902.[42] The British Officer Corps had also spent time studying the examples from the Russo-Japanese War (1904-1905). The Indian Corps were specialists in hill warfare which

41 Edmonds, *1915,* Vol. 1 fn. 2. p. 22.
42 Thomas Pakenham, *The Boer War* (London: Weidenfeld and Nicolson, 1979) p. 402.

the Western front offered little opportunity for them to demonstrate. However, many of Edmonds other criticisms could have equally been levelled at the BEF in 1914. The seven British divisions which had fought at Ypres had been reduced to a mere skeleton. The 7th Division had been 'battered almost out of existence' and 'reduced to a mere wreck of the fine force which had landed in Belgium'.[43] The BEF was short of shells and bombs and other equipment and, by the end of 1914, much of the reserves had been swallowed up. The Sappers and Miners had been used inappropriately and their accumulated skills were very difficult to replace. However, their ability to improvise has already been noted. Similarly, the accusation of over manning the front-line trenches which caused many preventable casualties can be questioned since this lesson had already been learned by November 1914. Many of the criticisms which Edmonds levelled had the roots in the parsimony of the Indian Government towards its troops. This is understandable given its usual enemies and the fact that it was the Indian government which was responsible for the Army's upkeep without any support from the Home government.

43 Richard Hughes, 'Tommy Capper's Immortals – How effective was the 7th Division at the First Battle of Ypres?', MA Thesis, University of Birmingham, 2015).

14

Finding out the Weaklings

On 26 December 1914 the BEF in France and Flanders underwent a major reconstruction into two armies, the First Army under General Sir Douglas Haig and the Second Army under General Horace Smith-Dorrien. The politics of the British Army at this point was somewhat tortuous. Lord Kitchener, who was now Secretary of State for War, had provided Sir John French with somewhat contradictory instructions to cooperate fully with the French whilst maintaining the BEF's independence and to avoid heavy casualties.[1] The nature of the fighting in 1914 prevented Sir John, who found it difficult to permit his troops to remain idle even if that it was possible, successfully managing both the military and diplomatic balance. Such was Kitchener's disapproval of Sir John's efforts to do so that, in November 1914, he made an offer to Marshal Joseph Joffre, Commander in Chief of the French Forces on the Western Front, to replace Sir John with Sir Ian Hamilton. Joffre declined the offer, but the appalled Sir John, in order to defend his reputation and Command was further anxious to support Joffre's plans, even though this may have been at the BEF's expense.

The creation of the First and Second Army required a level of command which was previously not known in the British Army. Sir John strongly disliked Smith-Dorrien ; a dislike which began before the beginning of the War.[2] Smith-Dorrien was chosen by Kitchener to replace Sir James Grierson, whose sudden, unexpected death had left the command of the BEF II Corps vacant; Sir John's own choice as Grierson's replacement was Sir Herbert Plumer. Kitchener knew of the animosity between French and Smith-Dorrien and knew that Smith-Dorrien would stand up to the Field Marshal. The fact that Smith-Dorrien openly kept a diary of events in

1 Edmonds, 1914, Vol 1, p. 499.See Stephen Badsey, 'Sir John French and the command of the BEF' in Spencer Jones, *Stemming the Tide: Officers and Leadership in the British Expeditionary Force 1914* (Solihull: Helion and Co. 2013), pp 40-42. For the complexity of Sir John's position.

2 Spencer Jones & Steven J. Corvi, 'A Commander of rare and unusual coolness, General Sir Horace Lockwood Smith-Dorrien', in Jones (ed.), *Stemming the Tide*, pp. 157-158.

order to inform the King of the BEF's activities further worsened the relationship between the two.[3] Sir John constantly interfered and criticised Smith-Dorrien to such extent that in May 1915 Sir Horace offered to resign but the offer was ignored by French who preferred to sack him.[4] Smith-Dorrien was, in French's opinion, 'quite unfit to command of an Army.'[5]

Sir Douglas Haig, on the other hand, was something of a protegee of Field Marshal French and was given something of a free hand and some of his offensive actions had little input from GHQ.[6] It has been suggested that French deliberately removed Smith-Dorrien in order to improve Haig's standing. The Indian Corps was attached to the First Army and so Willcocks came under the direct command of Haig, who, until that point, had been his subordinate in rank. Willcocks was deeply hurt by this as he argued that it would be seen by the Sepoys of the Indian Corps as an insult and a criticism of Willcocks as well as their performance. Although Willcocks generously writes that Haig's promotion was well deserved for his performance as a corps commander at Mons and the First Battle of Ypres, it was the fact that a junior was elevated into a superior position which galled him. Had the Indian Corps been attached to the Second Army, Willcocks argues, no implied criticism would be seen since Smith-Dorrien was already Willcocks' superior. In good grace, Willcocks argues that, with regard to his loyalty to Haig, No 'man ever rendered more loyal or wholehearted service and support to his superior officer.'[7] This may be the case, but Haig only receives this one mention in Willcocks' account.

Haig was, to say the least, diffident towards his new subordinate. On a visit to the Indian Corps Headquarters on 21 December 1914, he noted in his diary that Willcocks' confidence and joviality had declined since they had last met. At this meeting, a desperate Willcocks argued that his Corps was 'quite tired out and unable to fight any more'. Relief should be immediate or disastrous consequences would result. Haig wired the CGS, General Archibald Murray, recommending the immediate relief of the Indian Corps and move I Corps to Béthune the following day in order to gradually replace the Indian Corps.; this was the day he formally became GOC First Army.[8] By evening the Lahore Division had been completely withdrawn and by the

3 Richard Holmes, *The Little Field Marshal: A Life of Sir John French* (London, Weidenfeld & Nicolson, 2004), p. 212.
4 See C. R, Ballard, *Smith-Dorrien* (London: Constable, 1931, pp. 296-313.
5 Conversation with Field Marshal French recorded by Douglas Haig in Haig and Bourne, *Douglas Haig*, p. 219.
6 Nick Lloyd, 'With Faith and Without Fear': Douglas Haig's Command of First Army during 1915', The *Journal of Military History,* Vol. 71, No. 4, 2007, pp. 1051-1076.
7 Willcocks, *With the Indians,* p. 178.
8 Sheffield and Bourne (eds.), *Douglas Haig: War Diaries and Letter,* Entry for Monday 21 December 1914, p. 86. the editors also point out that Haig had previously made adverse comments on the Indian Corps HQ after a visit on 29 November 1914.

27 December, the whole of the Indian Corps had gone into reserve.[9] Willcocks admits that he thought that his days as Commander of the Indian Corps were numbered.[10]

Haig's diffidence may be thought to extend to the majority of the senior Commanders of the Indian Corps. Senior officers in both the BEF and the Indian Corps were equally inexperienced in modern war but, in spite of probably seeing much active service, the senior officers of the latter were, perhaps because of their age, less flexible than their Home Army counterparts, whose training for a European War was better as the 'pre-war organisation of the Indian Army having been based on the requirements of the frontier campaign only'.[11]

Major General Henry D'Urban Keary.

The axe was wielded by Haig by thinning out officers which he considered to be dead wood. Major General Watkins, the 54 year old Lahore Division GOC, was replaced by Major General Henry D'Urban Keary. Keary had been Commander of the Garhwal Brigade when it arrived in France and had displayed 'good initiative and tactical judgment' during the first few months of the War.[12] Lieutenant Colonel Charles Blackader, took over the Garhwal Brigade replacing Keary. having previously been Commander of the 2nd Battalion Leicester Regiment. The latter two changes could be interpreted as natural career progress for these senior British Indian Officers.

Changes in Senior Command in the Indian Corps, January 1915

Original Commander	Command	Replacement
Lieutenant General Watkins	Lahore Division	Major General Keary[13]
Major General Keary	Garhwal Brigade	Lieutenant Colonel Blackader[14]

9 For a detailed description of the changes which Haig made see. Edmonds 1915, Vol. 1 p. 22.
10 Willocks, *With the Indians,* p. 184.
11 TNA MUN 5/176/1143/16: Memorandum on India's contribution to the war in men, material and money, p. 7.
12 Morton-Jack, *The Indian Army on the Western Front,* p. 273.
13 After the withdrawal of the Lahore Division from the Western Front, Keary commanded it during the Mesopotamia Campaign. He was promoted Lieutenant General in 1917 and commanded 7th Meerut Divisional area in India in 1917 and commanded the Burma Division in 1918. He retired in 1919.
14 Major-General Charles Guinand Blackader in January 1916 was to command the 177th (2/1st Lincoln and Leicester) Brigade, in Dublin which was part of the 52nd (Midland)

Major General Carnegy[15]	Jullundur Brigade	Lieutenant Colonel Strickland[16]
Major General Brunker[17]	Sirhind Brigade	Colonel Walker[18]
Brigadier General MacBean[19]	Bareilly Brigade	Lieutenant Colonel Southey[20]
Colonel Jacob[21]	Dehra Dun Brigade	Brigadier General Johnson[22]

Willcocks was very critical of the War Office which, he claimed used the Indian Army as a 'dumping ground' for senior officers whom it had wished to reward but for which it did not intend to find a place in the British Army. Willcocks continues that, although this method involved good soldiers with good records, 'they were generally passed the age of Brigade command'.[23] The result of this custom meant that when the BEF and the Indian Corps were involved in combined operations it was the senior

Division during the Easter Rising and later the 38th (Welsh) Division until May 1918 when he retired through ill health.

15 Major General Philip Mainwaring Carnegy retired on health grounds.

16 Lieutenant Colonel Edward Peter Strickland was promoted Brigadier General on 10 January 1915 on taking over the Jullundur Brigade. He commander of the 98th Brigade from late 1915 and then as General Officer 1st Infantry Division on the Western Front from 1916 until the end of the War. He was then G.O.C. of the Western Division of the Rhine and then the G.O.C. of the 6th Division in Ireland and assumed the military Governorship in 3 Counties. His career continued as GOC 2nd Division and then G.O.C. of British troops in Egypt. He retired as a Lieutenant General in 1931

17 Major General Sir James Milford Sutherland Brunker commanded his Brigade at Givenchy on 22-23 December but was replaced two weeks later. He was 60 years old and spent the rest of his career as Inspector of the Royal Horse and Royal Field Artillery.

18 Colonel, later Major General, William George Walker VC was 52 when he took over the Sirhind Brigade. He later became G.O.C. 2nd Division until 1916 when he relinquished command retiring from the Army in 1919.

19 Brigadier Forbes MacBean retired at the age of 58 and died in 1919.

20 Lieutenant Colonel William Southey promoted Brigadier General on taking over the Bareilly Brigade. He was previously commander the of the 129th Baluchis when meant of all the replacements he was unique in coming from an Indian rather than British Battalion. He was to command the new 44th Ferozepore Brigade from October 1918 to December 1919. Serving on the North West Frontier as part of the 16th Division.

21 Colonel Claud Jacob was to have a distinguished career, After commanding the Dehra Dun Brigade, he commanded the 21st Brigade of the 'New Armies' in November 1915, and then II Corps of the Fifth Army in September 1916 with the rank of temporary Lieutenant General. After commanding II Corps during the occupation of the Rhine, he became Chief of the General Staff in India in January 1920 and was then both promoted to full General and appointed Aide-de-Camp to King George V on 31 May 1920. He returned home to England in 1924, and in November was given Northern Command in India. He took up the appointment of Military Secretary to the India Office in April 1926 and was promoted Field Marshal on 30 November 1926.

22 Brigadier General (temporary) C. E. Johnson is described as having 'ceased to be employed' on 27 December 1916 in the *Indian Army List* July 1919 p. 149

23 Willcocks, *With the Indians,* p. 13

officers of the Indian Corps which out ranked the officers of the BEF. Clearly as situation which was untenable given the size of the Indian Corps

John Bourne sheds further light on the replacement of senior officers in the BEF. He suggests that there were 1255 offers of Brigadier General or above in the BEF from 5 August 1914 to 11 November 1918 and they represented ten percent of those on the active Army List of 1914. A few of these were 'dugouts'; those officers who had previously retired but, like Colonel Ravenshaw of the 1st Connaught Rangers. were brought back into active service as war broke out.[24]

Bourne lists the reasons for replacing senior commanders during the war as:

i. Age (especially of 'dug-outs' early in the war).
ii. Scapegoating especially during the first two to two-and-a-half years of the war.
iii The 'new broom' phenomenon.
iv Rest and recuperation.
v. General reordering after specific campaigns.

In the case of Senior Officers of the Indian Army, the reasons for the reshuffle in January 1915 seem to be mainly that of age and rest and recuperation. The fact that, as in the BEF, officers within the Corps were promoted to take additional commands suggests that, at this stage in the War at least, similar criteria were applied. Condemnation of the Indian Army commanders was made by such as Greenhut, who wrote that 'a more severe criticism of the process of the (Indian Army) would be hard to find' than the dismissal of five senior officers of the Indian Army[25] and Haig, it seems would have agreed with this assessment when he wrote;' The War has proved that the whole of the senior officers on the Indian establishment are too old for their work'.[26] Such arguments ignore that 'the British Army (itself) also clearly suffered no complacency concerning Battalion command' and 'it was an organisation committed to quality control' in which a 'new broom philosophy was very prevalent.[27] The careers of Blackader, Carnegy Strickland, Jacob and, perhaps, Keary, suggest that talented and competent Indian Officers were also able to reach great heights. It is true that the original Brigade Commanders were probably too old to adapt to the industrial warfare into which they led their men, but their close subordinates were often to prove both flexible and talented. On the whole, one feels that the Senior Indian Commanders in 1914 suffered from the view that India was a backwater and their successors were able to 'shine' in the spotlight of the Western Front.

24 J. Bourne, 'Hiring and Firing on the Western Front' talk presented to the Lancashire & Cheshire Branch Western Front Association, 7 April 2011 <https://www.youtube.com/watch?v=qSOHzMjobvs> (accessed 30 August 2020).
25 Greenhut, Imperial Reserve. p. 62
26 TNA: WO 256:4: Haig, Western Front Diary 9, April 1915
27 Peter Hodgkinson, *British Infantry Battalion Commanders in the First World War* (PhD Thesis) University of Birmingham August 1993, pp. 143-155; published as Peter. E Hodgkinson, *British Infantry Battalion Commanders in the First World War* (London: Routledge, 2020).

15

Refit and Supply

The months between December 1914 to February 1915 were a period of re-adjustment, recuperation and supply of both materiel and men. The whole of the BEF, including the Indian Corps, was short of the basics needed for trench warfare. Picks and shovels required for excavating and improving trenches were hard to find. The delight when a few such essentials arrived in the Indian Corps has already been noted. The lack of hand grenades and trench mortars had been severely felt and Brigadier General Edmonds is complimentary about the Indians' ability to improvise such weapons.

However the new year did see important improvements. The Indian Corps began to receive better weaponry in January 1915. Battalions received additional machine guns, some of which were the latest Vickers models.[1] Genuine hand grenades were issued and replaced the home made jam tin bombs.[2] Their improvised trench mortars were replaced by British manufactured ones[3] and, equally as useful, they received better entrenching tools with which to dig in.[4] With greater experience and better weapons came greater confidence; 'No more hastily dug trenches full of slime and water but model breastworks constructed with skill and defended with care.'[5] As an unperturbable man of 47th Sikhs observed, 'There was a little fear at first, but essentially, it wasn't too bad.'[6]

The BEF made great effort in its attempts to replace the junior officers who had been killed or wounded in the early months of the war through entrants in the Officer Training Corps, The Inns of Court, the Honourable Artillery Company together with a cadet school created at Baillieu in December 1914 as part of the Artist Rifles which Sir John French converted into and Officer Training Corps when it arrived in France.[7]

1 Edmonds, 1914, Vol. 1 p. 58
2 Corrigan, *Sepoys*, p. 134.
3 Ellinwood, *Between Two Worlds*, p. 391.
4 CUL/MD: Hardinge Papers, Willcocks Letter to Hardinge, 2 September 1915
5 CUL/MD: Hardinge Papers, Willocks letter to Hardinge, 26 September 1915
6 Sardar Bahadar Suran Singh quoted in Morton-Jack, *The Indian Army*, p. .228
7 Edmonds, 1915, Vol. 1 p. 11.

Unfortunately, for the Indian Corps, it was hard if not impossible to use such methods The qualifications required by British Indian Officers have already been described.[8] Replacements could only come from those who had been released from the home country's training schedule or by officers who were transferred from a Battalion which had remained in India. Clearly, these were in short supply. The replacement officer needed to speak the appropriate language and the ability to build a relationship with the men prevented the easy recruiting of officers for the Corps.

Similarly, suitable rank and file reinforcements for the Indian Battalions were scarce. They too could be found from Battalions which had not embarked for France but the problem of Class Companies or Class Battalions further complicated matters. The lack of a well-developed recruiting system was also a problem as was the fact that, unlike the Home Country, there was no method of establishing 'New Armies'. The Martial Race Theory, since it was used as a measure of an ethnic group's fighting capabilities, also limited the number of prospective recruits at least early in the War.

The importance of *Rizzat has* already been discussed; Indian troops had certain important expectations from their British masters. With *Rizzat* came a guaranteed pension, a possible grant of land and the expectation that, when wounded, they would be returned to India with honour and reward. This had been the usual practice in previous wars in India and, when this policy was partially abandoned in France, it caused considerable resentment.[9] As Sir Walter Lawrence, wrote, the wounded Sepoy 'believes that he has done his duty, and that having been wounded it is his right to go home.'[10] The reasons for this change were the shortage of fighting troops in the front line; the difficulty of increasing recruitment and that many of the replacements who were obtained were unsuitable, unfit or only partially trained. Field Marshal French, was so concerned with the state of Indian replacements that he argued that unless the quality of reinforcements improved, such drafts should be stopped as they served no useful purpose.[11]

Given the shortage of troops, French's view demonstrates the genuine unsuitability of Indian recruits and why the slightly wounded were returned to the trenches. Townshend, in Mesopotamia, remarked that his Indian replacements were the most wretched class of recruits he had ever seen.[12] The resentment of wounded Indians being returned to the front line is easy to appreciate and, together with criticisms of medical care, was regarded by them as a serious break in the bargain between the Sepoy and the King Emperor. As Olusoga observes, to the Indian soldier it was inconceivable that a wounded Sepoy, who had acquired *Izzat* by fighting bravely, should

8 See Chapter 1.
9 David Olusoga, *The World's War* (London: Head of Zeus, 2014), p. 77.
10 IOR/MSS. EUR F143/65: Sir Walter Lawrence to Lord Kitchener 27 December 1915.
11 Merewether and Smith, *The Indian Corps*, p. 455.
12 Latter, 'The Indian Army in Mesopotamia', *Journal of the Society for Army Historical Research*, Vol. LXXII Nos. 290-292 1994 p. 171,

be returned to face mortal danger.[13] It was rumoured, probably incorrectly, that even the VC winner, Subadar Mir Dast, had made a request to the King Emperor that men who had been wounded should not be sent back to fight.[14] Some hospitalised Indians attempted to feign further illness by putting red dye in their urine and using other deceptions to fool the medical staff, who took strong action against these malingerers when they were exposed.[15] Brighton Council, which hosted the Indian Pavilion Hospital, and aware of the need to reassure wounded Sepoys, did its best to show that the treatment they received was both excellent and religiously correct.[16] The care of Indian wounded was no different from that of other Empire Troops but caused more resentment because of their different expectations.

An example of this difference can be found in a letter written by Private Joseph Lavenne, a member of the Australian Imperial Force who was wounded on 8 August 1916 at Poziéres. In a letter to a friend back home he observed:

> They took a piece of shell weighing 9½ ounces out of my shoulder. They joined the muscles together and then sewed up the whole show. I thought I would go mad for a couple of days with the pain. The stitches seemed as though they were tearing the flesh. It is now well joined up, but I was left with an awful scar. I don't think that I will join up with my Battalion again as I haven't the use of my left arm. I don't think my shoulder could stand any more soldiering. I reckon I was lucky.[17]

This was Joseph's second wound; he was sent back to the front despite the fact that his left arm had healed one inch shorter than his right and was killed in September 1918 during an attack on the Hindenburg line. His stoicism reflects that of the Sepoys who were in a similar situation but his letter does not reflect the resentment which is found in similar letters from wounded Sepoys and Sowars.

The Indian Corps was strengthened by the inclusion of four additional Battalions: The 2nd Battalion Connaught Rangers, the 4th (Territorial, City of London) Battalion, the 4th (Territorial) Battalion of Suffolk Battalion and the 4th (Territorial) Battalion of the Seaforth Highlanders. It was the 4th Battalion (City of London Regiment), which was allocated to be part of the Ferozepore Brigade which remained under the command of Brigadier General Egerton.

13 Olusoga, *The World's War*, p. 77 Omissi, *Indian Voices*, pp. 61-62
14 IOR L/MIL/5/825/2: Reports of the Censor of Indian Mails in France, Letter from Ragbir Singh to Gajander Singh.
15 A.T. Jarboe, Soldiers of the Empire: Indian Sepoys in and beyond the imperial metropole during the First World War (Ph.D. Thesis. North-Eastern University, April 2013), p. 119
16 Brighton Council, *A Short History in English, Gurmukhi & Hindu of the Royal Pavilion, Brighton and a Description of It as a Hospital for Indian Soldiers* (Brighton: King Thorne and Stace, 1915), pp. 5, 9
17 *The Dubbo News*, Joseph Lavenne to Mrs Picaud correspondence.

16

Divisional Expansion

The 4th Battalion (City of London), London Regiment (Royal Fusiliers) was a volunteer force created under the Haldane Reforms of 1906-12 and had mobilised on 3 August 1914. Initially, it was sent to do garrison duty in Malta where it arrived on 14 September. It commenced coastal defence and guard duties as well as training the 250 new recruits in its ranks. On 2 January 1915 the 1/4th Battalion was relieved by the 2/4th Battalion (leaving issued obsolete rifles and equipment for the newcomers) and embarked on HMT *Avon* for Marseilles. The Battalion was re-equipped with the Charger-loading Long Lee-Enfield (CLLE) rifles which had been adapted to fire the standard .303 ammunition. It derived its name from its ability to be loaded with five rounds from a charger clip rather than with a single bullet at time. This CLLE was an upgrade of the Lee Metford rifle and cheaper to manufacture than the standard SMLE service rifle which was distributed to Regular Army Battalions. The Battalion was also equipped with four Vickers water cooled 303 machine gun, the 1914 pattern webbing equipment replaced the 1903 leather pattern webbing since it proved to be more durable in the damp trenches. Like the Indian Battalions the 1/4th London's initially had eight companies but, on arriving in France, these were reduced to the Regular Army's four. Having arrived at Marseilles on 25 January 1915, the 1/4th London's. joined GHQ Reserve at Saint-Omer for further training

This training seems to have begun on 1 February 1915 when the Battalion marched to Belle Croix in north-eastern France where they received training in digging trenches. Other training, including practising attacks, rifle and machine gun drill, was to continue for the next seventeen days. All of this preparation was supervised by the Inspector of Infantry, Brigadier-General Oxley. During this early period in France the Battalion was forced to move its billets because of an outbreak of measles.[1] Clearly some of the soldiers of the 4th Londoner's found the change from civilian to military life difficult, as, during the first three weeks in France, there were four General Field Courts Marshall with sentences ranging from 6 months imprisonment to 56

1 F. Clive Grimwade, The *War History of the 4th Battalion The London Regiment (Royal Fusiliers) 1914-1919* (London. Headquarters of the 4th London Regiment, 1922) p. 21.

Field Punishment No. 1.

days No. 1 Field Punishment.[2] One suspects that conditions at the Front would came as a shock to the men after the relatively quiet days in Malta and the 4th London's War Diary records that on three days the weather was so bad that no outdoor activity was possible.[3] On 20 February, the 4th London's, commanded by Lieutenant Colonel G.P. Botterill, joined the Ferozepore Brigade with a strength of 25 officers and 828 other ranks and their training continued and including route marches and bayonet practice. The 4th London's were posted as Divisional Troops where, according to the Battalion History, they rapidly became friends with the Indian troops, especially the Gurkhas, for whom they had great admiration.[4] Unlike most British Battalions, this would be the first occasion when these Territorials would come into close contact with Sepoys. One suspects that the talented but amateur Territorials would be impressed by the professionalism and experience of their new Indian colleagues. On 22 February the Battalion received four lieutenants as reinforcements.

In late December and early January the Indian Corps having received additional numbers of machine guns it became necessary to train more men in their use. Lahore Division headquarters issued detailed instructions as to how this was to be done. The Ferozepore Brigade Headquarters decreed, that it was important to ensure that each Battalion had two officers, at least one of whom was a British officer, five NCOs of no lower rank than full corporal or Naik and twelve other ranks who were trained in the use of the machine gun. Training, which was to last four weeks, was to be given by the Brigade Machine Gun Officer assisted by existing machine gun section commanders.

2 FP. 1 consisted of the convicted man being placed in fetters and handcuffs and attached to a fixed object, such as a gun wheel or a fence post, sometimes int he crucifix position, for up to two hours per day.

3 TNA WO 95/3923: 3rd Indian (Lahore Division), 7 (Ferozepore) Infantry Brigade, London Regiment. 1/4 Battalion City of London Regiment War Diary, 1-15 February 1915.

4 Grimwade, *The War History of the 4th Battalion*, p. 23. The admiration for the Gurkhas was such that it appears that battalion members played a dangerous game with their bayonets which was known as 'Gurkha'.

Whilst 1/4th Londons were involved in their preparations, the Ferozepore Brigade was involved in activities of its own. Merewether and Smith point out that the months spent in the trenches with their appalling conditions had weakened the men of the Indian Corps and 'their feet had suffered to such an extend as to render hard marching an impossibility for a large proportion of the troops' as a result of water and mud in the trenches. This, Merewether and Smith optimistically commented, would impair the efficiency of the men if there was a prolonged advance after a successful attack.[5]

The Ferozepore Brigade on 29 January 1915 designed a 'Work Rota' with which to solve this decline.

Unit	Work Proposed	Time	Place Using 1:4000 Béthune Map	Remarks
1st Battalion Connaught Rangers	Attack on trenches by a Company at a time	10 am to Noon 2 pm to 4 pm	Square 10 d	The Route Marching programme was curtailed since the Brigade was under orders to be ready with two hours' notice
57th (Wilde's) Rifles				
129th Baluchis				
9th Bhopal Infantry				

On the 31 January 1915, the Ferozepore Brigade marched to new billets in the area of Ham -Guarbecque in the Pas de Calais and marching practice was now able to be undertaken according to the Work Rota. Egerton became concerned when it was observed that the 125th Baluchis' ammunition Mules were being led in threes by a follower driver. These animals were vital when the Brigade was on the move and it is clear that Egerton's concern was that three mules to a follower would be too much responsibility if they came under fire. The drill was changed to one mule of three to be led by a driver and the other two by Sepoys. The next week was spent training, marching and being inspected in preparation for a return to the trenches. The 1/4th London's state of readiness was of particular interest and they were inspected by both Egerton and Wilcock within a few days of each other.

The month of February 1915 was a relatively quiet one and, although, there were a number of artillery duels, the Lahore Division spent much of its time in training, assisting engineers and hardening their feet after their previous time in the trenches of the front line. The weather was wet, windy and on occasions, freezing. Towards the end of the month a large number of new men, most of whom were from the Indian Battalions stationed on the North West Frontier, joined the Division to fill the gaps made by injury or illness.

5 Merewether and Smith, *The Indian Corps,* p. 201.

17

'We taught the Huns a very sharp lesson'[1]

In March 1915 the British decided to go on the offensive again and attempt to break through the German lines in order to reach the Aubers Ridge which was some 2000 yards beyond the British Front Line and, somewhat over confidently, possibly reach enemy occupied Lille. It was the first occasion on the Western Front when the British both outgunned and outmanned their German opponents and British High Command hoped that it would be the beginning of a major offensive which would be 'the first systematic British attack since the commencement of trench warfare.'[2] The attack was planned to be coordinated with a similar French attack on Vimy Ridge which was to the south of Neuve Chapelle, but General Joffre subsequently decided that this would not be in the French Army's best interests.

During the early days in March, in preparation for the attack, there were a number of conferences for the senior officers of the Indian Corps and the Divisions were ordered to set up report centres in the area by 9 March. The Lahore Division's centre was at Lestrem, around 8 ½ miles north of Béthune. However, the First Army headquarters warned that, since there were more centres involved in the communication of messages, greater care had to be taken in their recording and transmission. Making sure that the correct address was recorded on any order was of particular concern. There were examples of operational orders arriving at the wrong Division or taking over six hours to reach the right Battalion or Battalions. This was in spite of them being carried by motorcycle messenger whose delivery time was extremely variable because they were in short supply. To the 'delight' of the armchair generals, all War Diaries were now to be submitted in triplicate.[3] On 6 March the Lahore Division's mining tools were collected together and transported to by train to Croix Marmuse at La Couture for storage which indicated that digging was to be put on hold for a

1 Willcocks quoted in George Morton Jack, *The Indian Army on the Western Front* (Cambridge: CUP, 2014) p. 233.
2 Homes, *The Little Field Marshal*, p. 271.
3 TNA WO 95/3914: 3 Indian (Lahore) Division Headquarters, Branches and Services, General Staff War Diary, 1 March 1915.

time. The Divisions were preparing for a major battle which became known as Neuve Chapelle.

In some ways, Neuve Chapelle set the example for many subsequent battles as it began with a heavy bombardment of artillery. The artillery of both the Meerut Division and the Lahore Division began their bombardment at 0730 hours on Wednesday 10 March which lasted 35 minutes.[4] The battle plan hoped that the guns would demolish the German wire, destroy the enemy in his forward trenches and put a curtain of fire behind the German front line which would prevent reinforcements reaching it.

The British and Indian force had a major advantage over their German opponents. They initially outnumbered them by roughly 15 to 1 but it was believed that an additional 4,000 Germans would arrive from nearby divisions within the first 12 hours of of the attack and, in addition, approximately 16,000 troops would arrive by train from Lille by the evening of the second day. This made it essential that the first day of the battle was successful as possible since, as a general rule, smaller numbers of defenders in properly prepared positions could hold off a larger number of attackers.

The Germans were not entirely unaware of the preparations being made for an assault. Early in the morning of 10 March, in spite of Haig's claim that the Royal Flying Corps had driven the enemy from the air, a German reconnaissance plane flew over the assembled Garhwal Brigade which was preparing to attack and noted that the trenches were crowed with troops.[5] Consequently, thirty minutes before the planned British bombardment, German artillery opened up on the 2nd Leicester's causing heavy casualties and destroying the telephones of the 1/39th Garwhalis which clearly made communications difficult.

The attacking infantry began its advance at 0805 hours as the guns changed their targets to the village of Neuve Chapelle which had been partly destroyed in October 1914. The Garhwal Brigade advanced and were supported by the 3rd Battalion London Regiment (Territorial) in reserve. The initial attack was successful in spite of two companies of the 1/39th Garhwal Rifles losing their direction and attacking German trenches which were fully manned since they had not been bombarded and consequently suffered heavy losses especially amongst their British Officers. In spite of this particular loss, the Garhwal Rifles held on under the command of their Indian officers and resisted German attacks in spite of being short of ammunition and bombs.

Their drift to the right caused a gap in the advancing British line which enabled the German 16th Infantry Regiment to improve its defences, so the Garhwal Rifles were unable to capture this trench which was on their left flank. It was eventually captured

4 The original plan was to bombard Neuve Chapelle (by compartments) for a period of four days but Haig felt that the lengthy barrage would be better to increase the ferocity of the gunfire for a shorter period, see Peter Wyatt, 'Douglas Haig and the planning of the Battle of Neuve Chapelle' in Spencer Jones (ed.), *Courage Without Glory. The British Army on the Western Front 1915* (Solihull, Helion & Co 2015) p. 194.

5 Merewether and Smith, *The Indian Corps*, p. 218. See also Field Marshal French's Seventh Despatch, Section 6, *London Gazette*, 14 April 1915.

by the 1st Seaforth Highlanders, but its defence slowed down the advance in that sector until nightfall. Field Marshal French was very pleased with the progress on this first day of battle regarding it as a 'splendid success' as the enemy had been 'completely surprised' through the 'magnificent determination' of all involved.[6] French somewhat over optimistically hoped for greater things the following day. The Germans, however, regained their composure and commenced counterattacks in strength which caused many casualties amongst the British and Indian attackers. The Garhwal Brigade continued to consolidate its position through the night of 10 March and into the following day.

Whilst their comrades had been involved in the attack, the Ferozepore Brigade had been in their billets in the villages some eight miles from the front line. On 11 March a company of the Bhopals were put on guard duty for the captured German prisoners and some spent time unloading ammunition. During the evening the Lahore Division was ordered to relieve the Meerut Division and the Ferozepore Brigade moved to billets in Richebourg St Vaast[7] and La Couture.[8]

On 12 March Haig mistakenly thought that the success of the attack had 'demoralised' the enemy and ordered that the Indian Corps should push through the barrage of fire regardless of loss using their reserves if necessary.[9] Consequently, Willcocks ordered the Lahore Division to advance at all costs but the Ferozepore Brigade was to remain in reserve at a position some two miles behind the front line. It was then ordered to advance towards Neuve Chapelle, and Brigadier Egerton was placed in command of all three Brigades in the Division.

Egerton was under some pressure to relaunch an attack that evening and was asked when he would like the preliminary bombardment to take place. His original suggestion was 2030 hours but, when he discussed a possible advance with Brigadier General Walker of the Sirhind Brigade he found that Walker's Brigade had lost more than a quarter of its fighting strength either killed or wounded and those who remained were exhausted.[10] Realising that it would take time to reorganise the brigades, Egerton ordered the Lahore Division to delay the bombardment until 2230 hours but also argued that, in his opinion, the attack which he had been ordered to make would fail. His opinion was shared by General Willcocks who cancelled the attack completely as he believed that it would be impossible to launch an attack with such a large number of troops hors de combat. The Indian Corps' Headquarters' Diary comments, with gentle criticism, that the men spent much of the day marching from point to point over unreconnoitred ground in the dark. The Ferozepore Brigade together with the Jullundur Brigade were withdrawn and the Sirhind Brigade took over the front line.

6 TNA WO 95/3913: 3 Indian (Lahore) Division. Headquarters, Branches and Services, General Staff War Diary, 10 March 1915.
7 Headquarters, the Connaught Rangers and the 57th Rifles.
8 4th Londons and 129th Baluchis
9 Edmonds, 1915, Vol 1. p. 143.
10 There were some 800 casualties. See Edmonds, 1915, Vol 1. p. 144.

Willcocks' decision to call off the offensive was courageous as it was in direct disobedience to Haig's order to maintain the offensive and it forced Haig to call off the attack. 'Willocks is no support whatsoever when operations are in progress.' he wrote, 'but appears as pleased as he can be' of the performance of the Garwhalis and Gurkha's success on the morning of the 10 March.[11]

The Ferozepore Brigade heard the bombardment begin at 0730 hours and was ordered to be in constant readiness from 1000 hours and a reserve of two companies was created under an officer of the Connaught Rangers. Though not actually involved in the direct fighting at Neuve Chapelle, the 129th Baluchis spent their time repairing roads often under fire. On 12 March, together with the 57th Rifles, they marched towards Neuve Chapelle. The 1/4th City of London troops spent their time working on the lines of communication. On 12 March they were engaged in a long circuitous march and, like the 89th Punjabis, spent much of the period of the battle marching from billet to billet. The fact that the battle was called off made these marches a waste of time.

The official end of the Battle of Neuve Chapelle could be considered to be 2200 hours on 12 March when Haig decided to end operations and consolidate the gains which had been made and during the evening the Ferozepore Brigade was withdrawn from the firing line.

The Neuve Chapelle offensive gained around 1,000 yards on a two-mile front and straightened out the Port Arthur Salient which posed a threat to the British divisions. There was also an effect on German strength and morale. It was estimated that over 2,000 Germans were killed, and Field Marshal French believed that almost 12,000 German wounded were removed by train and Merewether and Smooth suggest that 65 German officers and 1,625 other ranks were captured during the offensive.[12]

However, the British and Indian losses were also significant; 190 Officers and 2337 other ranks killed with 359 Officers and 8,174 other ranks wounded. One must remember that the Indian Corps and the BEF were small organisations and such losses especially for the Indian Corps had greater significance. Merewether and Smith record these as 63 British and Indian Officers killed, two thirds of which were British together with 772 British and Indian other ranks and roughly 2,800 other ranks wounded, over half of whom were Indian troops. As French subsequently telegraphed to the Viceroy Lord Hardinge:

> I am glad to be able to inform your Excellency that the Indian troops under Sir James Willcocks fought with great gallantry in the capture of Neuve Chapelle...

11 George Morton Jack, *The Indian Empire at War* (London. Little Brown, 2018) p. 276.
12 See Field Marshal French's Seventh Despatch, Section 5, *London Gazette,* 14 April 1915. Merewether and Smith, *The Indian Corps,* p. 268.

> their tenacity, courage, and endurance were admirable and worthy of the best traditions of the soldiers of India.[13]

Hardinge was quick to reply to Willocks with his own words of congratulations.

It did not take the Germans long, however, to recover and in the days following the battle subjected the British and Indian troops to very heavy shelling to which, because of the 'shell shortage', the British artillery found it difficult to respond. Despite the quick enemy recovery, Edmonds suggests Neuve Chapelle forced the Germans to take the BEF more seriously and caused them to strengthen their defences and garrisons opposite the British front. It also improved the attitude of the French who had previously doubted the BEF's ability to go on the offensive as opposed to line holding duties whilst they went on the offensive.[14]

However, there was a caveat in the commendations for the Indian brigades involved in Neuve Chapelle. General Haig, GOC of First Army to which the Indian Corps was now attached. was asked to inform the India Office the names of the Indian units which had done well at Neuve Chapelle. Although Haig did so, he wrote that. 'In order to prevent misconceptions [in India]'and false conclusions,' he wrote, it should be stated that although Indians had done very well, the tasks accomplished by them had not been so difficult as that of the British.'[15] In spite of the Indian Corps being one of the most experienced of the BEF's Army Corps by 1915, Haig was beginning to question its contribution to the fight.[16]

13 Willcocks, *With the Indians*, p. 235.
14 Edmonds, 1915, Vol. I, p. 154.
15 Sheffield and Bourne (eds.) *Douglas Haig*, entry for 5 March 1915, p. 110.
16 Morton Jack, *The Indian Empire*, p. 266. For a full account of Neuve Chapelle as produced by Haig's First Army, see TNA WO95/1093: Headquarters Branches and Services, General Staff Indian Army Corps, Narrative of Operations Near Neuve Chapelle, March 10-13, 1915.

18

Second Ypres

The rest of March 1915 was relatively quiet for the Ferozepore Brigade. Some of the other Indian Brigades were reorganised but the Ferozepore remained with Brigadier General Egerton in overall command with its constituent Battalions as before. During April, the 40th Pathans arrived from China and joined the Jullundur Brigade and on 12 April the Lahore Division was replaced in the front line by the Meerut Division.

Most of the first three weeks of April were reasonably uneventful, on Friday the 23rd, the Lahore Division received orders from First Army to hold itself in readiness for departure to an unknown destination and, on the following day, under the command of Major General Keary, they moved to establish their headquarters at Godewaersvelde, which was situated between Hazebrouck and Poperinghe. The journey took two days and as Merewether and Smith recorded, 'the men arrived footsore and tired after a plodding march of about thirty miles.[1] For the third time units of the Indian Corps was being urgently summoned to close a gap in the line; the first occasion was during the first battle of Ypres in October 1914 and the second in the same month when it was rushed forward to relieve the 2nd Corps. This third occasion transpired as a result when on, 17 April the 5th Division's 13th Brigade occupied Hill 60 after engineers had exploded seven mines after using experienced miners from Northumberland and Wales to tunnel beneath the enemy trenches in the Hill. Hill 60 had been captured by the Germans during the First Battle of Ypres Although the mound did not really deserve the description 'Hill' it offered the Germans an excellent view from which artillery observers could direct fire. The Hill was easily taken with only a few casualties but the fighting which ensured was vicious. 'The 5th Division are having an awful time. The men who are lucky enough to come back say that it is the worst fighting of the war.'[2]

1 Merewether and Smith, *The Indian Corps,* p. 280.
2 Captain Billy Congreve VC quoted in Terry Norman (ed.), *Armageddon Road: A VC's Diary 1914–1916* (London: W Kimber, 1982), p. 124.

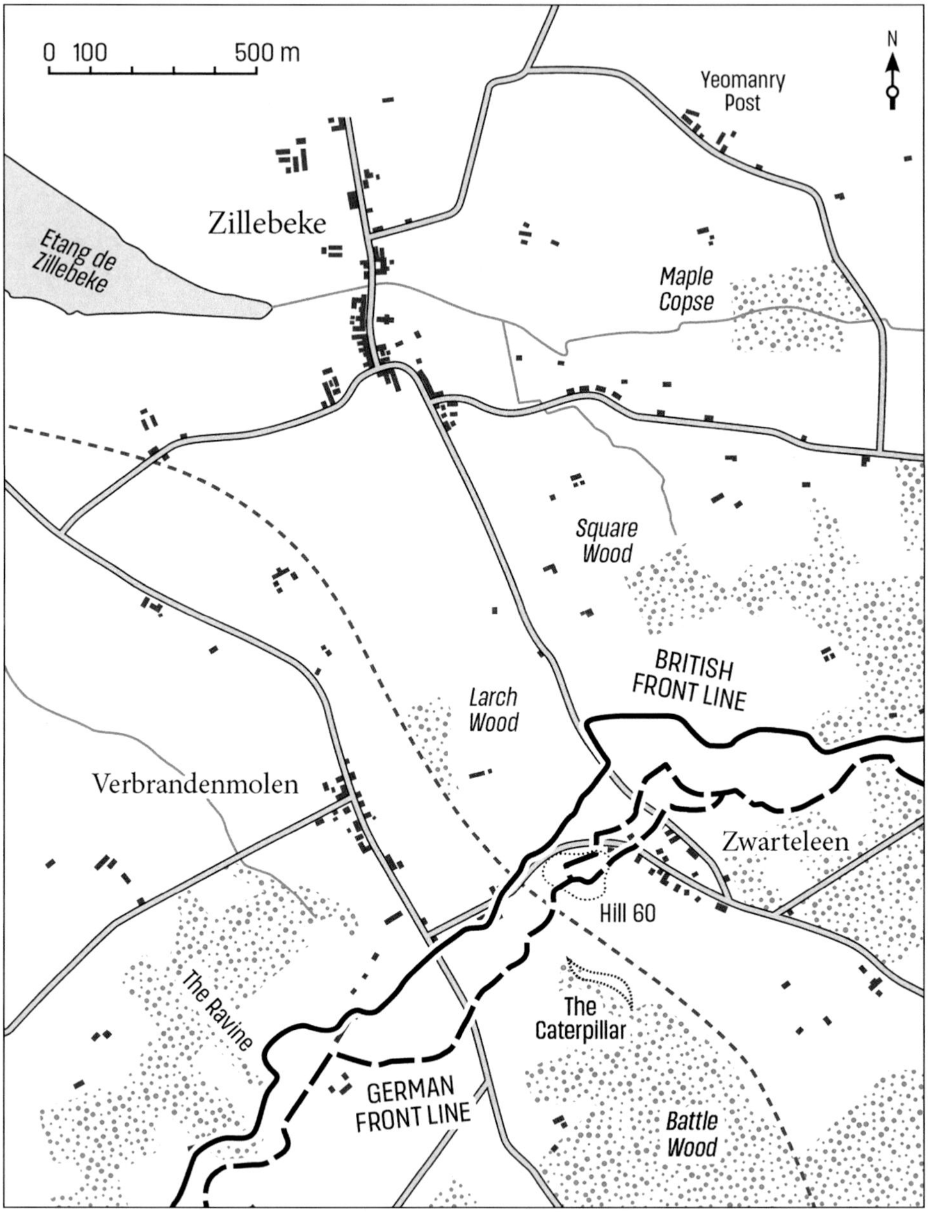

Map 5 Hill 60 and vicinity.

The fierce struggle to retain and capture the hill lasted from 17 April until 5 May when it was recaptured by the Germans after furious fighting with the use of many bombs and poisonous gas.

The deployment of the Lahore Division was a result of the furious fighting on the 22 April when, after a heavy bombardment, the Germans launched an attack using chlorine gas. During the German attack the French Colonial African Division, on the left flank of the British V Corps, were taken completely by surprise by the German's use of gas. They had not been issued with any form of protection and within a short time, 'hundreds of men were writhing in agony' and the Division broke. Sir John French described the use of gas as treacherous and believed that no blame could be attached to the French Colonials' sudden collapse.[3]

The gap left by the retreating French caused the Canadian Division which was on their right flank to perform a fighting withdrawal whilst the Germans advanced over the now vacant French trenches. Eventually the Canadians were able halt their withdrawal and join with the French in an over extended line A number of reinforcements, including the Lahore Division were pushed forward to help strengthen this line in order to prevent the Germans breaking through and capturing the town of Ypres. A counterattack involving the Ferozepore Brigade was organised for the 26 April. The weather was extremely cold, and the Brigade was organised with the Baluchis on the left flank, the 57th Rifles in the centre and the Connaught Rangers, supported by the Londoners, on the right. The Bhopals were in kept as support troops.

A forty-minute bombardment was planned and as soon as the guns opened up at 1320 hours, the men began to slowly advance as the German front line was some distance away and the ground was difficult to cross. Once again, one of the Indian units, the Jullundur Brigade, drifted from the designated route and crowded into the right flank of the Ferozepore Brigade and intermingled with the Connaughts. The advancing troops were met by withering German fire and many acts of gallantry were performed. The 129th Baluchis advanced steadily but this was impeded by the confusion caused by the Jullundur Brigade' s drift. As the Baluchis advanced up the slope towards the enemy front line they suffered heavy losses in killed and wounded as they were easy targets for the defenders. The 57th Rifles had a relatively easy initial advance until they came to the top of the slope and walked into into 'an absolute' inferno of fire.[4] Casualty numbers began to grow, particularly amongst the British officers, but the Baluchis pressed on and came to within 80 yards of the German front line. By this time the casualties had greatly increased and only two British officers remained active, one of whom was wounded and the other severely affected by the gas but he continued to try to bring his machine guns into action. During the advance of the attack the Battalion suffered three British officers killed and four wounded, and 3 Indian officers

3 Sir John French, Eighth Despatch, 15 June 1915, Section 4.
4 Merewether and Smith, *The Indian Corps*, p. 299.

killed and seven wounded. Thirty-six other ranks were killed and 215 wounded, many of whom had been attached from a Battalion of the Guides.

The Connaught Rangers had been shelled as they advanced through the northern outskirts of Ypres and their Commanding Officer, Lieutenant Colonel S J Murray was wounded, and his horse had to be destroyed.[5] Once at the jumping off point for the attack, they found that their advance was hindered by thick hedges through which there were only a few gaps. The speed of their advance was consequently delayed, and they had not reached cover by the time the 40-minute bombardment had ended, which meant that they were exposed to the withering fire of the enemy. During their advance, 15 of the 20 Connaught officers were either killed or wounded. The rank and file fared little better, three hundred and sixty one of the 900 men involved were either killed or wounded.[6] Their chaplain, Father Peal, showed considerable courage in administering to the Connaught wounded at the First Aid Post which had been established at La Brique even though it was constantly shelled.

The Jullundur and Ferozepore Brigades reached a point as close to the enemy as possible and attempted to construct defensive positions. The wandering direction of the advance meant that the troops were jumbled together and confused. The supporting Battalions had followed behind at a distance of 400 yards and reached the furthest point of the advance with slightly fewer casualties. The 4th London's were very fortunate to have only two men killed and one officer and ten men wounded.

The Germans then released gas in greater volume and the Ferozepore Brigade was greatly affected because of the wind blowing it in their direction. The only protection the Indians had were urine-soaked handkerchiefs or pagris which they pressed to their noses and they tried to press their faces against the parapets they had tried to construct.[7] Such attempts were useless and soon the ground was covered with writhing bodies which enabled the Germans, who were under less fierce fire, to increase their own. The French, who were exposed to even greater waves of gas, were forced to withdraw and the British line was swept back with them in a jumble of French, British and Indian soldiers desperately trying to escape the chlorine. Only a small number, including 60 Connaught Rangers together with a few of Sepoys from the 129th Baluchis and 57th Rifles were able to cope with gas and hold their position. It did not take the Germans long to counterattack this forlorn band and they too were driven back some 80 yards where they were able to establish another defensive position which they were able to hold until relieved at 0230 Hours on the 27 April by a group of 1st Battalion Highland Light Infantry of the Sirhind Brigade. At around 0300 hours the Ferozepore Brigade finally withdrew to La Brique.

5 TNA WO 95/3923: 3 Indian (Ferozepore) Division, Infantry Brigade, 1st Battalion Connaught Rangers. Entry for 26 April 1915.

6 TNA: WO95/3923: 3 Indian (Ferozepore) Division, Infantry Brigade, 1st Battalion Connaught Rangers. Entry for 26 April 1915.

7 Pagri = turban cloth.

The exact position and deployment of the Germans had been hard to determine because of their use of gas and the disorganised nature of both the advance and retreat. Captain Nosworthy of the Sappers and Miners, whose bravery has been mentioned in Chapter 5, made several attempts at reconnoitring the German positions and was able to sketch their front line.

However, taking one risk too many, on the 28 April Nosworthy was badly wounded.[8] Another officer, Captain Frederick Kisch who was also wounded, made similar reconnoitring expeditions and, together with Nosworthy's information it was possible, to produce a fairly accurate picture of the German defences.[9] With this information a further plan was devised to attack the German positions on the afternoon of the 27 April, The attacking troops included the French Moroccans on the left flank, the Sirhind Brigade to their right and the Ferozepore to their right in order to extend the line. Before the advance, the combined artillery of V Corps, the Sirhind Brigade and the Canadian Division were to shell the German front line.

The bombardment commenced at 1230 hours and the Ferozepore Brigade, which had been stationed at La Brique, immediately advanced to join the Sirhind Brigade which was holding the front line. The plan meant that the Ferozepore would arrive alongside the Sirhind at 1315 hours and, at the same time, the bombardment would

8 Francis Poitiers Nosworthy had been educated at Exeter School and the Royal Military Academy, Woolwich and commissioned into the Royal Engineers in 1907. He took part in the Abor and Mishmi expedition to India in 1912 and having recovered from his wounds served as a General Staff Officer in France. Returning to India he took part in the Third Anglo-Afghan War in 1919 He then the Staff College, Quetta from 1919 to 1920, and was appointed second-in-command of the Sudan Defence Force in 1926. He later attended the Imperial Defence College in 1931. In 1935 he was appointed to command the 5th Infantry Brigade. In 1938 he returned to India as Deputy Chief of the General Staff. He served in World War II as Commander of IV Corps which was envisaged as a counter-attack force since it Corps contained most of the armoured reserves and was preparing to face the expected German invasion of Britain after Dunkirk. He continued as Commander of IX Corps in Tunisia from 1942 and as Commander-in-Chief of West Africa Command from 1943. Nosworthy retired in February 1945.[4]

9 Frederick Kisch was born to a British-Jewish family in Darjeeling on 23 August 1888, where his father was head of the Indian Postal Service. The family later moved back to Great Britain where Frederick attended the Clifton College and subsequently the Royal Military Academy Sandhurst. Kisch joined the Royal Engineers in 1909 During his war service, he was wounded three times, and awarded the DSO. As a result of his wounds, he was declared temporarily unfit for frontline service and was subsequently transferred to the Military Intelligence Corps, where he served for the rest of the war. He also served as general staff officer to General Sir George Macdonogh. During the war reaching the rank of lieutenant colonel. In 1919 he was appointed to British delegation to the Paris Peace Conference. An active Zionist, Kisch served as Commission head for the Jerusalem region but in 1939 he was recalled to the Army, appointed to the rank of Brigadier and assigned to Eighth Army as CO Royal Engineers. He was killed in Tunisia on 7 April 1943 after stepping on a landmine during the Battle of Wadi Akarit. Kisch is buried at Enfidaville War Cemetery.

lift and target the German second line. The Ferozepore forward units were the 9th Bhopal Infantry who were on the right of the 1/4th London's. Following behind the Bhopals, at a distance of 400 yards, were the Connaught Rangers. The remaining Battalions of 57th Rifles and 129th Baluchis, both of which had suffered heavily on the previous day, were to act as reserves.

Contrary to the plan, the Sirhind Brigade, without waiting for the Bhopals to arrive, began to advance as soon as the bombardment began. It's commander, Brigadier General Walker, may have thought that reaching the German front line just as the bombardment lifted was more important than waiting for the Bhopals' support. The Sirhind Brigade came under heavy German fire but was able to find some cover behind hedges and ridges in the ground as they advanced on a two-Battalion front. Reaching the ridge, where there had been heavy casualties on the previous day, they came under heavy crossfire from both rifles and machine guns and the sepoys also had to endure heavy accurate artillery fire as the enemy had previously zeroed their guns on every likely place for advancing troops to take shelter. The Sirhind Brigade suffered very heavy casualties and failed to reach its targets, but it was able to dig in some distance from the German front line.

The 4th London's and the 9th Bhopals advanced towards their designated target, a farm on the right of the attacking line but they were also subject to shattering fire from artillery, machine guns and rifles. Their losses were high and sufficient to break up their attack, but they were able to finally come into line with the Sirhind Brigade. Similarly, the French Moroccans had advanced in the face of heavy fire and their attacking line, though much slowed down, remained continuous. Despite these setbacks, General Horace Smith-Dorrien, Commander of the Second Army, ordered that the advance be continued and provided 1,300 extra supporting troops for the Lahore Division to enable it to bolster the Sirhind Brigade if it decided to do so.

With increased vigour, the Sirhind Brigade attempted to advance in the face of withering fire but could only do so with French Moroccan's support and who had begun to advance again at around 1900 hours. This advanced was short lived, however, and the French began to retreat when the Germans began to use chlorine gas against them and this left the Sirhind Brigade exposed and without support. They too were forced to retreat.

Over the next few days, the British and Indian Brigades planned further attacks but most of these simply became artillery duels. Stalemate had been achieved and during the 29 and 30 April both the Ferozepore and Jullundur Brigades, having come under the overall command of General Sir Herbert Plumer,[10] were withdrawn to billets at Ouderom and their participation in Second Ypres was over. The remainder of Second Army continued to defend the line but, after a number of delays and heavy attacks by the Germans, it withdrew to the environs of Ypres by 4 May.

10 Plumer was appointed GOC Second Army after Smith-Dorrien's unceremonious sacking by Field Marshal French.

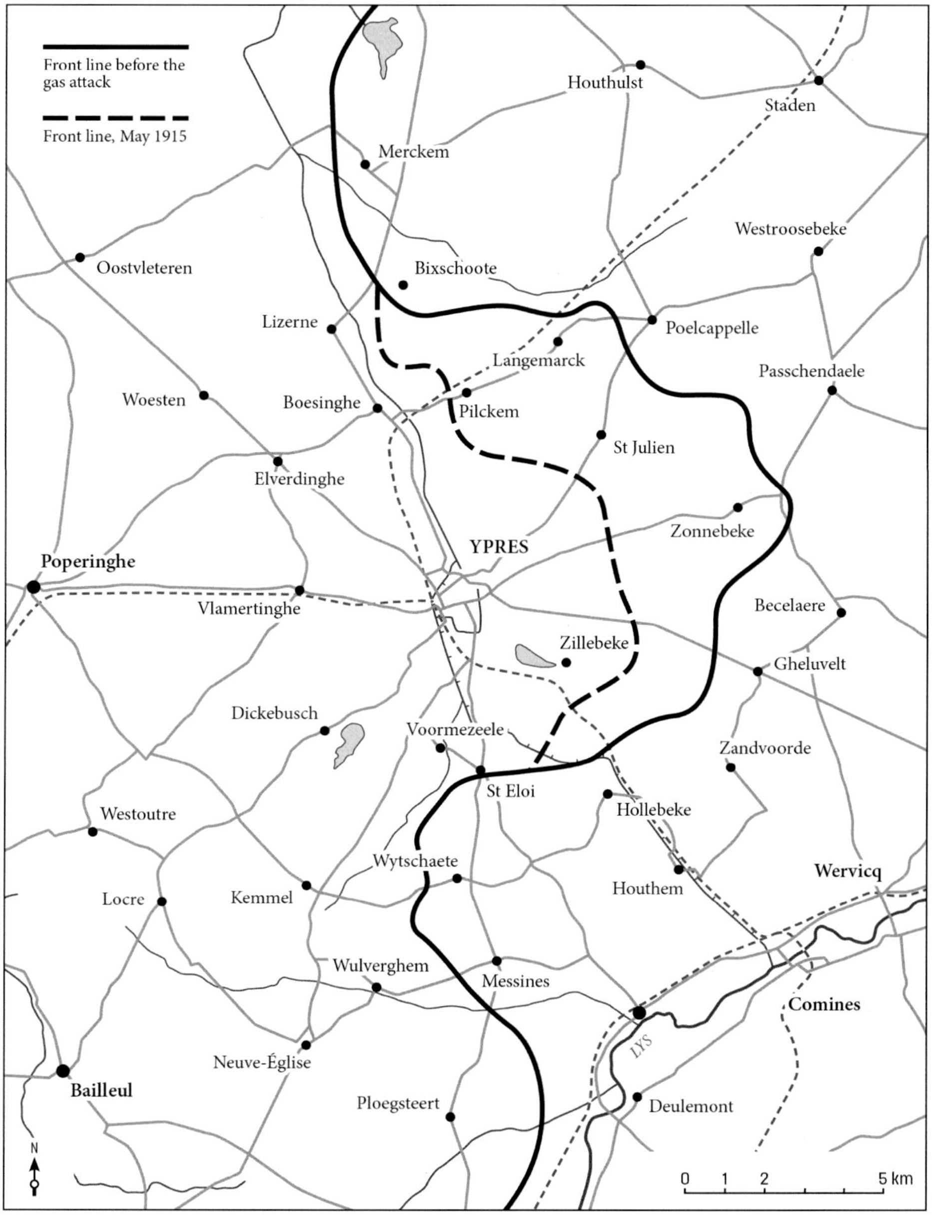

Map 6 German Map of the Battle of Second Ypres.

Edmonds put failure at the Second Battle of Ypres down to German superiority in artillery and the surprise use of gas. He believed that the involvement of the Colonial Battalions and inferior 3rd line French troops, who had recently replaced élite French troops, as a further reason for the Allied failure. However, he also believed that the outcome could have been much worse had the Germans taken advantage of the unexpected success.[11]

11 Edmonds, 1915, Vol 1, pp. 296-297.

19

Aubers Ridge

On 2 May 1915 the Ferozepore Brigade moved to new billets north of Meteren. and took the opportunity to evaluate its remaining strength after the ordeal of Second Ypres which was estimated to be as follows:

	Number on Strength			Capable of Fighting		
	British Officers	Indian Officers	Other Ranks	British Officers	Indian Officers	Other Ranks
Connaught Rangers	11		698	9		698
1/4 London	15		553	14		538
129th Baluchis	8	7	222	5	7	123
57th Rifles	9	7	308	7	6	263
9th Bhopals	9	8	334	8	7	291[1]

The dramatic reduction in strength, particularly within the Indian Battalions was obviously very serious. The difficulty in replacing the killed and wounded has already been discussed and the inability to provide recruits of the right calibre would have significant consequences for the Indian Corps as a whole.

On 3 May the Ferozepore Brigade marched again to new billets and together with the rest of the Lahore Division, re-joined First Army. They received visits from staff officers, the General Officer Commanding and Sir Douglas Haig, Commander of First Army. Although the Headquarters diary does not over-elaborate, it is likely that these distinguished visitors were trying to evaluate brigade fighting capabilities and morale after suffering such heavy losses. Fresh drafts were arriving to fill the ranks, but the battalions were no longer the tight knit units which had arrived in France

1 TNA WO 95/3922: 3 Indian (Ferozepore) Division, Infantry Brigade Headquarters War Diary, 2 May 1915.

in 1914. The 9th Bhopals, for example, received a total of 94 replacements made up from the 17th Infantry (The Loyal Battalion), 18th Infantry, the 16th Rajputs (The Lucknow Battalion) and the 96th (Berar) Infantry.[2] Similarly, the 57th Rifles received a draft of 150 reinforcements from various other Battalions.[3] The inclusion of men from other units began to weaken the family nature on which they the original Indian battalions depended for their cohesion. General Willcocks was particularly critical of the condition of recruits who had been sent from India, the quality of which by June 1915, he thought, ' was a humiliation.'[4] Willcocks blamed those officers in India who were endorsing sending these recruits but were ignorant of Western Front requirements and, being so far away from France, felt that they would be safe from criticism for their lack of rigour in selecting new reinforcements.[5] Whilst GHQ as demanding that the Indian Corps 'put forth its strength'.[6] Willcocks felt it was reaching its limits.[7]

The Indian Corps was to become involved in the next First Army offensive at Aubers Ridge. It took over 1500 yards the front line occupied by the British I Corps which together with a similar relief by of the 47th (London Division) enabled the Corps to reorganise. The Meerut Division had been chosen to take part in the assault and was assembled in depth for 800 yards of the front line adjacent to 1st Division.

The plan was for the I Corps and parts of the Indian Corps to attack side by side south of Neuve Chapelle, and for IV Corps to attack to the north with the intention that the two forces to join together having created a large gap in the German front line as well as encircling up to seven German Battalions and a number of artillery pieces. It was hoped that the British/Indian advance would continue onwards to the Haute Deule valley. The attack was to be preceded by a short 40-minute artillery barrage which, it was hoped would destroy the German wire and demoralize the troops.[8] In order to prevent the advance being stalled by enemy strong points, as had happened at Neuve Chapelle, 'infantry artillery' was to be attached to the various Divisions. This artillery consisted of 'Bomb guns' Hotchkiss and Indian mountain guns which were at last to prove to be of use.[9] However, the Germans had occupied their line for some months and had time to construct semi-permanent defences which could only be destroyed by heavy artillery.

Although the British made extensive preparations for the battle it, appears that the Germans had not noticed the significance of this activity. However, they had,

2 TNA WO 95/3923/4: 3 Indian (Ferozepore) Division, Infantry Brigade, 9th Bhopal War Diary, 2 May 1915.
3 TNA WO 95/3923/4: 3 Indian (Ferozepore) Division, Infantry Brigade, 57th Wilde's Rifles War Diary, 2 May 1915.
4 Willcocks, *With the Indians,* p. 309.
5 Willcocks, *With the Indians,* p. 310.
6 *Promite Vires.*
7 *Ultima Thule.* See Willcocks, *With the Indians,* p. 310.
8 British guns were suffering from worn barrels and lack of ammunition
9 'Bomb guns' or trench mortars.

having also learned from the experience of Neuve Chapelle, reinforced their front-line trenches by increasing their troops from two to three Divisions. The weather delayed the start of the attack and so it was decided that the British and French assaults would be made simultaneously with a barrage beginning at 0500 hours on the 9 May. It was, however, hardly any heavier than that delivered at Neuve Chapelle and although the artillery had been zeroing the agreed targets in the previous days, many of its barrels were worn and the shells frequently fell short, or even fell in the British trenches. Although the German wire was mangled, the parapets of their trenches were hardly affected. As Major General Richard Hawkins was to remark. 'it requires a great number of guns and a great deal of ammunition both to demoralise the defenders and, still more, to destroy his wire entanglements'.[10]

At 0525 hours the Dehra Dun Brigade climbed out of their trenches and formed a line in readiness for the time when the artillery increased its range. It had been hoped that the men would be able to sneak forwards, unnoticed by the Germans, who would be keeping their heads down. This tactic proved impossible and the Sepoys had to remain in the trenches because so many of the British shells were falling short making the area just outside their trenches unsafe. and it was only after the guns elevated their range at 0540 hours that an advance was possible. As the Dehra Dun Brigade began its advance, the Germans, no longer under fire, were able to defend their trenches using 'appalling machine-gun and rife fire.[11] Both first and second assaulting lines were decimated; especially in the case of British officers who were leading from the front. In spite of the rising number of casualties the attackers were able to reach a ditch in front of the German parapet but were unable to climb over it because of the intense fire above their heads. It quickly developed into a stalemate and, eventually, the men were ordered to return to the British trenches as best as they could.

By 0600 hours it was obvious that the attack had failed. Men were lying down in the ditch before the parapet, taking cover in shell holes or simply by laying down on the ground. Matters were made worse when the German artillery opened heavy fire on the British trenches which added to the number of casualties. It was observed that the Germans seemed to be assembling large number of troops close to their front line and it was assumed that this was in preparation for a counterattack. This meant that the British front line needed reinforcements which, because of the damage done to the communication trenches and the disorganised state of the returning attackers was very problematic. It was decided that the Dehra Dun Brigade should launch a second assault to thwart the German attack and, in preparation, howitzers opened a barrage at 0745 hours on the German trenches which was to last an hour. The second assault was postponed when news came that the attack by the 1st Division had also failed, and its Brigades had suffered heavy losses and therefore would not be fit to launch a second attack for at least two hours.

10 TNA WO 95/1228: 'Lecture on the Attack', 1st Division War Diary, April 1915.
11 Merewether and Smith, *The Indian Corps* p. 355.

It was decided that the Bareilly Brigade would relieve shattered Dehra Dun and the attack would begin at 1400 hours. The state of the British communication trenches has already been mentioned and when the Brigades began to move, the trenches were so congested that it became obvious that the Bareilly Brigade would not reach the front line by the designated time. Consequently the synchronised attack by the 1st Division and Meerut Division was postponed until 1600 hours which would be preceded by a bombardment commencing at 1520 hours.

Meantime, the Germans continued to reinforce their front line and Willcocks received reports that the various artillery barrages had not weakened the German position and consequently, their machine gun fire had not slackened. Despite this information, Willcocks was not willing to change the plan of attack and ordered that the assault should take place as planned and should be carried out at all costs. The relief of the Dehra Dun Brigade by the Bareilly Brigade continued slowly, hindered by the congestion in the trenches and under heavy artillery fire and this again delayed the preparations for the proposed assault. The planned British bombardment began at 1520 hours and the assaulting troops left the trenches 10 minutes later and began to advance only to be met by enemy heavy and accurate small arms and machine gun fire. To their front was a waterlogged ditch which ran parallel from 10 to 30 yards from the British front line and many troops were killed or wounded before they could reach it. So high was the casualty rate that the advance was paused, and the remaining assaulting troops were ordered to remain in the front-line trenches. During this phase, Lance Corporal David Finlay of 2nd Black Watch was awarded the Victoria Cross for saving the life of a wounded comrade.[12] Such was the casualty rate caused by the German fire that it was obvious that no further advance was practical. The British artillery bombardment had been too little and too ineffective. It had merely given the enemy a warning to stand to to receive an assault which was now expected.[13] The so-called 'Shell Scandal' was also a major factor as was the poor quality of the artillery ammunition; many of the fuses were defective and the shells failed to explode when they hit the muddy ground.[14] The Bareilly Brigade had suffered such a high casualty rate that it too had to be relieved which by the Garhwal Brigade and completed by 0100 hours on the 10 May. Temporary Brigadier General Southey, GOC Bareilly Brigade, was justifiably proud of his men's attempts, even though they

12 Finlay had been leading a bombing party of 12 men during the attack, 10 of whom were killed or wounded. After ordering the two survivors to return Finlay went to the assistance of one of his wounded men and carried him over a distance of 100 yards of fire-swept ground into cover. Sergeant David Finlay was subsequently killed in Mesopotamia when his regiment was taking part in the attempted relief of Kut. He is commemorated on the Basra Memorial.

13 Edmonds, *Military Operations France and Belgium 1915*, Vol. II (London, John Murray, 1928) (Henceforth, Edmonds 1915, Vol II) p. 41.

14 Edmonds refers to the poor levels of inspection in munition factories. See Edmonds, 1915, Vol II 1915, p. 41. It was a case of the haste in producing ammunition outstripping available quality control.

had not increased the British front line by one yard. He reported to Willcocks that 'British and Indian ranks alike did their level best to reach the enemy's line.' Brigade moral remained unshaken and if order to attack again, 'they would have undertaken it in the same spirit.'[15]

The Lahore Division's War Diary records the failure of the Meerut Division's attack through a series of telephone messages which clearly traces the fate of their Indian Colleagues. By the 10 May it was obvious that the British assaults had failed, and the Lahore Division consequently was stood down from its condition of 'constant readiness'. Trenches were deepened, but the men had to bail them out as rising surface water caused flooding.[16]

15 TNA WO 95/3947: Report of the action of the Bareilly Brigade during the period 8-10 May 1915', 7 Indian (Meerut) Division, 21 (Bareilly) Indian Infantry Brigade Headquarters War Diary.

16 TNA: WO95/3913 3 Indian (Lahore) Division, Headquarters, Branches and Services, General Staff, Appendix 11: 1500 hours 10 May.

20

Festubert

The Ferozepore Brigade was not involved in the next major operation. On 13 May Haig's First Army headquarters issued orders for a new offensive on the following day. The plan was to continue to press forward and establish both a defensive flank on the La Bassée Road on the left with the right flank resting on Givenchy. Once this line was established, the troops should continue their advance and establish on a further line from Festubert via La Quinque Rue, the Tourelle crossroads and Port Arthur. To assist the advance a lifting bombardment should be maintained eventually concentrating on the next objective, the Rue d'Overt to Rue de Marais line. Haig realised that this would not be a surprise lightening attack but rather a deliberate and persistent advance. As Edmonds claimed, Festubert was to be the beginning of the policy of attrition, 'the wearing down of a stubborn foe by the resolute use of superior numbers.'[1]

It was intended that a reconstituted Meerut Division and British 1st Division would simultaneously attack at 2330 Hours on 14 May.[2] The preparatory bombardment during 13 and 14 May took place during heavy rain and many of the shells again failed to explode because of the muddy ground. Failure of the shells to explode coupled with heavy rainfall made it difficult for observers to identify where the shells had actually landed. Even those high explosive shells which did work correctly were rendered less effective because of the mud and caused less damage to the German defences than was hoped.

The rain eased on the morning of the 14 May and Haig sought the opinions of commanders in the field as to the state of the German wire and trench parapets. The British commanders suggested that although the effects of the bombardment had been satisfactory, but the mud would slow the troops advance. Lieutenant General Anderson, commanding the Meerut Division, was much less confident. He reported

1 Edmonds, 1915, Vol. II, p. 52
2 The Dehra Dun Brigade was removed from the Meerut Division and replaced by the Sirhind Brigade.

to General Haig that he did not feel that sufficient damage had been done and that the wire cutting by artillery, which was essential for a successful assault, had not yet begun. Haig was convinced by Anderson's arguments and postponed the attack for 24 hours.

The weather on morning of the 15 May was much better but the shortage of guns and shells meant that the barrage could only be directed at the German line which was to be attacked and this alerted the Germans as to which part of the font line they would have to defend. The attacking forces hoped that they might be able to gain some element of surprise by deceiving the Germans as to when the actual advance would begin by bombarding the enemy trenches on both the 14 May and the morning of the 15th.

The night attack, planned for 23.30 hours, was to be made by the 5th and 6th Brigades of the British 2nd Division on a 1,300-yard front. The Garhwal Brigade, on the left flank of 5th Brigade, was to advances on a 400-yard frontage. The attacking British brigades would have the 4th Guards Brigade in support and the Garhwal Brigade would be supported by the Sirhind Brigade of the Lahore Division, which had temporarily taken the place of the Dehra Dun Brigade. The Bareilly Brigade was to be held in reserve at Croix Barbeé. The three attacking Brigades would outnumber the opposing German forces by a ratio of roughly 5:1. Indian battalions of the Meerut Division had an impressive six machine guns each but this number had only been achieved by scavenging the total resources of the Indian Corps.[3]

The assault opened by the light of a very new moon and, in order to distinguish friend from foe, the British and Indian attackers had a white patch on their backs and fronts. Beyond the breastwork was a dyke which was 12 feet wide and filled with four feet of water. As it ran parallel to the British front line it had to be crossed using light bridges and once across the troops lay down on the ground. They were some three hundred yards from the German front line and the intervening ground was covered by grass and weeds a foot high but through this verbiage there were the remains of furrows which led directly to the German parapet which should prevent the attacking force losing direction as had happened at Neuve Chapelle.

The 6th Brigade, on the right of the line, advanced silently at a walk with bayonets fixed and captured the German forward trench with almost no opposition. The supporting troops passed through and occupied the German supporting trench and the Brigade consolidated in preparation to continue the attack at daylight.

The 5th Brigade and the Garhwal Brigade were not so fortunate. In order to mislead the Germans as to where the attack would take place the Lahore Division, north of the attacking front had been ordered to support the attack by attempting to mislead the Germans by bursts of rifle or machine fire. Consequently, the Jullundur Brigade fired controlled five-minute bursts at roughly 45-30-minute intervals beginning at

3 See Robert Williams, 'The Battle of Festubert' in S Jones (ed) *Courage without Glory: The British Army on the Western Front 1915* (Solihull, Helion and Co. 2015), p. 267.

2030 Hours until 22:30 hours. Such unusual behaviour alerted the Germans and they began to send up flares under the light of which they saw the 6th and Garhwal Brigades laying the bridges with which to cross the dyke. The two brigades crossed the dykes with few losses and, as the 6th Brigade had done, lay down on the enemy side. As Merewether recorded, the Germans were now in a state of readiness and 'the moment our men advanced, the enemy opened a murderous fire from rifles and machine guns.'[4] The Germans used even more flares and a 'specie' of grenades which burst into flames when they hit the ground. The result was that No Man's Land was a bright as day and made even brighter by the use of a search light. The defending troops used mortars and shrapnel to target the advancing British and Indian troops and so intensive was this barrage that Edmond suggested that the Germans were not only aware of the pace of the attack but also the hour it was to be launched.

Only part of the Inniskilling Fusiliers, the battalion closest to 6th Brigade, successfully reached the German front line. Attempts were made to support this success by the 2nd Battalion Oxford & Buckinghamshire Light Infantry, but these were soon checked by the enemy. By 2400 hours, the advanced had ground to a halt and it was obvious that the attack on this part of the German line had failed. A renewed attack was made after a second bombardment at around 0315 hours. The Germans, however, had over three hours to reorganise and the assault was repelled. Haig, realising that the advance of the 5th and the Garhwal brigades had petered out, directed that the attack should concentrate on the advances made by the 6th Brigade and those troops of the Inniskilling Fusiliers which had been able to join them and the 5th and Garhwal Brigades would convert their attack into a defensive action.[5]

During the night of 16/17 May, The Garhwal Brigade was relieved by the Bareilly Brigade, and the British artillery continued to fire on the German trenches but scouts sent out from the British front line were unable to spy on the German position because of heavy rifle fire and the enemy's constant use of flares. On 17 May the Sirhind Brigade moved into the German trenches captured by the 5th Brigade. This was a difficult manoeuvre since the communication trenches were blocked with wounded and knee deep in mud and water and the heavily laden troops of the Sirhind Brigade found it difficult to move towards the front. So slow was their progress that the complete relief had not been completed by dawn of the 18 May. Noticing the confusion, the Germans attacked the front line, the parapet of which had been flattened in many places, but they were beaten back by rifle fire.

The trenches which the Sirhind Brigade occupied were also filled with dead and wounded and 104 were buried during the night. To make matters worse, whilst occupying these trenches the Germans had buried many of their dead within the parapets, but these had become dislodged because of the British shelling which had preceded

4 Merewether and Smith, *The Indian Corps*, p. 359.
5 TNA WO 95/3943: 7 Indian (Meerut) Division, 20 (Garhwal) Indian Infantry Brigade Headquarters War Diary, 15-16 May 1915.

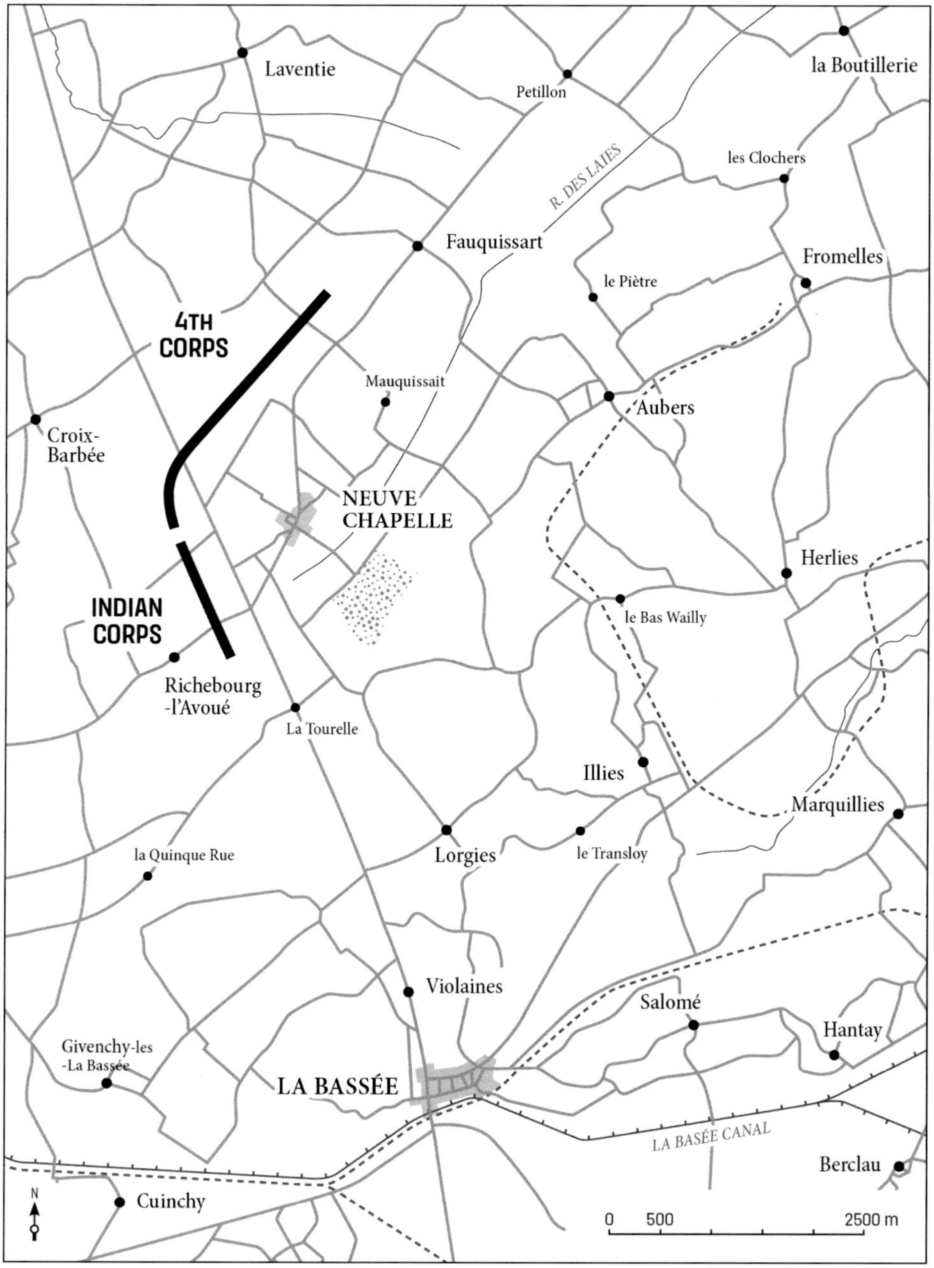

Map 7 Festubert, May 1915.

the attack. The remains of the corpses were trampled into the mud at the bottom of the trench and it took some days for them to be removed.

Throughout the following week, the British, Indian and Canadian divisions attempted to gain further ground but were frequently beaten back by enemy artillery, the condition of the ground over which they had to advance and the weakening effect of their rising casualties. The stocks of artillery shells, vital to assist attack, were almost reduced to nothing. Eventually these attempted assaults ground to a halt and the British and Indians were forced to consolidate the ground which they had gained but they remained under very heavy German artillery fire, which was far superior to that which the British could bring to bear. Casualties were very high considering the small amount of ground gained, First Army lost 16,500 killed and wounded. The Indian Corps suffered over 21,000 casualties with almost 4,500 men missing. A total of 270 British officer were killed, wounded or missing, which given their importance to the organisation of the Indian Army was calamitous.

21

Many Changes

May and June 1915 saw considerable changes within the Indian Corps. The Indian battalions had arrived at the front in 1914 with a strength of around 17,000 but at the beginning of June 1915 their strength, including the artillery, had risen to approximately 60,000 officers and men.[1] In the first week of the May, the 89th Punjabis arrived and replaced the 9th Bhopals in the Ferozepore Brigade, The Bhopals were to be posted to Mesopotamia together with the 125th (Napier) Rifles from the Bareilly Brigade which had been replaced by the 69th Punjabis.

The weather was balmy and there were fears that the warm weather might cause an outbreak of typhus as often occurred in the area even without the increased risk from the large numbers of troops which had now arrived. However, the Indian Medical Services proved up to the job and there was no epidemic. Militarily, things were also quiet, but Naik Ayub Khan, a Mahsud of the 129 Baluchis, had an adventure which brought him to the notice of high-ranking Officers of the Indian Corps which included Sir James Willcocks.[2]

Naik (Corporal) Ayub Khan, originally of the 124th Baluchis had arrived in France in early 1915 as one of the casualty replacements for 129th Baluchis. Unlike some of his companions he had nor deserted when it became known that they were to leave for Europe. It had been a common practice for warriors of the North West Frontier to enter British Army camps under the pretext that they were deserting from their own bands. Once admitted to the camp, they acquired useful information before slipping away. Ayub Khan, among a number of other Sepoys had volunteered to use similar tactics in order to gain information of the Germans. They had been refused as it was considered too risky and likely to end in their deaths. Not daunted, Ayub Khan, whilst part of a patrol in No Man's Land on 21 June 1915 went missing before it had returned

1 Merewether and Smith, *The Indian Corps,* p. 377.

2 Willcocks, *With the Indians,* pp. 304-308. Willcocks was resentful that the censor did not allow his version of Ayub Khan's exploits to appear in print.

to the British front line.[3] The Naik was close to the enemy wire and it was feared that, in the darkness, he had been captured. or even killed. It was similarly wondered by some if he had taken the opportunity to desert even though this was much harder to do than it had been in India. Given, Ayub Khan's character, his officers refused to believe that such a good soldier, who had vowed 'that he would either die in France or return an Indian officer', would desert to the enemy.[4] The following day. General Willcocks visited Khan's Battalion and his section officer, Lieutenant Harold Lewis requested permission to go out after dark as he was sure that Khan was either dead or wounded and laying in No Man's land. Willcocks, though sympathetic, refused to be persuaded as he considered that such a venture was too dangerous. They need not have worried as at 2330 hours on the 22 June the wandering Naik returned to the British trenches unarmed.[5] His story was that he had decided to try and find out details of the German deployment by pretending to be a deserter. After hiding his rifle and ammunition he walked up to the German wire and called out 'Musalman'.[6] A German officer called out to him and told him to enter the trench and after convincing its suspicious occupants, Ayub was conducted to the Bois de Beitz and then on to the local German divisional headquarters. The resourceful Naik is said to have made mental notes of all he saw during the journey.[7] He was interrogated in Hindustani by a German officer who attempted to obtain details military information from the Naik who was equally anxious not to give anything away. It seems that the Germans made much of the fact that Ayub Khan's fellow Muslims, the Ottomans, were fighting on the Germany's side and this meant that the Indians in France were being duped into killing the allies of to their coreligionists.

The interrogators were keen to question Khan as to the morale of the members of his Battalion and he encouraged the Germans to believe that there was a great deal of dissent against the war. Ayub Khan even promised that, if he was allowed to go back to his Battalion, he would quickly return with at least 20 other deserters. The delighted captors, having heard what they wanted to hear, offered him 20 marks a head if he could do so. The Naik remained with the Germans through the 22 June and was subjected to much interest and kindness from the German soldiers who clearly saw him as a useful tool. Merewether claims that the cunning Indian even took care to remember the numbers on the Germans' shoulder straps.[8] That night, he was taken back to the section of the German Front Line where he had earlier entered, and they

3 TNA WO 95/3925: 3 Indian (Lahore) Division, 7 (Lahore) Infantry Brigade, 129 (DCO) Baluchi War Diary, 21 June 1915.

4 Ayub Khan quoted in George Morton-Jack, *The Indian Empire at War*, p. 248.

5 TNA: WO95/3925: 3 Indian (Lahore) Division, 7 (Lahore) Infantry Brigade, 129 (DCO) Baluchi War Diary, 22 June 1915.

6 Merewether and Smith, *The Indian Corps*, p. 381.

7 Merewether and Smith, *The Indian Corps*, p. 381. Merewether conjectures that this was the 13th Division of the German VII Corps.

8 Merewether and Smith, *The Indian Corps*, p. 382.

then let him go. Retrieving his rifle and ammunition which he had hidden before 'surrendering', Naik Ayub Khan returned to the Indian Corps line where he gave an account of the information he had gained, the accuracy of which Merewether claims was verified by other sources.[9] Ayub Khan was promoted to Jemadar and decorated with the Indian Order of Merit, 2nd Class, for his daring, courage and skill.[10]

In July 1915, the Ferozepore Brigade, as part of the Indian Corps, occupied a line of roughly 2 miles in length. The 1/4th London's acted as the reserve for the Jullundur Brigade and the 89th Punjabis were the Sirhind Brigades reserve. On 9 July instructions were received by the Indian Corps, to temporarily vacate a portion of their front-line trenches in favour of the 1st Corps to allow the Indians to undergo a badly needed reorganisation. The serious casualty rate and the paternalistic nature of the Indian Army was a source of concern for High Command. Replacements of all ranks arrived from India and joined battalions in which they were strangers. The nature of fighting in France and Belgium was just as alien to these newcomers as it had been to the original battalions who had arrived in 1914. They required intensive training so that they could take their place in the depleted ranks. Willcocks, knowing how to boost his men's morale, suggested that the reorganisation took place during the Muslim festival of Ramadan which began on 1 July and this was agreed. Withdrawal from the Front Line meant that the Muslims in the Corps would have a less difficult time in following the rule to fast than if they had remained active at the Front.

On 7 July, the Indian battalions of the Ferozepore Brigade were withdrawn to allow this reorganisation to take place. The Connaught Rangers and the 1/4th London's remained and were joined in the line by the 2nd and 4th Battalions of the Black Watch, both of which had fought at Neuve Chapelle.[11] British officers returned to Great Britain for short periods of leave but it was not possible to offer such a luxury to their Indian troops. Rumours that this might happen circulated even towards the end of the war, were common.[12]

However, conditions for the Sepoys did improve somewhat. The 57th Rifles war diarists mentions very good billets where Sepoys were able to bathe. Although the 57th moved in and out of the trenches, their conditions were described as being very peaceful, the weather was very fine, and the health of the men was good.[13] The strength of each Lahore Division brigade was increased by roughly a thousand Sepoys

9 Merewether and Smith, *The Indian Corps*, p. 383.

10 Jemadar Khan was decorated again in Kenya in December 1916 with the Indian Order of Merit 1st Class with the unit citation: Acted with great gallantry in a bombing attack against an enemy position on night of 15/16 December 1916. See Edward Paice, *Tip and Run: The Untold Tragedy of the Great War in Africa* (London: Weidenfeld & Nicolson, 2007) p. 260.

11 TNA WO 95/3922: 3 (Lahore) Division, 7 (Ferozepore) Infantry Brigade Headquarters War Diary, 9 July 1915.

12 Omissi, *Indian Voices*, pp. 15-16.

13 TNA WO 95/3923: 3rd Indian (Lahore) Division 7 (Ferozepore) Infantry Brigade, 57th Rifles War Diary, 1-31 July 1915.

who were transferred from their linked Meerut Division brigades. On 24 July the 19th (Western) Division, a New Army formation, joined the Indian Corps thus increasing its available numbers by some 17,000 officers and men. Given the mounting numbers of British units within the Indian Corps and the difficulties in replacing Indian casualties, it was increasingly clear that the Corps' contribution to Western Front operations was being reduced as the 6th Jats, 15th Sikhs and 51st Dogras embarked for Egypt and Mesopotamia which was nearer to subcontinent bases for supply and replacement draft purposes.

22

'A niche in the temple of fame'

In September 1915 the Indian Corps had mostly returned to its more normal functions and the Ferozepore Brigade was again in the front line. The weather was very changeable and, early that month, the trenches were again flooded despite Sepoy attempts to improve drainage. Worse was to come: General Willcocks was replaced as GOC Indian Corps.

Relations between Willcocks and Haig had never been easy. On 3 September Willcocks attended an interview with Haig, Commander of First Army and Willcocks' superior. Haig, in his diary recorded that Willcocks suggested that he lacked Haig's confidence and, if this was the case, he would rather go.[1] It is true that Haig had a less than complimentary view of the senior commanders of the Indian Corps. When he visited the Indian Corps' Headquarters on 29 November 1914, Haig recorded a feeling that all was not well and on 21 December, after another visit during which Willcocks had suggested that the Indians were tired out and unable to fight, Haig had recommended the Corps' immediate relief.[2]

Haig regarded Willcocks' attitude as overprotective of his Sepoys but one would suggest that, in spite of Haig's experience in India, he did not make sufficient allowance for the impact which the changes in fighting, high casualties, especially amongst the British Officers, and the generally overwhelming experience of modern warfare had upon the Sepoys. Willcocks was certainly protective of his men. He had been with the Indian Army for 37 years and had been victorious in a number of campaigns. When he arrived in France, he was the third senior officer next to Field Marshall French and General Smith-Dorrien and clearly felt affronted when men such as Haig were appointed over his head. Willcocks was not the only Indian Senior Officer to be treated in this way.[3] Things came to a head when, during the planning the next British offensive, which will be discussed later, Haig proposed that the Indian Corps

1 Sheffield & Bourne, *Douglas Haig*, diary entry for 3 September 1915.
2 Sheffield & Bourne, *Douglas Haig*, diary entry for 21 December 1914.
3 Willcocks *With the Indians*, p. 52.

should take part in a diversionary operation, the details of which Willcocks consequently formally objected to in a memorandum, Haig regarded this memorandum as a most discouraging document and felt that the Indian Corps must still do its share.[4] Shortly afterwards, Haig's Senior Staff Officer, Richard Butler, received a letter from Willcocks expressing delight that the Indian Corps had been ordered to go into battle. The suspicious, and perhaps perceptive, Haig felt that the letter was meant to counterbalance the negativity in Willcocks' memorandum and did not truly reflect the attitudes at the Indian HQ.

Willcox claimed to have received mixed messages regarding as to his own future and that of his Corps. It seems that Kitchener had visited Willcocks in August and pledged that it was his intention to keep the Indian Corps in France until the end of the war even though it had been suggested to him that they be relieved. The quality of drafts from India had improved and earlier in that month, King George V had presented Willcocks with the badge of the order of St Michael and St George.[5] In spite of these positive signs, however, Willcocks' fate was sealed and on 5 September 1915, Willcocks was told he could go on leave. It was exactly a year to the day since he had been appointed Commander of the Indian Corps. Unsurprisingly for a man who was convinced that he had done his best, Willcocks was very bitter about his 'sacking' which he solely laid at the feet of Haig. He, at first, protested that he only received verbal instructions to go on leave. Even the Indian Office did not receive any information of the dismissal until Willcocks notified them. Sir James also claimed that even Kitchener, the Secretary of State for War, had also heard of Willcocks' fate by word of mouth and had asked to receive an official report. Willcocks was convinced that, had Kitchener not died in sinking of HMS *Hampshire*, he would have ensured that he did not end up on the 'scrapheap'.[6] He was convinced that senior officers of the Indian Corps were undervalued and failed to be recognised in the way the British officers were.[7]

Willcocks was courteous enough to praise his successor, Lieutenant General Charles Anderson. Anderson was Commander of the Meerut Division during the battles of Neuve Chapelle and Festubert. Willcocks described Anderson as a 'most earnest fighting soldier 'but, earlier, Haig had criticised him for packing too many men in the front and support trenches at the battle of Festubert who were to become casualties

4 Sheffield & Bourne, *Douglas Haig*, diary entry for 30 August 1915.
5 At the same ceremony Willcocks' ADC, his only son, Lt. J.L. Willcocks, Black Watch was awarded the Military Cross.
6 Willcocks *With the Indians,* pp. 322-323.
7 In May 1917 Willcocks was appointed Governor and military C-in-C of Bermuda (where a large Bermuda Garrison protected the Royal Naval Dockyard and other strategic assets) a post in which he served until 1922. He was appointed Knight Grand Cross of the Order of the Bath (GCB) in the 1921 Birthday Honours. Willocks memoirs, *The Romance of Soldiering and Sport,* were published in 1925. He was later to return to India and died at Bharatpur in 1926

Lord Kitchener, Secretary of State for War 1914-16.

through friendly fire. Willcocks had defended his colleague by claiming that it was hard to tell whether it was British or German artillery which had caused the casualties.[8] Anderson went on to command the Corps until its departure from France and then went on to command XXII Corps and later I Corps; one of the few Indian Officers to raise to such prestigious commands.

Merewether described Willocks as having the firmness of Kitchener, the patience of Job and the tact of Talleyrand.[9] Willcocks' knowledge of the Indian Army may have not been unique but was certainly extensive and in great depth, and the Corps continued to retain its unique identity on the Western Front. Willcocks had, like his Sepoys, much to learn about the new way of fighting a modern industrial war but there is no doubt that his performance as GOC Indian Corps was, on balance, successful. The organisation of the Indian Army had not been constructed for the type of warfare into which it was forced to engage in the battles of 1914 and its methods of recruiting, equipping and commanding made it vulnerable to the cost incurred on battlefields of France and Belgium. Alongside these criticisms it must not be forgotten that, at the outbreak of the First World War, the Indian Army was the only large force outside the Great Britain which could be swiftly called upon to fight. A call which it answered to the best of its ability and with considerable success. Willcocks was both the head and heart of the Corps, but he also found it difficult to adopt the unswerving determination necessary to defeat the Germans. His paternalism and tendency to think of himself as head of a family rather than the head of a ruthless war machine was a weakness but an understandable one. The desperate situation in which the BEF found itself in 1914 which forced it to use a make do and mend strategy in merely holding back the Germans was one which Willocks could support with a clear conscience. The ruthless attrition which had begun in 1915 with increasing loss of life was one which, on behalf of his Sepoys he could not support. Nevertheless, one must agree with Merewether's prediction that Willcocks should not be counted as the 'least of the heroes who stood for England in the autumn of 1914.'[10]

8 Sheffield & Bourne, *Douglas Haig*, diary entry for 10 May 1915.
9 Merewether and Smith, *The Indian Corps*, p. 394.
10 Merewether and Smith, *The Indian Corps*, p. 395.

23

A Final Throw

The offensive which had concerned Willcocks would take place in the French black country about Loos. The British had prevaricated for some time with regards to taking the offensive again, as its experiences at Neuve Chapelle and Festubert had not been positive ones. General Foch, the Allied Supreme Commander, was determined that the BEF should support the French Tenth Army's planned offensive at Artois. This support was to be provided by the I Corps and IV Corps of Haig's First Army. Once again, the lack of artillery and sufficient ammunition was a problem for the BEF. There were insufficient shells for the type of whirlwind bombardment that had been delivered at Neuve Chapelle and, consequently, a four-day slow bombardment was planned together with the release of gas at the beginning of the actual attack in order to help the British reach the German trenches. However, it had been calculated that 1,100 gas cylinders were needed to make its use effective but only 160 were actually available. This meant that gas could only be directed at the German salient rather than across the whole line of attack.

The First Army assault was partially successful. Loos was secured but breakthrough of German second line of defence was not achieved. This was to some partially a result of Field Marshal French retaining British reserves too far to the rear and even when they did arrive, the Germans who, by that time, had also been able to bring in their reserves, halted their advance. First Army casualties of 50,500 were over two and a half times that of the enemy. It was the failure at Loos which led to the resignation of Sir John French and his replacement by Haig who had used his connections to bring about the change.[1]

The Indian Corps had been instructed to take part in one of a series of secondary actions which were designed to keep the enemy engaged whilst the main attack was made at Loos. In this way it was hoped that the Germans would be unable to reinforce their line at Loos as they, themselves, were being attacked elsewhere. In total, there were four of these secondary attacks which were as follows

1 Sheffield and Bourne, *Douglas Haig'* pp. 153-173

Sir Patrap Singh and Sir Douglas Haig discuss events with Marshal Foch.

Allenby's V Corps augmented by the 14th (Light) Division was to attack at Bellewaarde Farm, which was situated east of Ypres:

> Pultney's III Corps was to attack near Bois Grenier,
> The First Army's 2nd Division was to launch an attack near Givenchy.
> The Indian Corps was to attack near Neuve Chapelle.

The Indian Corps assault was to be delivered by the Meerut Division led by Anderson's replacement, Brigadier General Claud Jacob who had formerly led the Dehra Dun Brigade. The Lahore Division alongside the 19th Division were to hold the front-line trenches whilst the attack was delivered.

Ferozepore Brigade Operational Order No, 51 described the part which it was proposed it would play in the secondary and diversionary attack.[2] It was to provide a smoke cloud for 34 minutes using Threlfallite Grenades.[3] These Grenades were produced by Albright and Wilson, a company based in Oldbury, then in Shropshire,

2 TNA WO 95/3922: 3 Indian (Lahore) Division, 7 (Ferozepore) Infantry Brigade, Operation Order No. 51, 23 September 1915.

3 This bomb was a tin of 5 inches in length and contained red phosphorus, which produced a radius of 12 yards of dense smoke. See Bertram Smith, *Bombs and Hand Grenades* (New York: E.P. Dutton and Co, 1919), p. 11.

and which was originally created to produce phosphorous chlorate for the match industry. The grenades were to be distributed three to every four yards of trench and a total of 2,050 were distributed to the Brigade.[4] The smoke caused by these grenades, which burned for roughly ten minutes, were to be supplemented by smoke candles which were to be thrown into No Man's Land from every 25-yard sections of trench at two-minute intervals The Brigade was ordered to be prepared to take advantage of any weakening or withdrawal of the enemy caused by the main attack by the Meerut Division. During the initial bombardment, the Ferozepore Brigade in common with those occupying the from line, were to use rifle and machinegun fire in order to prevent the Germans from attempting to repair damage which it had caused.

Order No 51 set out in great detail the preparations which were necessary for the attack, setting out the number of rounds to be issued per man, the flag which were to be used to identify each brigade and the one-way system to be used in the communication trenches. In an Appendix the possible outcomes of the Meerut and 19th Divisions' attack were listed and these stressed the importance of officers being familiar with the ground across which they would lead their men. A further Appendix listed action if or if not gas and smoke were used. In the former situation a mine, situated close to the enemy salient near the Winchester Road would be exploded. This was done at 0548 hours on 24 September and produced a crater which was 92 feet across.

On 22 September the Lahore Division attempted a feint by pretending to attack. There was a five-minute bombardment on the enemy's front line followed by a similar bombardment on the support trenches. Bayonets were displayed above the Lahore Division's front trench and dummy heads were also raised above its parapet. The Sepoys contributed to this ruse by shouting loudly. The object of this feint was to draw the Germans into the front trench where they would be subjected to a heavy shrapnel bombardment. The ruse failed as did a similar strategy by the 19th Division on 23 September. In fact, none of the planned subsidiary attacks achieved their objectives. They all ended with the British troops back at their starting lines and no German reinforcements other than those in the immediate area were drawn into the diversionary actions.[5] However, Haig, in his report on the offensive dated 26 September 1915, stated that he was very pleased with the manner with which … [the] Indian Corps carried out the role assigned to (it) of retaining the enemy on their front.'[6]

4 TNA WO 95/3922: 3 Indian (Lahore) Division, 7 (Ferozepore) Infantry Brigade General instructions regarding the action for forming a smoke cloud and a smoke screen during bombardment and assault, 18 September 1915.

5 Edmonds, 1915, Vol. II. p. 259.

6 Merewether and Smith, *The Indian Corps*, p. 449.

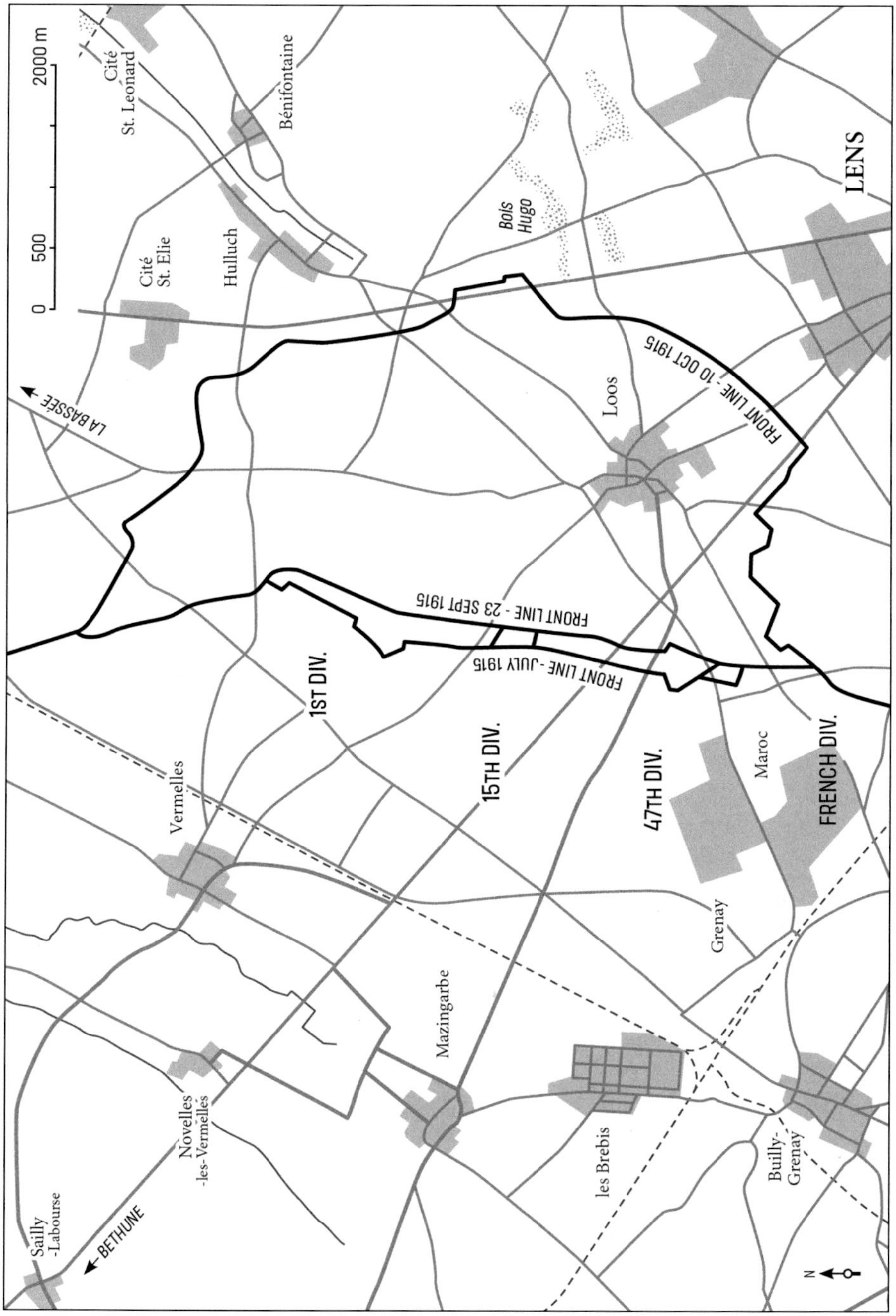

Map 8 Battle of Loos, September 1915.

24

Departure

Loos was Field Marshal French's last real battle. His behaviour during the battle was reminiscent of an earlier age of combat. Indeed, French was observed riding behind the lines, sometimes alone, watching his troops, with whom he was popular, as they advanced towards the front. The high casualty rate, especially the loss of senior officers, affected and depressed him.[1] He oscillated between hope and despair and, in the words of Major John Charteris of Haig's staff, 'Sir John French is played out … The show is too big for him and he is despondent.'[2] French did not help the BEF by agreeing to this attack in the first place and his holding back the reserves on the first day was even more unhelpful. 'He was indecisive, emotionally volatile, and had little regard for the niceties of staff work.'[3] French subsequently offered his resignation on 8 December after experiencing great pressure to do so, and he was replaced by his onetime friend, Douglas Haig.

Loos was also the last of the Indian Corps' major Western Front engagements. The high number of casualties of both officers and Sepoys were impossible to replace. The recruiting system in India, which required each Battalion to have its own recruiting depot, which were trying to recruit, and train reinforcements for their own home-based battalions, was not sufficiently developed enough to rapidly replace Sepoys.[4] Special requirements, such as the ability to speak an Indian language, prevented the speedy replacement of officers. The number of British nationals in India was small and most were engaged in government service and officer recruitment was based on the

1 Richard Holmes, *The Little Field Marshal,* pp. 305-306.
2 John Charteris, *Field Marshal Earl Haig* (London, Cassell, 1920), p. 116
3 Dan Todman, The Grand Lamasery revisited: General Headquarters on the Western Front, 1914-1919 in Gary Sheffield, and Dan Todman, *Command and Control on the Western Front* (Staplehurst: Spellmount, 2004), p. 45.
4 Alan Jeffreys, The Expansion of the Indian Officer Corps during the First World War in Alan Jeffreys (ed.), *The Indian Army in the First World War* (Solihull: Helion & Co., 2018), p. 176..

demands of frontier campaigns rather than a European war.[5] Gurkhas, for example, only spoke Gurkhali and could only be directed in their native language rather than Urdu which served as a default language for communication within the Indian Army. Merewether mentions an Indian battalion on the Western front which had no less than 70 British officers in its ranks over the period of its service when the normal compliment was thirteen.[6] Such incidences undermined the close-knit family character of the IFEA when it left India for France. The 59th Rifles had arrived in France with 13 British officers, 18 Indian officers and 810 other ranks. In November 1915 it had none of its original British officers and only four original Indian Officers with 75 men still with the Battalion. By October, the Indian Corps had suffered over 20,000 casualties.

On 31 October the Headquarters of the Indian Corps received Operation Order G. 239 which stated that the Corps would 'probably' shortly be required to set off from Marseilles.[7] The Front occupied by the Meerut and Lahore Division would be taken over by the formations of the IX Corps which was commanded by Lieutenant General Sir Richard Haking. Consequently, the relief of the Indian Corps began on 3 November 1915 but Haig had decided that the Indian Cavalry Corps would remain on the Western front in the hopes of a decisive breakthrough. As the Indian Corps prepared to leave, the Cavalry Corps sent a message praising their countrymen's 'staunchness and gallantry on many memorable occasions.'[8] The Indian Infantry corps thanked the Cavalry Corps for its good wishes and hoped that there would be an opportunity for the cavalry to uphold the best traditions of the Indian Army. This proved to be something of a forlorn hope as the Indian cavalry was mainly used to provide dismounted parties for trench duty. Casualties amongst the Indian cavalry compared with those of the Infantry were relatively light because they were held back from action on many occasions. The 1st Indian Cavalry Division's only major battle was Cambrai during the German counter-offensive of 30 November to 3 December 1917. The 2nd Indian Cavalry Division was deployed in support of attacks on the Bazentin – Longueval Ridge in July 1916 and Flers-Courcelette in September prior to eventual transfer to Egypt.

Similar messages of goodwill were sent by Field Marshal French who wrote that the combat in Europe had cost the Indian Corps many courageous lives which had required replacements from unconnected Battalions. During its time on the Western Front, the Indian Corps had shown 'the most praiseworthy courage under novel and trying conditions, both of climate and fighting, and have not only upheld, but added

5 TNA MUN 5/176/1143/16: Memorandum on India's contribution to the war in men, material and money, p. 7.

6 Merewether and Smith, *The Indian Corps*. P. 457.

7 TNA WO 95/109: Indian Corps Headquarters Diary Operational Order G. 239, 31 October 1915.

8 TNA WO 95/109: Indian Corps Headquarters Diary, 19 November 1915.

to the good name of the Army which they represent'.[9] King George V also praised the Indian Corps; in referring to his confidence in summoning it to France and Belgium, the King concluded that it had been fully justified by the Corps' sense of duty, chivalry and courage. However, Indian Corps was now required in another field of action but before they left the Prince of Wales would visit the Corps and thank the Indians on behalf of the King.[10] The date of this letter, 25 October, is interesting as it precedes operation Order G 329 by a week.

The units of Ferozepore Brigade commenced their entrainment to Marseilles. In the case of the 57th Rifles, the journey began on 8 November and, having marched to Lillers in the Pas de Calais, they boarded a train on 8 December.[11] The Battalion arrived at the port in the afternoon 11 December and immediately boarded the SS *City of Glasgow,* which had brought the Headquarters section to France in 1914. The 57th Rifles were joined on board by the Veterinary Corps, the Meerut Casualty Clearing Station staff and the Supply and Transport Corps. Some men were left at Marseilles in order to bring the Battalion's animals on another ship. The *City of Glasgow* sailed at 10 am on 12 December and, as the War Diary of the Rifles states, they had been in France for one year and 77 days. Sailing was a dangerous affair and the *Glasgow* was armed with a 12 pdr gun and the Battalion's machine guns were erected for further protection with two at the bow of the ship and one on each side. A party of 60 rifle men were also assembled on the upper deck in case of attack from German submarines which had been reported to be active in the area.

Th City of Glasgow arrived at St Paul's Bay, Malta on 16 December and entered Malta's harbour on the following day. The ship re-embarked on the 18 December and arrived at Alexandria, Egypt on 22 December and it then travelled to Port Said where, on Christmas Eve, the troops disembarked and bordered a train for Suez where they arrived on the same day. On Christmas Day the 57th Rifles handed over their mules and carts to the 129th Baluchis. The Battalion was further depleted when three Indian officers and 140 members of the 28th Punjabis, who had been transferred to the Rifles during their time in France, left to return to their own Battalion. These numbers were partially replaced by 35 new recruits who had come from the regimental depot in India. The ability to increase an Indian Battalion's strength in this way was one of the benefits of it being closer to home.

The duties of the 57th Rifles including patrolling the line of the Suez Canal to prevent enemy patrols from placing mines near its banks. In order to identify possible enemy activity a 12-foot-wide track beside the canal was swept daily and examined each day for suspicious footprints, a primitive but effective method of detection. These

9 Field Marshal Sir John French, Special Order of the Day, 22 November 1915.

10 George V, Message of the King-Emperor to the British and Indian Troops of the Indian Corps in France, 25 October 1915.

11 The details of the 57th Rifles departure from France and activities in Egypt are recorded in the Battalion's War Diary. TNA WO 95/3922/5: 3 Indian (Lahore) Division, 7 (Ferozepore) Infantry Brigade, 57 Rifles War Diary.

S.S. *City of Glasgow*: Transport of the 120th Baluchis.

duties continued for the whole of January 1916 and one is left with the impression that the war diarist felt that they were extremely tedious.

Indian Expeditionary Force D had advanced along both the Tigris and Euphrates for most of 1915 with the initial objective of defending the Shatt Al Arab waterway and the port of Basra in order to protect the important British oil fields. This force gradually fell foul of mission creep as local commanders saw the possibility of demonstrating the fame of British Arms in the Muslim world. The 9th Bhopal Battalion, which had formerly been part of the Ferozepore Brigade, joined the Tigris Force. The Lahore Division, together with the Meerut Division, was also to form part of the Tigris Corps Force commanded by Lieutenant Sir Fenton Aylmer.VC. The Tigris Corps was sent to relieve Townshend's 6th Poona Division which was besieged at Kut-al-Amara. Its mission turned out to be an abject failure and the disaster resulted in a complete reorganisation of the Indian Army. The Tigris Corps was under the direction of the Indian Government and its military headquarters at Simla and this structure of command continued until the fall of Kut. The result of this organisation and its defects in administration and excessive parsimony effected the Indians in France and even more so the IEFD in Mesopotamia. Its supply route was from India via Egypt and the success of its campaign depended on the resources of India rather than those of Britain which were to prove inadequate.

Unfortunately for IEFD, the lessons learned in the modern warfare of France were either forgotten or unknown to commanders in Mesopotamia. It arrived with the old-style Indian administration, its transport was traditional and its medical services completely inadequate to cope with large numbers of casualties. Staff officers had not learned how to manage large bodies of men and did not have the example of a BEF staff to copy. The mission creep, encouraged, by the Viceroy, put greater strains on the IEFD and small-scale attack followed small scale attack incurring heavy casualties. By the time of the Battle of Ctesiphon, the Force had become overstretched and its support services were on the verge of collapse.[12] Although the IEFA faced many initial difficulties it never came as close to administrative collapse as did IEFD, partially because it was close to the BEF from which it could learn.

Despite these deficiencies, there were still some senior officers who were prepared to defend of the Indian Army administration such as William Birdwood, Commander of the I Anzac Corps, and a self-confessed protégé of Kitchener whose creation it was. Birdwood rightly pointed out that India had been 'milked' of its resources when called upon to assist the European Theatre of War but Mesopotamia was 'by far a more difficult undertaking than any contemplated in Europe.'[13] However, it was the mission creep which increased operational difficulties. Birdwood's protested that the fault was not with the system but the failure of General John Nixon the commander of IEFD to ask for resources until it was too late.[14] It is a moot point as to whether the resources could have been provided quickly enough to have made a difference. It is hard to disagree with the Mesopotamia Commission's conclusion that the problem with IEFD was 'not the fighting capacity of the combatant forces of the Indian Army but the system of military administration in control of the Army.'[15]

12 A. Syk, The 1917 Mesopotamia Commission, *RUSI Journal,* No. 154 2009, pp. 94-101.
13 Australian War Memorial Records: Letters written by Field Marshal Lord Birdwood to various correspondents, 19 July 1916-16 September 1918: Letter to Major General Ernest Dunlop, 19 July 1916, p. 3.
14 Birdwood to Dunlop p. 5.
15 BL/IOR/L/PS/20/57: Mesopotamia Commission. p. 115.

25

Performance of the Indian Corps on the Western Front

Criticisms of the Indian Corps' performance on the Western Front can be divided into six primary categories. First, the Indian troops were of poor quality and extremely inferior to their British counterparts.[1] Second, the reliance of Indian troops on their British officers which meant that without them the Indians were 'like sheep without a shepherd.[2] Third, the Indians were unable to cope with the climate in Flanders, especially during the winter of 1914-15.[3] Fourth, the inability of the Indian units to withstand the strain of shellfire and remain resolute unlike the ability of British battalions.[4] Fifth, such was the Indian inferiority, lack of moral fibre and resolve that they were prone to wounding themselves in great numbers in order to be withdrawn from the front.[5] Sixth, that the divisions of the Indian Corps 'did not turn out to be a great success' and were, in fact, 'failures'[6] These criticisms could be summarised by the claims made by Frank Richards whose well-publicised but mistaken comments about the Indians 'They suffered from cold feet, and a few enemy shells exploding round their trenches were enough to demoralise the majority of them ... [They] were no good at fighting.'[7]

1 John Charteris, *At GHQ* (London: Cassell, 1931), pp. 66-67.
2 B. Brice & W. Pulteney, *The Battles of Ypres* (London: John Murray, 1927) pp. 102-103
3 Austen Chamberlain, Secretary of State for India, cited in G Morton-Jack, *The Indian Army on the Western Front*, p. 157. Vedica Kant, *If I die here,* p. 41.
4 Nickolas Gardner, *Trial by Fire*, pp. 174-175
5 Jeffrey Greenhut, 'The Imperial Reserve' pp. 57, 59–60,
6 John Terraine, *Douglas Haig, The Educated Soldier* (London: Cassell, 2000 [1963]) pp. 48-49 and Greenhut, The Imperial Reserve pp. 68, 70
7 Frank Richards *Old Soldiers Never Die* (London: Faber and Faber, 1933), pp. 38-39. It is likely that Richards had mistakenly identified French colonial troops as Indians.

In recent years many of these assertions have be found to be either untrue or exaggerated and historians such as Morton-Jack[8] Jeffreys,[9] McClenaghan[10] and Basu[11] have done much to set the record straight and to counteract the apparent racialism which can be found both in contemporary and more recent accounts.

The original Sepoys in the Indian Corps were professional soldiers, often with years of service as were the members of the BEF. They were committed to serving the King Emperor and were experts with the somewhat antiquated weapons with which they had been issued. Their employment of artillery was not extensive and the machine-guns with which they arrived in France were greatly inferior to those in the BEF and when upgraded to the Vickers Mk II. the tripods with which they came equipped proved useless.[12] It was only a result of the ingenuity and engineering skills of a British officer that a workable tripod was cobbled together.[13] The original tripods were described by Major General Watkins, GOC Lahore Division[14] as being practically useless as they were too big for the saddles used by mules to transport them and too heavy to be manhandled. Moreover, Watkins complained there were no spare parts for their original machine guns and they were prone to jamming at the most perilous time.[15] He was anxious they were replaced by the more reliable Vickers and provided an example of how defective Martini-Henry rifles materially affected the outcome of an attack by the 129th Baluchis.[16] By 1915 the problem of the lack of suitable machine guns had eased but the damage to their fighting reputation had been done.

The Indian Army had no experience similar to that which the British Army gained in the Boer War. Indian combat experience was mainly against inferiorly armed tribesmen who resisted pitch battles but preferred to sally forth and retreat after exchanging shots. They were suddenly flung into battle during First Ypres with little opportunity to acclimatise and opposed by a larger and better equipped force of the enemy.

The reliance on their British officers has already been discussed and there were many occasions when Indian Officers and NCOs proved their worth in the absence of their British Officers. It is not surprising that the average Sepoy was at a loss without the Officer Sahib since this is how they were trained. When, in such circumstances, the Sepoy showed a decline in their morale it was a self-fulfilling prophecy and not a measure of their courage.

8 George Morton-Jack, *The Army in India.*
9 Alan Jeffreys (ed.), The *Indian Army in the First World War.*
10 Tony McClenaghan, *For the Honour of My House* (Solihull, Helion & Co. 2019)
11 Shrabani Basu, *For King and another Country* (London, Bloomsbury, 2015).
12 TNA WO 95/3911: Telegram No. 67-G, 9 October 1914, GOC Lahore Division to the General Staff Indian Army Corps, Appendix No 1 (2
13 TNA WO 395/3911: Major Caldicott AOD, 16-17 October 1914.
14 Message from G.O.C., Lahore Division to General Staff Indian Army Corps, p. 1
15 Message from G.O.C., Lahore Division to General Staff Indian Army Corps, p. 2
16 Message from G.O.C., Lahore Division to General Staff Indian Army Corps, p. 2

The accusation that the Indians could not cope with the climate on the Western Front is generally untrue. The decision to send the IEFA to France was taken in haste and men landed in France in the Autumn of 1914 attired in summer uniforms. They did not receive the appropriate serge khaki uniform until December having struggled through temperatures as low as -10o C.[17] The struggle to provide the Sepoys with the correct winter dress was complicated by a 'one size fits all' mentality which required Gurkha officers to purchase safety pins to enable their men make their newly issued British' long johns' fit correctly. The failure to issue every Sepoy with an extra blanket on their arrival in France required them to improvise with eiderdowns and curtains.[18] Rather than the Indian Corps being unable to cope with the European climate, it was the lack of suitable winter gear which was the real problem.

The allegation that the Indians were unable to stand up to heavy shelling would also seem to be unfounded. The expectations placed on the Indian Corps, when it was so deprived of troops, was an additional area of concern for Willcocks. He complained that as far as *some* were concerned, 'An Army Corps (no matter its fighting strength in numbers) was [regarded as] an Army Corps.'[19] One would suggest that the '*some*' referred to Douglas Haig, Commander of First Army. Smith-Dorrien commented on the bravery shown by the Indians in face of murderous fire but criticised them for foolish behaviour in failing to conceal their presence whilst advancing.[20] They simply advanced towards the enemy without making use of the terrain. British Battalions had learned this skill during their experience in the Boer War. The Indian Army's last major campaign had been on the North West Frontier in 1908 and some of the new recruits would have had no active service experience until their arrival in France. Rather than lacking resolve, the Indian Corps demonstrated determination and tenacity which compared extremely well to the troops of the BEF.

The accusation concerning self-wounding has some credibility as has already been discussed but one must agree with Doherty and Donovan when they write that 'the continued effectiveness of Indian Army Units would be all the more remarkable if large numbers of them were choosing self-harm to avoid the firing line'.[21] The percentage of Sepoy casualties in the Indian Corps was greater than the those of the British Battalions which they fought along-side, The following table, from Merewether and Smith, indicates the casualties in the Indian Corps up to 19 November 1915. Calculations such as this are notoriously difficult to make but there is little reason to believe that these figures are wildly inaccurate.[22]

17 Corrigan recounts how the Lahore Division's Sirhind Brigade did not receive its winter clothing until January 1915. Corrigan, *With the Sepoys* pp. 43-45.
18 Corrigan, *With the Sepoys* pp. 43-45.
19 Willocks, *With the Indians,* p. 7.
20 H. Smith-Dorrien, *Memories of Forty-Eight Years' Service* (London: John Murray, 1925), pp. 456-458.
21 Doherty & Donovan, *The Indian Corps on the Western Front*, p. 44.
22 Merewether and Smith, *The Indian Corps,* p. 430.

	Killed	Wounded	Missing	Died	Total
British Units					
British Officers	124	363	37	?	524
British ORs	1,806	8,388	2,089	?	12,283
Total	1,930	8,751	2,126		12,807
Indian Units					
British Officers	150	294	49	3	496
British ORs	4	34	?	9	47
V.C.O.s	103	336	50	6	495
Indian OR	2,345	14,221	3,148	661	20,375
Total	2602	14,885	3,247	679	21,413
Staff Casualties					
British Officers	2	8	–	–	10
British ORs	1	15	–	–	16
Indian ORs	4	2	–	–	6
Grand Total	4,539	2,3661	5.373	679	34,252

The final criticism that the Indian Corps' component divisions were failures is unproven by the facts. The BEF, which had fought itself to a standstill, was saved by the arrival of the Indians. Conan Doyle, having compared the arrival of the Indians with a 'Tiger on an Icefloe' commented 'that they made head against the fierce German assaults is a wonderful proof of their adaptability.'[23]

In truth, the Indian Corps in France was an experiment with both successes and failures. The Corps had not been trained for the war into which it had thrown. Unlike the BEF, it had not had the opportunity to learn lessons from fighting the Second Boer War. It had rarely fought pitched battles against well-armed enemies. Its cultural composition, its emphasis on officer-sepoy relations and the concepts of *Izzat* and *Rizzat* were somewhat unique and led to bewilderment and self-wounding. However, these concepts also brought about the desire to come to the aid of the King Emperor, their ingenuity and make do skills and their sheer bravery together were able to counterbalanced much of these weaknesses. As Rob Johnson has observed, 'We should remember that the Indian Army was pitched hastily into a conflict without the luxury of preparation in order to hold the line in France, replace shattered divisions or secure vulnerable parts of the empire.'[24]

23 Arthur Conan Doyle, *The British Campaign in France and Flanders 1915* (London: Hodder & Stoughton, 1917), pp. 329-30.

24 Rob Johnson, I shall die Arms in hand; wearing the warriors' clothes: Mobilisation and the initial operations of the Indian Army in France and Flanders in Alan Jeffreys (ed.), *The Indian Army in the First World War* (Solihull, Helion, 2028), p. 51.

Sepoy; 129th Duke of Connaught's Own) Baluchis.

Appendix I

Lahore Division Order of Battle 1914

Ferozepore Brigade
1st Battalion Connaught Rangers
129th Duke of Connaught's Own Rangers
57th Wilde's Rifles (Frontier Force)
9th Bhopal Infantry

Jullunder Brigade
1st Battalion Manchester Regiment
15th Ludhiana Sikhs
47th Sikhs
59th Scinde Rifles (Frontier Force)

Sirhind Brigade
1st Battalion Highland Light Infantry
1st Battalion King George's Own Gurkha Rifles
1st Battalion 4th Gurkha Rifles
125th Napier Rifles

Divisional Troops
15th Lancers (Cureton's Multanis)
Headquarters Divisional Engineers
No. 20 Company Sappers and Miners
No. 21 Company Sappers and Miners
Signal Company
34th Sikh Pioneers

Artillery
Headquarters Divisional Artillery
5th Brigade R.F.A and Ammunition Column
11th Brigade R.F.A and Ammunition Column
18th Brigade R.F.A and Ammunition Column
109th Heavy Battery

Appendix II

Ferozepore Brigade's Linked Battalions

Indian Corps Battalion	1st Linked Battalion	2nd Battalion
57th Wilde's Rifles	55th (Coke's) Rifles	58th (Vaughan's) Rifles
129th Baluchis	127th Baluchis	130th Baluchis
9th Bhopal Infantry	–	–

The routine practice of linking battalions with one another was a method which the Indian Army used to substitutes casualties with trained replacements was adopted as a way of overcoming the shortage of Sepoys in the early part of the Indian Corps' time in France. It was particularly useful in providing British officers who were at least familiar with the way in which Indian battalions functioned. However, as we have seen the casualty rate was so high that the link battalions could not cope, and it became necessary for replacements to be found wherever they could.

Appendix III

The Indian Soldiers' Fund

On 1 October 1914 the Indian Soldiers' Fund was created by a committee chaired by Sir John Prescott Hewett, the then Conservative Member of Parliament for Luton, in order to support the Indian troops who were fighting in France and Flanders. Hewett was a British Indian civil servant who served as Lieutenant Governor of the United Provinces of Agra and Oudh. Hewett had spent a great deal of his career in Indian in famine relief, improving Indian education as well as organising great state occasions such as the Delhi Durbar of 1911.

The Committee, which was under the auspices of the St. John's Ambulance Association, consisted of men and women who had connections with India and wished to do what they could to improve the comfort of the Indian soldiers. Lord George Nathaniel Curzon, a former Viceroy provided the Committee with facilities for their meetings at his house at No. 1 Carlton House Terrance in Central London. It was later moved to South Kensington and the position of Chair passed to Sir Trevedyn Wynne, the Managing Director of the Bengal Railway Company.

The Fund was set up to provide medical and other comforts for Indian soldiers through either gifts or donations of money.[1] Individuals such as Canon Henry Lonsdale of Corbridge on Tyne, who was anxious to provide winter clothing for the 500 Indian Christians who made up the 30th Indian Labour Corps contacted the Fund which would ensure the distribution of such items.[2] Initially, there was some argument as to the status of the Fund but eventually it was agreed that it should be entirely responsible for dealing with offers of help and the distribution of comfort to Indian Troops since it had the best information regarding their needs. Appeals for donations were made to the general public and by November 1915 a total of £151,762 had been received. Gifts of clothing were also received which included over 200,000 items.

1 IOR/L/MIL/7/17264: Formation of the Indian Soldiers' Fund 1914-1921, p. 1.
2 IOR/L/MIL/7/17264: Formation of the Indian Soldiers' Fund 1914-921, pp. 6-8.

The Fund was also charged with supporting the Lady Hardinge Hospital at Brockenhurst Park, near Southampton. Built by the Government, the hospital had 500 beds and was staffed by 10 Indian Medical Services officers, a matron and assistant matron and 19 nurses who had been selected because of their knowledge of Indian languages. The Fund also support hospitals in France and Egypt as well as nine hospital ships. It also attempted to provide comfort for Indian Prisoners of War. Merewether reports that 480 tins of condensed milk, 100 lbs of sweets and 10,000 cigarettes together with bread making flour for t hose Indians who would not eat bread made by Europeans due to caste requirements were despatched every week.[3] The items supplied to the Corps run into the tens of thousands and included:

78,000 socks 12,00 Balaclavas 22,000,000 cigarettes
40 gramophones 7,000 religious books 85,000 handkerchiefs
125,000 lbs of sweets 850,00 envelopes 130 footballs.[4]

3 Merewether and Smith, *The Indian Corp*, p. 503.
4 Merewether and Smith, *The Indian Corps*, p. 503

Bibliography

Primary Sources

British Library: Indian Office Records

L/MIL/5/825/1f.66, Memorandum from Censor of Indian mail re Indian troops' dissatisfaction with pay. 12 February 1915

Reports of the Chief Censor, to General Sir Edmund Barrow, 15 February 1915. L/MIL/5/825/1. India Office to Evelyn Berkeley Howell, 15 Feb. 1915

L/MIL/7/1/17023/ Confidential Review Reports on Indian Army Units 1913-1924

L/ML/16/17/16/22 Collection of private Telegrams between the Secretary of State for India and the Viceroy, prior to the Outbreak of War with Turkey

L/ML/17/5/2402 Bruce Seton, An Analysis of 1000 wounds and injuries received in action, with special reference to the theory of the prevalence of self-infliction

L/Mil/7/120: Reorganisation, 1861-1936

L/MIL/7/17264: Formation of the Indian Soldiers Fund. 1914-1921.

L/PS/20/57: Commission Appointed by Act of Parliament to Enquire into the Operations of War in Mesopotamia

L/PS/20/57: Mesopotamia Commission, Wedgwood, Separate Report

MSS. EUR F143/65.: Sir Walter Lawrence to Lord Kitchener 27 December 1915

MSS Eur F 120 :Indian Soldiers Fund, Records including Proceedings, Proceedings and Bills

The National Archives/TNA (Kew)

WO 32/5110: Sir Walter Lawrence to Lord Kitchener, 27 Dec. 1915

WO 95/1093: Indian Corps, Deputy Director of Medical Services: War Diary.

WO 95:1134: 4th (Queen's Own) Hussars; War Diary.

WO 95/1187: 2 Indian Cavalry Division, Secunderabad Brigade, 34th (Prince Albert Victor's Own) War Diary

WO 95/3911: Telegram No, 959/1, From General Officer Commanding to General Officers Commanding 3rd Division

WO 95/3914: 34th Sikh Pioneers War Diary

WO 95/3917: 3 Indian (Lahore) Division, Headquarters Branches and Services, Royal Army Medical Services Assistant Director Medical Services

WO 95/3922: 3 Indian (Lahore) Division, 7 (Ferozepore) Infantry Brigade, Brigade Headquarters' War Diary
WO 95/3923: Connaught Rangers Medical Officer's Diary.
WO 95/3923: 3 Indian (Lahore) Division, 7 (Ferozepore) Infantry Brigade 9th Battalion Bhopal Infantry, War Diary
WO 95/3923/5: 3 Indian (Lahore) Division 7 (Ferozepore) Infantry Brigade: 57th Rifles. War Diary
WO95/3924: 3 Indian (Ferozepore) Division, Infantry Brigade, 129(D.C.O.) Baluchis, War: Diary
WO 95/3930: 7 Indian (Meerut) Division Headquarters. Branches and Services General Staff War Diary
WO 95/3932, Meerut Division, Headquarters Branches and Services, Adjutant and Quartermaster General: War Diary
WO95/3991: 3rd Indian (Lahore) Division, Headquarters, Branches and Services, General Staff: War Diary
WO 95/188: War Office Report on Changes in the Indian Amy Corps
WO 95/1093: Indian Corps, Deputy Director of Medical Services: War Diary
WO 95/1135: 2 Cavalry Division, 4 Cavalry Brigade, Headquarters.
WO 953923/4: 7 Indian (Lahore) Division, Ferozepore Infantry Brigade, 9th Battalion Bhopal Infantry, War Diary.
WO 95/3923: The General Officer Commanding 7th Indian Infantry Brigade. War Diary.
WO 95/3923: 3rd Indian (Lahore Division), 7 (Ferozepore) Infantry Brigade, London Battalion. 4th 1/4 Battalion City of London. War Diary.
WO 95/3927: 3 Indian (Lahore) Division, 8 (Jullundur) Infantry Brigade, 59 (Scinde) Rifles. War Diary.
WO 95/3929: 3 Indian (Lahore) Division, 9 (Sirhind) Infantry Brigade, 15th (Ludhiana) Sikhs, War Diary
WO95/3927: 3 Indian (Lahore Brigade, 8 (Jullundur) Division, 1 Battalion, Manchester's War Diary
TNA WO 95/3947: 7 Indian (Meerut) Division, 21 (Bareilly) Indian Infantry Brigade Headquarters, Report of the action of the Bareilly Brigade during the period 8-10 May 1915

Hansard
House of Lords Debates (09/09/14), Vol. 17, Col. 547

Imperial War Museum
Private Papers of Field Marshal Sir Henry Wilson
DS/MISC/2: Henderson Papers
HU 81657 Connaught Rangers in Mesopotamia, 1914-1918
MUN 5/176/1143/16, Memorandum on India's Contribution to the War in Men, Material and Money August 1914 to November 1918
Private Papers of R. Crude.

Cambridge University Library
CUL/MD, Hardinge Papers

Public Records Office, Northern Ireland
McCrory Papers, Diary Book 1.

Australian War Memorial
Field Marshal Lord William Birdwood to various correspondents, 19 July 1916–16 September 1918.
Field Marshal Lord William Birdwood to various correspondents, 19 July 1916 – 16 September 1918: Letter to Major General Ernest Dunlop, 19 July 1916

Official Publications
Anon., *The Army in India and its Evolution* (Calcutta: Superintendent of Government Printing, 1924)
Butler, Arthur Graham, *Official History of the Australian Army Medical Services, 1914-1918: Volume III – Special Problems and Services* (Canberra: Australian War Memorial, 1943)
Edmonds, James Edward, *Military Operations, France and Belgium, 1914*, Vol. I (London: MacMillan & Co, 1920)
—— *Military Operations France and Belgium 1914,* Vol. II (London, John Murray, 1925)
——*Military Operations, France and Belgium, 1915,* Vol. I (London, Macmillan, 1927)
——*Military Operations, France and Belgium 1915*, Vol. II (London, John Murray, 1928)
Government of India, *The Army in India and its Evolution* (Calcutta: Superintendent Government, Government Publishing, 1924)
HMG, *Commission Appointed by Act of Parliament to Enquire into the Operations of War in Mesopotamia* (London: HMSO, 1917)
Indian Army List, July 1919
London Gazette
MacGregor, Charles Metcalfe, *The Defence of India: A Strategic Study* (Simla: Government Central Branch Press, 1884).
Macpherson, William.Grant, *Medical Services General History: The Medical Services on the Western Front, and during the Operations in France and Belgium in 1914 and 1915* (London: HMSO, 1928)
Mobberley, Frederick. James, *The Campaign in Mesopotamia,* Vols. I-IV (London: HMSO, 1923-27).
Schwink, Otto, *Ypres 1914: An official account published by order of the German General staff. Translation by G. C. W. With introduction and notes by the Historical Section (Military Branch) Committee of Imperial Defence* (London: Constable and Company Ltd, 1919).
The Superintendent, *Census of India, 1911*, Vol. I (Calcutta, Government Press, 1913)
War Office, *Monthly Army List*

Published Primary and Secondary Sources

Abantika Chappals, Sandals Gosh, (ed.), *History of the Armed Forces Medical Services* (Hyderabad, Orient Longman, 1988)

Lord Anglesey, *A History of the British Cavalry: Volume 8. 1816-1919, The Western Front,* (Barnsley: Pen and Sword, 1995).

Shrabani Basu, *For King and another Country* (London, Bloomsbury, 2015).

Brice, Beatrice & Pulteney, William., *The Battles of Ypres* (London, John Murray, 1927)

Brighton Council, *A Short History in English, Gurmukhi & Hindu of the Royal Pavilion, Brighton and a Description of It as a Hospital for Indian Soldiers* (Brighton, King Thorne and Stace, 1915).

Brock, Michael, & Brock, Eleanor, (eds), *H.H. Asquith, Letters to Venetia Stanley* (Oxford: OUP, 1985)

Busch, Briton C., *Hardinge of Penshurst* (Hamden: Archon, 1980)

Cardozo Ian, *The Indian Army in World War I, 1914-1918* (London: Routledge, 2019)

Cato James P., *Solah Punjab: The History of the 16th Punjab Battalion* (London: Gale and Polden, 1967)

Charteris, John, *At GHQ* (London, Cassell, 1931).

Cooter, Roger, Harrison, Mark & Steve Sturdy (eds.), Medicine *and Modern Warfare* (London: Wellcome Trust, 1999)

Calder, Kent E., *The Sepoy* (London: John Murray, 1919)

Clutterbuck, L.A. and Dooner, W. T., *The Bond of Sacrifice: A Biographical record of all British Officers who fell in the Great War* (London: The Anglo-African Publishing Contractors, 1918)

Coleman, Frederic, *From Mons to Ypres with French: A Personal Narrative* (London: Sampson Low, 1916)

Collie, Robert, John, *Malingering and Feigned Sickness, with Notes on the Workmen's Compensation Act 1906 and Compensation for Injury, including the Leading Cases Thereon, 2nd ed, revised and enlarged* (London: Edward Arnold, 1917)

Corrigan, Gordon, *Sepoys in the Trenches, Gordon Corrigan, Sepoys in the Trenches, The Indian Corps on the Western Front 1914-1915* (Staplehurst: Spellmount 2006)

Doherty, Simon and Donovan, Tom, *The Indian Corps on the Western Front* (Brighton: Tom Donovan, Editions, 2014)

Arthur Conan Doyle, *The British Campaign in France and Flanders 1915* (London, Hodder & Stoughton, 1917),

French, Sir John, *1914,*(London, Constable, 1919)

—— *The Despatches of Sir John French,* (London: Chapman & Hall Ltd., 1914)

Fuller, J. F. C., *The Army in My Time* (London: Rich & Cowan 1935)

Gardner, Nikolas, *Trial by Fire: Command and the British Expeditionary Force in 1914.* (London: Greenwood Publishing Group 2003).

Gosh, A. (ed.), *History of the Armed Forces Medical Services* (Hyderabad: Orient Langman, 1988)

Grimwade, F. Clive, The *War History of the 4th Battalion The London Battalion (Royal Fusiliers) 1914-1919,* (London: Headquarters of the 4th London Battalion, 1922)
Gooch, John, *The Plans of War: The General Staff and British Military Strategy, 1900-1916*, (New York: John Wiley and Son Inc, 1974).
Woseley Haig, Thomas, The Indian Army 1885 to 1919, *The Cambridge History of India* (Cambridge, CUP, 1932) Vol. 6
Hardinge, Charles. *My Indian Years* (London, John Murray, 1948),
Heathcote, Tony, *The British Field Marshals 1736-1997* (Barnsley: UK: Pen & Sword, 1999)
Hodgkinson, Peter. E, *British Infantry Battalion Commanders in the First World War* (London, Routledge, 2020)
Farrar-Hockley, Antony, *Goughie: The Life of General Sir Hubert Gough* (London; Granada, 1975)
Harrison, Mark, *The Medical War: British Military Medicine in the First World Wa*(Oxford, OUP, 2010)
Holmes, Richard, *The Little Field Marshal: A Life of Sir John French* (London, Weidenfeld & Nicolson, 2004
Jack, George Morton, *The Indian Army on the Western Front* (Cambridge, CUP, 2014)
—— *The Indian Empire at War* (London. Little Brown, 2018)
Jones, Spencer, *From Boer War to World War: Tactical Reform of the British Army, 1902-1914* (Oklahoma, University of Oklahoma Press, 2013)
—— *Stemming the Tide: Officers and Leadership in the British Expeditionary Force 1914* (Solihull, Helion and Co. 2013)
—— *Courage Without Glory: The British Army on the Western Front 1915* (Solihull: Helion, 2015).
Kant, Vedica, *'If I die here who will remember me?' India and the First World War* (New Delhi, Roli Books, 2014).
Levine, Phillipa, *Prostitution, Race and Politics. Policing Venereal Disease in the British Empire* (New York, Routledge, 2003)
Mason, Philip, *A Matter of Honour. An Account of the Indian Army Its Officers and Men* (London: Macmillan, 1978)
MacMunn, George, *The Martial Races of India* (London: Sampson Low, 1933)
Maxwell, Robert, *Villiers-Stuart* (Edinburgh: Pentland Press, 1989)
McClenaghan, Tony, *For the Honour of My House* (Solihull, Helion & Co., 2019)
Menezes, Stanley L., Fidelity *and Honour. The Indian Army from the Seventeenth to the Twenty-First Century (*New Delhi: OUP, 1999)
Merewether, John W. B and Smith, Frederick, *The Indian Corps in France* (London, John Murray, 1918)
Montgomery, Bernard Law, *The Memoirs of Field-Marshal the Viscount Montgomery of Alamein, K. G.* (London: Collins, 1958
Moreman, Timothy, Lord Kitchener, the General Staff and the Army In Indian 1902-14, French, David, & Holden Reid, Brian, (eds.), *British General Staff: Reform and Innovation* (London: Routledge, 2004)

Norman, Terry, (ed.), *Armageddon Road: A VC's Diary 1914-1916* (London, W Kimber, 1982).
Olusoga, David, *The World's War* (London, Head of Zeus, 2014),
Omissi, David, *The Sepoy and the Raj: The Indian Army, 1860–1940* (Houndmills: Macmillan 1994)
—— *Indian Voices of the Great War* (London, Penguin Viking, 2014)
Paice, Edward, *Tip and Run: The Untold Tragedy of the Great War in Africa* (London, Weidenfeld & Nicolson, 2007)
Pakenham, Thomas, *The Boer War* (London, Weidenfeld and Nicolson, 1979)
Pollock, John, *Kitchener: The Road to Omdurman* (London: Constable, 1998)
Richards, F., *Old Soldiers Never Die* (London, Faber and Faber, 1933)
Sheffield, Gary, *Command and Morale: The British Army on the Western Front 1914-1918* (Barnsley: Praetorian Press, 2014),
—— *Douglas Haig. From Somme to Victory* (London: Aurum Press, 2016)
—— & Bourne, John, (eds.), *Douglas Haig. War Diaries and Letter,* (London: Weidenfeld and Nicolson, 2005
Singh, Gajendra, *The Testimonies of Indian Soldiers and the Two World Wars: Between Self and Sepoy* (London: A & C Black, 2014)
Smith-Dorrien, Horace, *Memories of Forty-Eight Years' Service* (London: John Murray, 1925)
Smith, A. *Four Years on the Western Front* (London: London Stamp Exchange, 1987).
Smith, Bertram, *Bombs and Hand Grenades* (New York: E.P. Dutton and Co, 1919).
Terraine, John, *Douglas Haig: The Educated Soldier* (London, Cassell, 2000).
Thapar, Daya, Ram, *Morale Builders: Forty Years with the Medical Services of India* (London: Asia Publishing House, 1965).
Thompson, G.H., *History of the 1st Battalion, 14th Punjab Regiment, Sherdil-ki-Paltan (late XIX Punjabis)* (New Delhi: Roxy Printing Press, 1946)
Townshend, Charles, *When God Made Hell: The British Invasion of Mesopotamia and the Creation of Iraq, 1914-1921* (London: Faber and Faber, 2011)
Travers, Tim, *The Killing Ground* (Barnsley: Pen & Sword, [1987] 2003),
Trench, Charles Chenevix The *Indian Army and the King's Enemies; 1900-1947* (London: Thames & Hudson, 1980)
Warner, Philip, *Auchinleck: The Lonely Soldier* (London: Buchan and Enright, 1981).
Willcocks, James, *With the Indians in France* (London: Constable and Co. Ltd., 1920)
—— *The Romance of Soldiering and Sport* (London: Cassell, 1925)
Ron Wilcox, *Battles on the Tigris: The Mesopotamian Campaign of the First World War* (Barnsley: Pen & Sword 2006)

Journals & Newspapers

Alexander, Caroline, The Shock of War, *The Smithsonian,* September 2010
Anon, Little Lives of Great Men, *The Illustrated War News*, Issue 14, 25 March 1915

Buxton, Hilary, Imperial Amnesia: Race, Trauma and Indian Troops in the First World War, *Past & Present*, Volume 241, Issue 1, November 2018

Crum, W. E., 'The Indian Army Reserve of Officers', *Journal of the United Service Institution of India,* Vol. XLV, 1916.

Ellinwood, DeWitt C., Ethnic Aspects of the Indian Army in World War I, Indian History Congress, *Proceedings of the Indian History Congress* (1978), Vol. 39, Volume I

Gardner, Nickolas, British Prestige and the Mesopotamia Campaign, 1914–1916 in *The Historian,* Vol. 77, Issue 2, Summer 2015,

Greenhut, John, The Imperial Reserve: The Indian Corps on the Western Front, 1914-15, *Journal of Imperial and Commonwealth History*, XII (1983)

Humphries, Mark, Wilfully and With Intent: Self-Inflicted Wounds and the Negotiation of Power in the Trenches, *Histoire sociale, Social History,* Vol. 97, Issue 47 June 2014

Johnson, Robert, 'I shall die arms in hand, wearing the Warriors' Clothes': Mobilisation and Initial Operations of the Indian Army in France and Flanders. *British Journal for Military History,* Vol. 2, Issue 2, February 2016

Kaushik, Roy, Race and Recruitment in the Indian Army 1880-1918, *Modern Asian Studies,* Vol. 47, No. 4, 2013

Latter E., The Indian Army, *Journal of the Society for Army Historical Research,* Vol. LXXII No 291, Autumn 1994

Lloyd, Nick, With Faith and Without Fear, Douglas Haig's Command of First Army during 1915, The *Journal of Military History,* Vol. 71. No. 4, 2007

Manimugdha, S. Sharma, For Indian Sepoys who served in WWI, the Army was like a University, *The Times of India,* 10 November 2018

Snape, David, 'With a master's eye he saw what was needed and did it': Kitchener's Indian Army Reforms 1902-1909, *Soldiers of the Queen: Journal of the Victorian Military Society*, Issue 170, May 2018

Sundaram, Chandar S., Arriving in the Nick of Time': The Indian Corps in France, 1914-15, *Journal of Defence Studies*, Vol. 9, No. 4 October-December 2015

Syk, A., The 1917 Mesopotamia Commission, *RUSI Journal,* No. 154 2009

Vogt, Karen F., Origins of Military Medical Care as an Essential Source of Morale. *Military Medicine,* Vol 180, Issue 6, June 2015

Unpublished Theses

Hughes, Richard, 'Tommy Capper's Immortals – How effective was the 7th Division at the first battle of Ypres?', (MA Thesis, University of Birmingham, 2015.

A.T. Jarboe, 'Soldiers of the Empire: Indian Sepoys in and beyond the imperial metropole during the First World War' (Ph.D. Thesis. North-Eastern University, 2013).

Index

PEOPLE

PLACES

FORMATIONS & UNITS